DEC 1 4 1993

MAR 3 0 1995
APR 1 4 1998

STRATEGIC TRENDS IN SERVICES

STRATEGIC TRENDS IN SERVICES
An Inquiry into the
Global Service Economy

edited by
ALBERT BRESSAND AND
KALYPSO NICOLAÏDIS

A SERVICES WORLD FORUM PROJECT

1817

Harper & Row, Publishers, New York
BALLINGER DIVISION
Grand Rapids, Philadelphia, St. Louis, San Francisco
London, Singapore, Sydney, Tokyo

International Standard Book Number: 0-88730-317-X

Library of Congress Catalog Card Number: 88-34168

Printed in the United States of America

Library of Congress Cataloging-in-Publication Data

Strategic trends in services : an inquiry into the global economy / edited
  by Albert Bressand and Kalypso Nicolaïdis for Services World Forum.
     p.   cm.
  Bibliography: p.
  Includes index.
  ISBN 0-88730-317-X
  1. Service industries. I. Bressand, Albert. II. Nicolaïdis, Kalypso.
III. Services World Forum (Association)
HD9980.5.S77   1989
338.4—dc19   88-34168
                                                         CIP

89 90 91 92 HC 9 8 7 6 5 4 3 2 1

in memoriam
Jacques Nusbaumer

CONTENTS

vii

LIST OF FIGURES

LIST OF TABLES

FOREWORD

This book was prepared by Services World Forum (SWF), an international association of scholars and decisionmakers with substantive interest and involvement in services issues.[1] SWF was founded as a nonprofit association in October 1985 by a small group of individuals working in government, business, international organizations, and universities but participating in its activities in their own right. The purpose of the SWF is to promote objective analysis of national and international issues in services and frank and open dialogue among its members, through an annual conference on services every spring in Geneva and the publication of an SWF book series on topics of concern to its members. SWF is open to anyone in the world wishing to and able to contribute to its aims and activities.[2] To quote one of its founders, Jacques Nusbaumer, "SWF's hope is that [its books] will encourage the exchange of ideas on the subject of services, and that [they] will be found a useful tool by all those in the private sector and government who are dealing with the issues in this area."

Starting with this second volume, the Services World Forum is adopting a new format which, if successful, could be replicated in future publications. The aim is to present an integrated perspective on the emergence of the global service economy by bringing together research reflecting the state of the art in each of five major areas of inquiry related to services. In addition, an introductory essay at the beginning of the volume surveys major developments on the world economic scene from a services point of view.

Five major areas of inquiry are investigated in this book. Part I, Corporate Strategies, Markets, and Regulations, covers business developments in services and analyzes regulatory frameworks from the corporate point of view. Part II, Development, Trade, and Economic Policies, covers macroeconomic issues, and analyzes services trade patterns and dynamics that policymakers had overlooked until very recently. Part III, the Uruguay Round Services Negotiations in Search of a Framework, presents an historical overview of ongoing negotiations and suggests elements of a service agreement. Part IV, Fundamental Concepts of a Service Economy, focuses on new analytical tools needed for understanding the service economy, with an emphasis on the various dimensions of risk. Part V, The Empirical Framework and the Methodological Challenge, reviews statistical and theoretical progress pertaining to the assessment and measurement of service activities at the national and international levels.

SERVICES: A NEW FAD OR A NEW WORLD?

The authors contributing to this book illustrate from various angles how the emergence of a service world economy is currently putting into question classical perceptions of economic dynamics, with answers yet to come.

Obsolescing Tools. Indeed, there is hardly a part of this book that does not question, in one way or another, the ability of traditional economic tools to accurately describe today's world economy. In this economy:

* Supply and demand, production and transaction processes can no longer be straightforwardly separated, what used to be considered costs (factors of production) are becoming assets (products), while networking relationships, such as corporate alliances or electronic interconnection, challenge the traditional boundaries of economic units (Part I).

* The ability to process information is becoming the major source of comparative advantage for nations around the world, and development strategies can no longer be based on traditional trade specialization patterns (Part II).

- Transborder transactions themselves are increasingly at odds with "trade" concepts as we understand them, thereby making international collaboration on "trade in services" a test of the adaptability of postwar international economic regimes (Part III).

- Mathematical and philosophical objects such as volatility, options, and risk are the ingredients of esoteric "products" bought and sold by the tens of thousands, and both corporations and government are becoming more preoccupied with acting upon levels of risk than levels of wealth (Part IV).

- The distinction between "prices" and "volume," at the heart of such concepts as real growth rate and inflation, is losing relevance, thereby making it increasingly hard to account for growth rates, the conventional measure of the wealth of nations (Part V).

And New Concepts. The last two decades may be remembered as one of those troubling historical periods when an old paradigm is irreversibly losing its grasp while another is yet to come. The many books that have been published during this period announcing the advent of the electronic or informatics age testify to the fact that never before have people been so prone to real-time analysis of the change at work within their own societies.[3]

While this has been illustrated in the realm of finance and capital allocation, major developments occurring in widely different realms— from information technology to worldwide monetary flows and transnational industrial restructuring—converge in bringing about a far-reaching transformation of economic interactions. This is one of the central themes of this book: actors are no longer simply engaged in producing, consuming, or managing but, rather, taking part in increasingly complex and shared processes of wealth creation. The term *service economy* indeed doesn't point to some postindustrial phase of economic development but rather to the emergence of more symmetrical relationships among economic actors.

This in turn implies or accelerates fundamental changes in the means through which actors can influence or control economic processes. Private and public decisionmakers around the world may still lack conceptual tools that would guide them in dealing with this new reality. This, however, does not prevent them from experimenting with new strategies, regulatory concepts, and technologies from which analysts will then be able to extract further insights on the underlying paradigm.

In Part I of this volume, the authors argue and illustrate the fact that networks are becoming the privileged modes of management and delivery of services and are therefore becoming the central means through which economic actors create and exchange value. In Part II, service-based development strategies are explored, information management often being at their core. Part III focuses on the dynamics of the GATT Uruguay Round of Multilateral Trade Negotiations and points to possible new approaches to international collaboration as governments are trying to cope with the internationalization of the "services logic." Part IV describes the multifaceted world of risk management and the complex web of tools and institutions pertaining to it. Finally, Part V reviews current efforts in trying to assess services activities in innovative ways. These are among the promising paths that an observation of today's world economy invite us to explore.

Services are no longer invisible, and ignoring this major change in the economic landscape can already be identified as a source of strategic and policy mistakes. The tip of the iceberg has emerged; a conceptual framework that could help us apprehend the whole is only beginning to take shape.

—Albert Bressand
Kalypso Nicolaïdis

NOTES

1. See SWF's earlier book, *The Emerging Service Economy* (New York: Pergamon Press, 1987), edited by Orio Giarini, SWF's first president.
2. See the Services World Forum membership list as of December 1988 at the end of this book.
3. A good illustrative overview is provided in James R. Beniger, *The Information Control Revolution: Technological and Economic Origins of the Information Society* (Cambridge, Mass.: Harvard University Press, 1986).

INTRODUCTION
The World's Back Office Takes Over

Albert Bressand

The 1980s may be remembered as the time when services ceased to be invisible.[1] At first glance, this development may appear paradoxical. After all, services have long accounted for more than half of economic activity, so why are they just now becoming visible on both national and international agendas?

FROM HAVANA TO PUNTA DEL ESTE

The launching of a new round of Multilateral Trade Negotiations under the auspices of the General Agreement on Tariffs and Trade (GATT), which culminated in the Punta del Este, Uruguay, declaration of September 1986, is the best-known example of the prominence acquired by service issues in the mid-1980s. Although it is described as a negotiation process, the Uruguay Round is more a self-education, research, and learning process. By tackling for the first time services matters as a policy priority, private and public decisionmakers have come to realize that the importance of services is not limited to their direct role in trade and employment. Beyond their direct, sectoral importance, services are indeed a major dimension of economic activity, even within the manufacturing sectors. The lack of a common worldwide approach to the workings of inter-

1

national markets for services is thus increasingly viewed as a major obstacle to further growth.

In the early 1980s, those proposing to address this concern in the context of international negotiations coined the phrase "trade in services" to facilitate discussion in the institutional and legal context that had made possible successful liberalization of trade in goods. It is gradually becoming clear, however, that the changing nature of the global wealth creation process must be reflected in a new international economic paradigm. Translating this still sought paradigm into an international regime is clearly beyond the agenda that can be addressed during a four-year round of multilateral trade negotiations. Unlike the eight postwar trade rounds, the Uruguay Round is probably better seen as the first step in a much longer, yet critical, process, comparable to the overall process of trade liberalization that began with the 1947 founding GATT conference at Havana and culminated in the 1973–79 Tokyo Round.

The splitting of the Uruguay round into two separate negotiation processes, where services are to be addressed free from direct reference to GATT rules, was mostly due to political considerations, and, notably, to the fear of some developing countries that they would have to make concessions on services as a quid pro quo for the removal of barriers facing their exports of manufactured goods. Yet, ex post, negotiators are awakening to the fact that this provides an opportunity for innovations in international rulemaking. Indeed, as some realize, by deciding to address "services," they have begun to pull a thread woven into increasingly complex patterns.

In many ways however, multilateral negotiations over services are only the tip of the iceberg. Other recent major economic developments must be brought into the picture, even when they are usually discussed under other headings than services.

FROM FINANCIAL SERVICES
TO FINANCE AS SERVICES

The financial scene is probably the most appropriate one in which to look for other clues to the 1980s services paradox. While oil shocks, inflation, and "stagflation" made headlines in the 1970s, and while the Third World debt was undoubtedly the most prominent global economic issue of the early 1980s, the mid-1980s were a time of spec-

tacular—and highly contrasted—developments centered on world
financial markets. These developments—and the opportunities and
risks they bring about—are symbolized by the two seminal events
marking the financial scene in the mid- and late 1980s—namely, the
London Big Bang of 1986 and the worldwide stock market crash of
1987.

The London Big Bang, as well as less spectacular small bangs and
quasi-bangs in countries as diverse as Canada, France, Denmark,
Germany, and Australia, illustrates the compelling need for regulators and market participants to adjust to these deep changes in the
nature of market interactions and organization, and, notably, to the
impact of information technology. The stock market crash of October 1987, which almost coincided with the first anniversary of the
Big Bang, nonetheless made clear that these new opportunities did
not come free of increased risks, largely consequence of computerized trading techniques. Although its actual economic consequences
later appeared more limited than anticipated at the time, the crash
put an abrupt end to five years of bullish atmosphere that had extended well beyond the stock markets to affect the political mood,
the regulatory cycle (in the form of a worldwide deregulation trend),
and our visions of the future.

Beyond headlines, however, the implications of the stock market
crash and of the deregulatory bangs have to be assessed in a long-
term perspective, of which the emergence of an information- and
service-intensive economy is an essential aspect.

Obviously, the role of financial markets in the economy precedes
by centuries the recent emphasis on services. Yet recent developments concerning the nature of financial interactions are increasing
the relevance of services and information concepts for the understanding of financial markets. In particular, the advent of electronic
networks represents a qualitative change in the working of financial
and other markets that can be compared to such seminal transformations in the history of markets as the development of fairs in
medieval Europe. Through watershed transformations of this magnitude, major changes have taken place in the ways in which supply
and demand can actually meet. Not only does this make possible
greater market efficiency, but it also makes for major changes in the
respective role and power of the various economic actors and influences the directions of market development. The medieval fair heralded the rise of the city and the merchants, while accelerating the

erosion of the power of the feudal warlords who previously controlled much economic activity. Today, the advent of the electronic market is redistributing functions and power among financial institutions. In particular, it is giving services an increased relevance well illustrated, in the financial realm, by the blurring of the time-honored distinction between financial services and the much broader field of finance and financial markets. This traditional distinction can be seen as one between the realm of "high finance"—namely, financial markets and institutions performing the crucial task of allocating capital, one of the fundamental factors of production—and the world's financial back office, in which a number of specialized activities (financial services) are carried out so that the financial system can effectively fulfill its function.

According to this distinction, the role of the financial back office was simply to expedite, in the most efficient and productive ways, a number of logistical tasks that did not have in themselves (except in case of gross malfunction) an impact on the higher order process of capital allocation. The notion of services was not seen as particularly illuminating outside of these back-office tasks, as the prestigious functions of high finance were discussed in terms of broad macroeconomic and policy forces. This division of labor found an expression at the institutional level with central banks, the Bank for International Settlement, the International Monetary Fund, and the International Development Bank granting little attention to trade in financial services. Before its inclusion in a multilateral round of trade negotiations, some specialized aspects of the latter subject were addressed, when at all, in highly technical bodies such as International Telecommunications Union (ITU), the International Civil Aviation Organization, and technical OECD committees.

What the events of the 1980s tell us, however, is that the back office is less and less limited to an ancillary role. This is true at the level of individual financial institutions, where technology and service innovation are recognized to play a strategic role: the fact, for instance, that John Reed was chosen to succeed Walter Wriston as the head of the Citicorp after presiding over the reorganization of Citicorp's multibillion dollar back office is telling. This also applies, in other forms, to the economic system as a whole. In particular, designing and servicing electronic networks has become the most critical and influential aspect of setting up and operating a new market, whether in existing instruments or in new products. In this sense, the London 1986 Big Bang as well as the October 1987 crash can be remembered as the time when the "invisible hand" at work in the world's financial market had to be recognized, with all policy implications, for what it has become: global financial services in an electronic glove.

FROM MARKETPLACE TO
SERVICE-INTENSIVE NETWORKS

The Big Bang of October 27, 1986, and its preparation represent a far-reaching effort on the part of the London financial community to maintain or expand its position as a center of the world's financial markets. This search for world competitiveness has had two major results.

First, and most obviously, competition has been promoted through the removal of some of the key barriers to entry and protections enjoyed until then by market participants. Following on earlier reforms at the New York Stock Exchange (NYSE), fixed commissions have been abolished and the traditional division of labor between brokers (who channeled customers' orders) and jobbers (who were active on the Stock Exchange floor) has come to an end.

The second result of this search for competitiveness may, however, be the more significant over the long term because it involves a *qualitative* change in the nature of the stock market itself. The relevant model here, rather than the NYSE, is NASDAQ (National Association of Securities Dealers Automatic Quotation), the U.S. market for over-the-counter stocks that pioneered electronic networking as an alternative to the traditional marketplace and has quickly established itself as the world's third largest financial "center" after New York and Tokyo.

Breaking away from the definition of a market as a physical place, where buyers and sellers would actually meet, was very much in line with London's previous success as the center of the global Euro-markets. Replicating this success in the brave new field of global equity trading was the biggest gamble behind the Big Bang. In the words of then chairman Nicholas Goodison: "The Stock Exchange recently took important steps towards becoming the first truly International Stock Exchange. . . . Big Bang was perhaps the first step towards a worldwide electronic market place for equities. . . . The screen is the new market place and computers backed up with new rules and surveillance measures have ensured that there is effective regulation and supervision of the market participants."[2]

Although the stock exchange floor has not been immediately abolished, it has become superfluous as the real marketplace in London became identified with the powerful set of electronic networks at the core of the new exchange and notably with the Stock Exchange Automated Quotation System (SEAQ) and with settlement networks such as Talisman and Taurus.

A number of exchanges have actually pushed this logic one step further than was initially the case in London doing away altogether with the exchange floor. This is the case of the Bermuda-based Intex as well as of the stock index options market created in Paris at the end of 1988 in cooperation among notably Credit Commercial de France and Sweden's OM company.

Moving from the concept of an exchange as a place to that of a network has far-reaching implications. This is true not only of the geographic reach of the exchange (which now extends to virtually the whole planet) but also of the role of services in the working of the financial system as a whole. Service providers, who previously acted simply as "facilitators," may now greatly increase the diversity, scope, and depth of their activities. In addition to the "facilitating" services that already existed (such as providing a place to meet and keeping records and statistics), new services can be offered through the network (such as real-time price quotation, and electronic settlement). Furthermore, operating and upgrading the network itself quickly becomes a major source of influence on the possibilities open to market participants regarding the definition and introduction of new products and the directions in which the market develops.

The most fundamental change at the heart of the London Big Bang is therefore that market participants interact within a network. This change in turn casts the stock exchange in the role of network operator and service provider instead of its traditional role as meeting place for exchange members.

Addressing a Euromoney seminar on September 11, 1986, just before the Big Bang, Peter Cox, International Market Manager of the London Stock Exchange, stressed that "London will now compete on the basis of the services it offers."[3] The qualitative change involved is vividly illustrated by the dominant role that service fees, as

opposed to membership fees, now play in the balance sheet of the
Stock Exchange.

	1977	1987
	%	%
Service fees	30	60
Member contributions	40	15
Other	30	25

Source: International Stock Exchange, London, September 1987.

Obviously, many of these services were already provided, in one form
or another, to stock exchange members. Nevertheless, the move toward electronic networking implies that stock exchanges—and capital markets in general—are becoming service-intensive and service-
driven in the following sense.

• Services can now be defined, in a precise and operational manner,
  as a set of clearly identified information-processing activities (or
  better, to borrow a phrase from Anthony Rutkowski, as a set of
  "shared processes" within a global information fabric).[4]

• Services that once were lumped together can be unbundled and
  sold separately by the exchanges as well as by independent service providers, thereby opening new opportunities for competition and cost cutting.

• New services can be designed either by rebundling existing services in a different manner or by taking advantage of new technological possibilities (such as real-time position management).

• Services provided by one stock exchange or capital market institution no longer need to be sold by that institution alone but can
  be made available through other networks, as illustrated by the
  agreements passed by SEAQ with Reuters, NASDAQ, and Tele-
  kurs for the distribution of its domestic equities prices in the
  United Kingdom and internationally.

As a result, what used to simply be described as capital flows must
increasingly be understood as a complex process in which the nature
and quality of services and the structure of networks—electronic as
well as traditional—play a major role in shaping resource allocation.

FROM BANG TO CRASH

While the Big Bang suggests that financial services and capital markets have now become one and the same reality, the stock market crash of October 1987 brought to light the deeper repercussions of the role of electronic networks as the modern equivalent of the physical marketplace. Obviously, the crash of October 1987 eschews simple, unambiguous interpretations. Official reports[5] have drawn widely differing conclusions, market authorities in New York and Chicago have argued among themselves, computers have been blamed for their role in precipitating the market break but also for having been disconnected in an effort to slow the pace of selling. This analytical confusion has allowed each shade of opinion to present the crash in the light that best suited its purpose. Supply siders have put the blame on congressional efforts to restrict mergers and takeovers. U.S. Democrats and European leaders have felt vindicated in their denunciation of President Reagan's legacy of budgetary red ink. Opponents of deregulation have pointed their fingers at the "casino society" set in motion, according to them, by free-wheeling financial markets. This state of confusion, however, is an invitation to take a fresh look at some of the analytical tools on which our understanding of markets rests. As in the case of the Big Bang, services and information economy concepts have an important role to play in this rethinking.

In an economy where the market is no longer a place but a set of electronic networks, the law of supply and demand and the price formation process are better understood in terms of interactions among three groups of actors—namely, users, service providers, and network operators[6]—than between buyers and sellers, the traditional dichotomy. While the underlying balance between supply and demand obviously remains the long-term driving force, the *process* whereby this balance is actually implemented and the services as well as network management strategies that make it increasingly "visible" cannot be assumed away in "invisible hand" metaphor. Understanding the dynamics of the market increasingly calls for an explicit analysis of such processes and strategies, whereby service providers and network operators influence the solicitation, transmission, and processing of both supply and demand.

What is new, obviously, is not the existence of service providers but the fact that their role is no longer simply that of "intermediaries" or "middlemen" that would do nothing else than channeling, aggregating or otherwise facilitating the buying and selling by others. Much more is taking place in today's complex markets than the straightforward transfer of property rights over well-defined products. Suppliers of supporting services as well as network operators must now be seen as full participants in the creation of "value-added."

In particular, innovation, the creation of new products, is now an integral aspect of the working of markets. A vivid example of this creative rather than intermediary role of service providers is the part played by portfolio insurance in the chain of events that led to a 508-point drop of the Dow Jones on Bloody Monday. The fact that $60–90 billion worth of stocks (representing under 10 percent of the stocks owned by pension funds) were "portfolio insured" meant that funds had not acted simply as intermediaries for their clients but had provided them with innovative packages combining investment and insurance functions. For better or for worse, they had added value to these transactions, thereby going much beyond their role as transmission belts between supply and demand.

Similarly, the *swap markets* represent a fundamental change not just in financial services as traditionally defined but in the working of the capital allocation process itself. They make it possible for investors to access and use hybrid instruments that combine characteristics from a number of currencies and markets (such as interest rates, liquidity, regulatory features, and currency denomination). The fact that instruments can be custom-fit to the needs of a given investor, rather than having an investor choose among a set of existing instruments, has profound repercussions on the relationship between the financial sphere and the so-called real economy.[7]

NETWORKED MARKETS IN SEARCH OF A REGULATORY FRAMEWORK

Financial services are not, by far, the only examples of the changes in the nature of economic interactions from which services derive their increased importance and salience. As in the case of the Big Bang,

many such changes are not usually addressed under the heading of
services but, rather, under the heading of deregulation, thereby ob-
scuring deeper changes in the role of services. Yet deregulation (the
word is quite misleading) is at heart an effort to adapt the regulatory
framework to the changing value-creation process.

It is no coincidence that most deregulatory efforts have taken
place in service fields: telecommunications, transport, broadcasting
and the media, finance. The only major exception is energy, although
even there service issues such as pipeline transportation also play a
role. In all or most of these cases, what is at stake is a shift from the
traditional view of services as fulfilling simple logistical functions to
the gradual realization that, under one name or another, services are
major economic activities in and of themselves.

As long as these various services were seen as logistical activities,
two consequences followed. First, their role in value creation tended
to be relegated to the back office, implying little interest on the part
of the top corporate leadership. Second, in this perspective, there
was no strong incentive to challenge the pervasive view that it was
natural for governments to intervene with the objective of providing
the economy—more generally, society—with the best logistic infrastructure support possible. In this sense, regulating and, in many
countries, assuming a direct operating role in transport, communication, financial services, and so on was a natural extension of the role
of the state in providing highways, bridges, justice, and other infrastructure or general support functions for the economy and the
society.[8]

This traditional view of services as logistic functions is less and less
in line with the nature of the new wealth-creation processes. Like in
the field of finance, the notion of back-office functions separate
from and subordinate to the core economic activities is being increasingly challenged by the deeper levels of interactions now developing
among consumers and producers as well as among firms. Bringing and
keeping the actors together—a task best understood in terms of service functions—is an essential part of an increasingly flexible and customized production process.

It is therefore becoming quite artificial to draw a line between
value-creating activities and the support services on which they rely.
The blurring border between so-called basic services and value-added
services in the field of telecommunication is a good case in point. It
is increasingly inadequate to distinguish between value-creating acti-

vities and the support services on which they would need to rely. The same is true in traditional transportation modes, where shipping or delivering complex goods by air calls for sophisticated skills and innovative "products" that are an integral part of the overall production scene. In today's complex and fast-changing markets, the innovative management of delivery systems is an integral dimension of value creation.

Manufacturing is not outside of such changes. On the contrary, the move from traditional market places to networked markets is a powerful force behind the growing integration of what used to be considered the "real" production process and a number of activities considered as purely supportive. The role of zero inventory management techniques is one of many illustrations of this convergence of so-called logistical functions and higher-order, value-creating functions into a tightly integrated, service-intensive production process. More generally, as the point is made in the first part of this book, the development of corporate networks (whether intracorporate networks or, to use the PROMETHEE categories, transcorporate networks such as Electronic Data Interchange and metacorporate networks such as user groups and standardization coalitions) has the same impact on the role of services in the production process as the development of electronic networks has on the working of markets.

There is no place in this brief introduction to review in this light the various fields mentioned, but PROMETHEE has presented an analysis of the deregulatory process in telecommunications that also brings to light the organic relationship between the role of information services and the development of networked markets.[9] When considering deregulation in air transportation and in finance, we see electronic networks such as computer reservation systems, payment systems, or the various value-added networks that connect users to traditional and new service providers acquiring a role well beyond that of black-office tools and actually serving as electronic marketplaces. A number of previously logistic services, such as the handling of reservations or the processing of payments, now assume key functions in the working of the market itself. One consequence is that problems of transparency, neutrality, and access are therefore emerging, creating a strong demand for a regulation of a new type: network based rather than sector based.

At this stage, the common elements in the various deregulatory/ reregulatory processes are not always clearly perceived. The significance of deregulation as the search for a new framework adapted to the changed nature of the value-creation process is still partially obscured by the early and somewhat naïve concept of deregulation as administrative simplification (remember the 1980 Bush commission and its efforts to reduce the number of pages of the *Federal Registry*). As years go by, the Big Bang, telecommunication deregulation, the deeply transformed nature of the transportation market, and a whole set of similar processes will gradually begin to be seen as part of one single, integrated transformation organized around the emergence of networked markets in which service providers, network operators, and users (buyers or sellers) join in new, powerful forms of value creation. Such is one of the key perspectives in which the "service paradox" mentioned at the beginning of this chapter will gradually be understood.

NOTES

1. This chapter has benefited from a discussion held at the Services World Forum general assembly meeting of February 5, 1988, and notably from comments by Geza Feketekuty and Kalypso Nicolaïdis.
2. International Stock Exchange, London, 1987.
3. Proceedings of the September 10–11, 1985 Euromoney Conference, "London After Deregulation."
4. Anthony Rutkowski, "The Global Information Fabric," *Project PROMETHEE Perspectives* no. 6, Paris.
5. The major reports concerning the stock market crash of 1987 are those of the Brady Commission and of the Securities and Exchange Commission (SEC) in the United States, of the International Stock Exchange in London, and of the Deguen Commission in Paris.
6. For a discussion of the distribution of roles within the "OSU triangle" (Operators, Service Providers, and Users), see Project PROMETHEE Perspectives 5, "Deregulation in the 1990s," Paris (March 1988).
7. For a discussion of "info-currencies" and financial engineering, see Albert Bressand, "Currency Chaos: the Ultimate Strategic Weapon," *The International Economy Magazine* I, no. 1 (October/November 1987).
8. This state of affairs was challenged earlier in the United States than in Europe, not because the views taken on these matters were very different but rather because the role of the judicial process in the United States allowed a number of small actors with high stakes in challenging the situation to obtain changes applicable to all potential participants and disproportionate with those immediate stakes. In Continental Europe, by contrast, such pres-

sures used to be dealt with on an ad hoc, case-by-case basis through discretionary administrative measures rather than through judicial decisions applicable *erga omnes*. It is not widely known outside of France for instance that the French telecommunications "monopoly" is only a de facto situation to which the minister is free to make a wide range of pragmatic exceptions.

9. Catherine Distler, ed., *La déréglementation dans les années 1990: Enjeux pour les télécommunications et l'économie d'information*, PROMETHEE, Paris. This report is also available as a special issue of *Le Communicateur* no. 5 (July 1988).

I CORPORATE STRATEGIES, MARKETS, AND REGULATIONS

INTRODUCTION, BY ALBERT BRESSAND

Is the service economy a change in nature of the economic system, or is it simply a change in semantics? After all, services have always accounted for the largest share of the gross national product of most developed and developing economies. If it were to be equated with the development of the "tertiary sector," the service economy would not be qualitatively different from the type of economy to which we are accustomed. We would simply be witness to a closing of the gap between economic reality and the language used to describe it.

Another, more demanding concept of a service economy is, however, that a deep transformation is presently taking place that cannot be adequately understood in the analytical framework inherited from the previous, industrial era. Seen in this light, services are important not because of their (large) share in GNP or in job statistics but because they offer critical insights into the changing nature of the economic system as a whole.

Reviewing some key developments in the field of corporate strategies, this first part of the book focuses on the role of networks in the creation of economic value and competitive advantage.

Chapter 1, based on the research carried out by PROMETHEE analyzes the new types of needs these networks respond to and the new types of products they serve to offer. This approach stresses the

15

increased pervasiveness of such means of organizing economic exchange in situations where the mastery of "mass customization" and new approaches to productivity are the key to corporate success.

Leif Edvinsson and John Richardson (Chapter 2) develop the same line of argument through a series of examples and show how increased attention granted to the management of "thoughtware" within the firm and customer relationship outside the firm is needed to ensure the efficient use of information networks.

The next two chapters are case studies focusing on the role of networks and networking in specific sector sectors. Chapter 3 examines how computer reservation systems have completely reshaped the relationship between airlines and their customers and have created a "networked market" for airline services.

Finally, Giorgio Spriano (Chapter 4) describes how the effective conduct of externalized R&D activities has usually implied setting up collaborative networks. This in turn points to key role of networks for the new types of economies of scale and scope called for by current technological developments.

1 NETWORKS AT THE HEART OF THE SERVICE ECONOMY

Albert Bressand, Catherine Distler,
and Kalypso Nicolaïdis

The emergence of a service economy can be interpreted in two very different fashions. The first approach, an intellectual dead end, is to employ descriptive indicators (such as the share of services in employment and production statistics), and to contrast manufacturing on one side with services on the other. Such an approach may have been useful a few years ago when services were truly invisible not just to economists but even to many service companies themselves. Today however, this descriptive approach encourages unproductive debates for or against services in which much energy is wasted on the straw man of "deindustrialization" or on restating the importance of manufacturing.

The alternative approach, which we adopt in this chapter, is based not on a dichotomy between goods and services but on an analysis of the wealth-creation process as a whole. This integrated approach had already led us, in previous work, to challenge the traditional concept of "products" and to suggest instead that corporations were actually engaged in the production and sales of complex packages ("compacks") in which goods coexist with services.[1] We turn our attention in this chapter to another major dimension of the wealth-creation process, productivity.

Without attempting to provide an exhaustive analysis of the new concept of productivity called for by the changing nature of economic activity (see Chapter 16), we show how corporations are exploring a new "productivity frontier" that calls into question the old dichotomy between manufacturing and services. We first present the case that exploring this productivity frontier implies a focus on relationship management rather than product-based strategies for creating wealth and competitive advantage. Next, we turn our attention to the impact of new information management techniques on the productivity of relationship management. Such productivity gains are discussed in the framework of new patterns of economic interactions that we briefly describe under the headings of mass customization and integration. The blurring of the boundary between production and transaction—or, more concretely, between their traditional locus (the "factory" and "marketplace")—leads, with proper definition, toward a new organizational and wealth-creation paradigm centered on networks and networking strategies. The last sections of this chapter present a concise typology of relationship management performed within different networks. In conclusion we present concrete examples to illustrate four levels of corporate networking that can serve to redefine productivity and competitiveness in the emerging global information economy.

RELATIONSHIP MANAGEMENT
AS WEALTH CREATION

Productivity has traditionally been measured in terms of output per unit of input. Jacques de Bandt points out in Chapter 16 how, in addition to raising many traditional difficulties particularly regarding product innovation, this apparently straightforward definition is poorly adapted to a service-intensive economy.

Nonetheless, it served as a satisfactory proxy as long as most productivity gains in the economy stemmed from, or could be understood as, more efficient methods to carry out the material-processing central to an industrial economy, such as automatization and robotization. Today however productivity gains are no longer confined to material processing but extend to nonmaterial dimensions of wealth creation, most notably the management of relationships.

Managing relationships has always been a key dimension of economic activity, both within companies and in the marketplace. Yet, changes in management or marketing styles took place at a far slower pace than did innovation material processing. Different concepts of corporate organization followed each other every few decades rather than every two to five years as was and remains the norm for manufacturing equipment. Accordingly, most companies are still organized around the pyramid, functional, or matrix models that were pioneered in the early and middle decades of this century.

The diffusion of information technology has dramatically altered the traditional timeframe in which we are used to thinking of structural change. We now see rapid improvements in the productivity with which relationships are managed, both in terms of quantitative and qualitative factors.

- *Quantitative* factors entail the ability to manage a greater number of relations by handling a higher number of parameters. The new generation of computerized reservation systems put in place by airlines for instance, allows handling up to 1,500 reservations simultaneously and can also be used as delivery channels for a variety of other services.

- *Qualitative* factors entail the ability to manage each of those relations with greater depth on the basis of real-time electronic interactions: Witness the customization of holiday packages or the fine-tuning of financial instruments to specific tax, currency, cash flow and risk preferences.

This capacity to manage more relations in greater depth and at higher levels of quality is reflected at various points of the economic process such as relationships between producers and suppliers, joint production systems, and distribution networks.

The strategies followed by a number of leading companies in making innovative and productive use of their distribution networks offer examples of such productivity gains. The networks developed by information service companies such as Reuters (previously an ordinary news service agency) are now used to support a much broader and more profitable gamut of activities ranging from computer services to trading. Similarly, the expertise developed by American Express in processing credit card slips finds new markets with travel agents and airlines in search of economies of scale in processing reservations. More generally, delivery systems that used to be perceived and managed as back-office functions are now seen as key strategic assets for global competitiveness and in some cases can become the raison d'être of a company. Creating value-added at the level of delivery networks, rather than simply viewing the network as a means to sell existing products efficiently, then becomes the key to success.

Such trends have major implications in the search for a conceptual framework adapted to economic analysis, as well as strategic planning. Whereas, for instance, economic theory routinely starts from the existence of a set of products with corresponding production and demand functions and then examines the relationships economic actors will set up (within firms and in markets) in order to allocate these products, the reality often appears to be quite the reverse: *relationships* constitute the independent economic variables, while products can serve to extract value from them. Indeed, at the heart of current changes in the economic system is the fact that it is increasingly difficult to describe products independently of actors who contribute in making them useful. As value becomes increasingly a function of utilization, the convergence of roles through coproduction progressively blurs the distinction between consumers and producers. Such trends have led some to identify a new breed of economic agent: the"prosumer."[2] Even this term, however, still conveys the old dual paradigm, and it would probably be more appropriate to speak of a spectrum of "contributors" to value creation, each performing a different function.

The emergence of a service economy has been looked for successively in the new characteristics of consumption, output, and social behavior. Yet a more fundamental change in paradigm is needed to go beyond the superficial and often misleading contrast between manufacturing and services. The observation of corporate strategies in services as well as manufacturing suggests taking as a starting point, in this challenging intellectual endeavor, the move from product-based to relationship-based processes of value creation.

CUSTOMER RELATIONS AS INFORMATION MANAGEMENT

Information—from market research to technology know-how—has always been a key input for production. Its growing importance can be seen through the rapid development of consulting services and technical publications. For many companies, however, information is even more. In the words of an insurance executive: "Information is our entire product. Data is a raw material. Those that are better at massaging and manipulating it will win out in the marketplace."[3]

Information management is a critical dimension of relationship management. In addition to allowing direct improvement in performance, the versatility of today's information technology and expertise facilitates transfer of experience, methodology, and innovations across sectors, as illustrated by countless examples, from the role of "quants" (hard sciences geniuses) in designing new financial products to the fact that the largest order ever for "engineering computer workstations" was placed by Citicorp.[4]

As access to, management, and control of information become priorities in the search for competitiveness, information systems are bound to attract substantial resources and attention. In the case of information-intensive activities like banking, financial services, insurance, and airline operation, while information systems typically represent more than 2 percent of total expenditures, this figure that could grow, according to a 1987 *Datamation* survey, to 5 percent by 1990 and 10 percent by 1995.[5]

But information management encompasses a much broader set of activities than the data processing operations for which these systems are typically used. On one hand, data can be thought of as a primary resource processed with increased productivity by computers; on the other hand, it is in the form of customized knowledge that information acquires value as a final product, in and of itself.

By the same token, the type and amount of information exchanged as part of value-creation go much beyond the price signals on which economists tend to focus their attention. The need for information is also qualitatively different from what would be assumed in economic models under the heading of "perfect information." What is at stake is not just the capacity of buyers and sellers to know what can be exchanged, with whom and at what price, but more fundamentally the ability to identify relationships that could become new loci for value creation. In this vein information exchange becomes the aim and not merely the means of interaction between economic actors.

MASS CUSTOMIZATION AND THE MOVE
FROM TRANSACTION TO INTEGRATION

The various aspects of relationship management converge in making possible a new type of productivity gains that we have labeled mass customization,[6] combining economies of scale from the point of view of producers and customized outputs as perceived by users. Obviously, it has always been the case that an object owned by someone could be thought as unique. But this was due to the proprietary relationship rather than to the intrinsic characteristics of the product. New possibilities of information transmission and processing now make it possible to adapt products to individual needs or preferences. In the case of services, the scope of adaptation is virtually limitless.

This type of value creation calls into question the clear-cut distinction between production and transaction, because relationships with customers are not necessarily confined to the realm of transactions but play an increasing role in product design and development. Rather than a set of bilateral relations, the economy must then be seen in terms of complex value-creation chains. The search for quality, defined by Japanese companies as "total customer satisfaction," as well as the increasing importance of liability considerations reinforce such trends, bringing the various contributors to wealth creation ever more tightly together across sectors as well as across borders.

The term *mass customization* is meant to remind us, however, that the challenge in designing these services is not only to increase their value through customization but also to keep the costs of managing each relationship as low as possible. Adaptation, that is, the process of "adding on" customized features to a core, mass-produced item, was the initial embodiment of mass customization. This skill distinguished profitable from nonprofitable data-base managers . . . or car manufacturers. While previous notions of "flexible production" tended to be based solely on this dimension, we want to stress here the second dimension, which we call generalization and which describes the reverse evolution from custom to mass. Ultimately, there exists a fine line between *generalizing* to a greater range of customer a service originally conceived and still sold as customized (such as an expert system) and transforming it into a standardized product as perceived by the customer: willingness to pay and relative value appropriation by each player depend on this line.

Beyond the focus on minimizing transaction costs (considered central in contemporary economic analysis), actors are engaged in optimizing the synergies between the various relationships in which they are involved. We refer to this process as integration. Mass customization must be seen against the background of this broader move from transaction to integration. Focusing on this qualitative change in the way economic actors relate to one another probably offers the most powerful insights into the emergence of what some have called, somewhat narrowly, a service economy and what we ourselves prefer to label a networked economy.

NETWORKS AS RELATION-MANAGEMENT FACTORIES

To illustrate vividly this shift in paradigm, one can analyze its implications in terms of the basic organizing concepts, or the ideal types, on which our intuitive understanding of the economy usually depends. While they may appear to model-makers and number-crunchers as lacking in sophistication, such basic concepts tend to have a fundamental influence on corporate strategies, national policies, and political visions.

Thinking about the industrial economy was often done, quite appropriately, with two central metaphors referring to the realm of production and to that of transaction. The first one was "the factory" (or even "the assembly line"). Although only a minority of the members of industrial societies actually worked in one, the "factory" provided a guiding metaphor for examining the value-creation process and the ways in which productivity gains could be achieved. For better or for worse, this paradigm was also a major inspiration of the political theories of the industrial age and of the broader visions of the world at the core of social interactions. The second, more abstract, metaphor that arose from industrial society had to do with representations of the market process through which transactions took place. The notion of a "marketplace," a place in which sellers physically interact with buyers as in the traditional village market or the medieval fair, neatly summarize these intuitions of what transactions are and how they can be organized. To be sure, theoreticians came up with more sophisticated descriptions of market processes, but even here central implicit references such as the famous "Walrass auctioner" illustrate the powerful role of these guiding metaphors.

A relationship-based process of value creation is no longer amenable to the insights that once went with the distinct metaphors of the factory and marketplace. It is becoming necessary to identify alternative organization models that could play the same role in facilitating our collective understanding of the integration processes at the heart of the new economy. In this spirit, throughout our work at PROME-THEE, we make the case that networks are bringing under one single notion and replacing the two fundamental ideal types associated with yesterday's industrial economy, namely the factory and the market.

The factory was the place and the social institution in which products were manufactured in the most efficient ways conceivable at the time. The marketplace was the locus of transactions. As production and transactions merge into more complex, information-intensive integration processes, networks—especially electronic networks—have become central to wealth creation. Understanding their dynamics can provide fundamental insights into a relationship-based economy.

Networks and the Networked Economy

The role of networks in today's corporate strategies is easily detected by even a cursory reader of the general business press and literature. To take just a few illustrations, a series of articles published in *Business Week* on deregulation used the word *network* several dozen times to describe the new competitive strategies followed by trucking, railroad, airline, and many other companies, in a deregulated environment.[7] *Networking*, in the more narrow meaning of interconnecting computers, is also covered in depth not just in the technical literature but in the general business press.

Actually, beyond technical connection, networks have come to play such a central role in the working of both the factory and the market that it is appropriate to speak of the emergence of a networked economy. A *networked economy* is one in which the dominant locus of value creation consists of interrelated and flexible architectures that allow for the aggregate management of individual relationships. *Network architectures* are characterized by the fact that the division of labor to implement mass customization processes cannot be defined a priori but stems from strategic interactions among participating actors. As networks expand, they will come to constitute markets for all actors as well as strategic tools for dominant actors. The spread of networks is witness to the fact that various categories of organizational arrangements previously seen as structural acquire the status of economic products, which can be created and exchanged on a relatively short time horizon.

Every network can be seen as a specific set of interactions among a number of actors who collaborate in extracting value from their relationships, while competing in shaping the network architecture. The involvement of those actors is based on nonexclusive functions rather than permanent structural positions. More specifically:

1. Networks must provide for a physical capacity to interact. They must therefore have access to proprietary or shared *infrastructure* through which interactions can be channelled. Such infrastructure need not be of a cables and connectors type since interpersonal links can develop without material mediators. Yet, the development of electronic infrastructures is a major factor behind the increasing effectiveness even of networks that used to be of an intangible nature.

2. Networks must also provide for ways in which to create mutual expectations and behavioral norms and to make possible orderly allocation of rights, pricing, and conflict resolution. We refer to this dimension as the *infostructure* of networks.

    In this light, a network can be defined *as a set of technical means—or infrastructures—and strategic norms—or infostructures—enabling actors with rights of access to set up and manage value-creating relationships among themselves.*

In short, we view the term *networked economy* as inclusive of what is usually thought of under the label *service economy.* Services constitute the economic dimension of networks, while infrastructures serve as delivery channels and infostructures as design rules for network-based services. Yet our approach puts greater emphasis on structural dynamics and attempts to go beyond debates related to the service label, which always ends up trying to situate services with regard to industrial production—whether services are viewed as "post-," "peri-," or "neo-" industrial.

There is an intimate link between networks and services. Seen as relationship-based wealth-creation activities, services can be delivered in different manners, including in the traditional interpersonal fashion associated for instance with hair-cutting or health care. But productivity gains in services provision can most efficiently be secured in the framework of networks. On one hand, networks are the mass-delivery and mass-processing channels central to productivity gains based on minimizing average costs. On the other hand, networks embody the means for *flexible product adaptation* central to maximizing the average utilization value for users. Together, those two characteristics point to networks as the optimal tools for efficient "aggregate management of individual relationships" at the heart of the networked economy.

CONNECTION MANAGEMENT AND CORPORATE NETWORKING

In a networked economy actors endeavor to shape network architectures to their advantage. They seek to enhance productivity gains generated through the network by focusing their efforts and those of all network participants on connection management. Altogether technical, strategic, and normative, *connection management* seeks to ensure the best fit possible among the infrastructures and infostructures of networks and the actors they are meant to serve. We will illustrate this vision by exploring the dynamic forces behind the expansion of four types of networks, identified as intracorporate, transcorporate, intercorporate, and metacorporate.

Intracorporate Networks

The main objective of intracorporate networks is to better coordinate day-to-day activities by enabling end users within the same company to share information and processing capacities. Electronic networks allow real-time transmission, processing, and distribution of information related to customers (technical connection). Meanwhile, remote interaction between plants makes it possible to arbitrate among different constraints (models and delays for example) and to manage global networks of plants as integrated production facilities (strategic connection).[8]

Available technology and prevailing management styles are the driving forces shaping the architecture of such networks. In this view, specialized networks that had been developed around specific needs (such as inventory management or production) are gradually being interconnected to create a global intracorporate network—both in terms of activity and location. Pioneered by Citicorp, the reorganization of banks' back offices around electronic networks is a classic example. So is Nissan's satellite-based network allowing for direct integration between regional technical centers and production facilities. A new frontier is that of real-time global corporate experience-sharing as provided by *Decnet* for Digital.

Transcorporate Networks

A second type of corporate network bringing productivity gains into the realm of relationship management takes the form of electronic links between a company and its closest suppliers, customers, and partners (technical connection). Typically it involves linking specific actors or parts of companies who gain by sharing a specified type of information. The search for better coordination through private networking now extends to customer/provider relationships that were previously conducted in the anonymous marketplace through general purpose networks (the telephone, telex, mail). In addition to reducing or eliminating paper transactions, extensive use of electronic networks makes possible coordination with customers and suppliers through the use of increasingly detailed and customized data flows. Better adaptation of the product to demand fluctuations, higher quality, and reductions in inventories and delays are typical objectives (strategic connection). Financial functions—from automated payments to customers' incentives programs—can also be incorporated.

A major cause as well as a major consequence of transcorporate networking is the process of progressive "deepening" of the interaction between supply and demand. Buyers and sellers, providers and users are all participating in the creation of value and are doing so in increasingly flexible fashions. The deepening of the relationship between buyers and sellers means that their interactions go much beyond exchange of products for payment to include 1) interactions *before* the production stage to identify products, either existing or to be developed, that would generate additional value, 2) interactions *during* the production stage to fine tune the product to the needs and possibilities of the customer and producer, and 3) interactions *after* the production stage to facilitate use (training, joint operation), to maintain and service the product, and to identify opportunities for a new round of product development and sales. While the existence of each of these levels of interaction is not an intrinsically new phenomenon, they are increasingly managed through the same technology within the same networks transcending corporate boundaries. Hence, the multiplication of transcorporate networks testifies to the fact that the emphasis of connection management moves from the technical to the strategic as it serves to integrate the efforts of actors who are not part of the same organizational and hierarchical structure.

A central example is that of electronic data interchange (EDI) systems. Their selling points center on cost savings and the speed of doing business, but their long-term, deeper impact will probably have to do with the qualitative change in supplier/producer/customer relationship, which they are gradually reshaping. General Motors in 1984 gave its suppliers until 1987 to adapt to EDI or lose its orders. Transcorporate networking can extend to a whole industry. In Europe for instance, automobile manufacturers and their suppliers are taking part in a major EDI initiative, called ODETTE (Organization for Data Exchange through Tele-Transmission in Europe), while 12 of the biggest chemical companies have set up a working party to create a pan-European EDI system.[9]

Finally, electronic information networks, such as Reuters, can be used to create networked markets in which not just information but property rights over assets is traded. By adding trade initiation and settlement functions, trans-corporate networks can become transaction networks. In such cases, the normative dimension of connection management becomes prominent: only networks who are able to send out clear and trustworthy signals about their operating norms can actually be successful in attracting participants into their networks (self-regulated stock exchanges are good examples).

Intercorporate Networks

Corporations tend to be overwhelmed with inadequate, obsolete, or fragmented data, while at the same time they search for relevant and up-to-date information on technology, customers, or markets.

Intercorporate networks developed on the basis of corporate alliances of all sorts, are a means of addressing these higher-order information needs, whereby strategic connection management becomes a central concern. The current wave of corporate alliances testifies to the fact that straightforward mergers are not the most efficient way to establish strategic convergence in a highly volatile and risky environment. Sharing strategic information in cross-licensing deals and R&D consortia, cooperating toward well-defined objectives within joint ventures, creating synergies among products within cross-distribution agreement, often represent the best—even if often temporary—avenues for flexible strategic repositioning.

At the international level, the creation of such intercorporate networks is too often perceived, notably by American companies, as a second best strategy that may have had to be substituted, for political reasons, for direct exports or the creation of a fully owned subsidiary. In many instances, however, international corporate agreements represent an effort by corporations to adapt to the blurring, rather than to the reinforcement, of national and sectoral borders. The erosion of sectoral and geographic borders has major implications for which traditional organizational and trade specialization models may often not offer the most efficient answer. Intercorporate networks help corporations meet with greater timeliness and efficiency than those traditional patterns the far more complex and demanding needs of sharing technological know-how, of customizing products to local demand, and of working toward compatibility of products.

Metacorporate Networks

A fourth type of network aims to affect the environment in which a group of firms operate. Lobbying associations are a traditional example. But such metacorporate networks, are now multiplying as a response to the need to set and implement common information technology standards. The Corporation for Open Systems (COS) is a good case in point. This nonprofit American consortium was designed to deal with conformity testing of the Open Systems Interconnection (OSI) standards put forward by a number of non-IBM information systems providers and users. In Europe, the ESPRIT (European Strategic Program on R&D Information in Technology) program, which has led to the setting of instruments to exchange information among

European companies and of rules of access to technological know-how,[10] is another example of the metacorporate network.

NETWORKS AND THE 'MARKET IN' CORPORATION

The four types of networks identified above are being set up to respond not only to specific but also to converging needs. Intra- and transcorporate networks can be seen as fulfilling "coordination" functions and as focusing mainly on a better management of data flows; connection is technical before it is strategic or normative. Actors involved have functionally complementary roles. As the networks expand, obvious synergies develop between the two types of networks while "outsiders" hook up with internal networks and while actors within corporations develop more intensive and continuous links with coproducers (so-called suppliers or customers) than with their own hierarchical structure.

Inter- and metacorporate networks, on the other hand, are initially set up to link actors with strategically complementary roles. They organize knowledge flows rather than data flows. They also have a tendency to converge as intercorporate networks start to serve as instruments to influence norms or rules of the game and as metacorporate networks working toward common norms serve to explore the corresponding markets. Figure 1-1 illustrates this evolving emphasis in terms of connection management. Ultimately, what we should increasingly observe is a convergence *between*, not only *within*, those two pairs: strategy-led networks will increasingly consolidate their infrastructure and standardize their information flows. Networks initially set up to optimize data management and promote cost efficiency turn out to be the basis for strategic alliances. (Chapter 3, Computer Reservation Systems, is a case in point.)

Capitalizing on the new networks to gain access to relevant technology and information is a key dimension of present corporate strategy. This strategic change is a fundamental aspect of the so-called service economy and can be summarized by the Japanese goal of moving from "product out" to "market in" strategies.

A "market in" approach is one in which products are not simply developed and, later, sold, but one in which the production system and the marketplace become one and the same. What this means

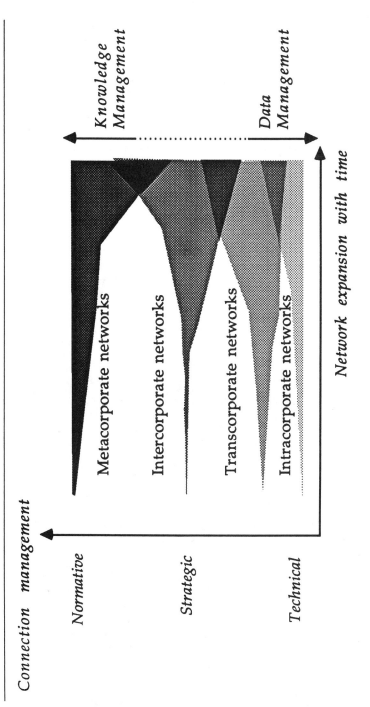

Figure 1-1. Network Expansion: The Evolving Emphasis of Connection Management.

in practice is that relations with suppliers and customers are a pervasive feature of the production process. In this sense, networks are not only somewhere on a spectrum between "markets" and "hierarchies," whereby the basic organizing principle would be to minimize individual connection (transaction) costs.[11] As the locus of mass-customization processes and "market in" strategies, they obey a different logic: integration, rather than production followed by transaction, is the process at the core of value creation.

NOTES

1. Albert Bressand, "International Division of Labor in the Field of Services: The Need for a New Paradigm," report to the European Commission, PROMETHEE Report no. 2, Paris, October 1986. Bundling and Unbundling are also addressed in J. N. Bhagwati, "Splintering and Disembodiment of Services and Developing Nations," *World Economy*, June 1984, pp. 133-44.

2. P. Eiglier and E. Langeard, "Eléments pour une théorie des services. Application à l'entreprise," *Economie et Société*, Paris (1979).

3. J. Sitkin, vice president for Corporate Administration, Aetna Life and Casualty, quoted in *Datamation*, November 15, 1987.

4. According to Dataquest Inc., 14 percent of the "engineering workstations" to be sold in the world in 1987 were expected to find their way to Wall Street's trading rooms.

5. Sitkin, quoted in *Datamation.*

6. For a more detailed analysis of mass-customization, see Albert Bressand and Kalypso Nicolaïdis, "Les services au coeur de l'économie relationnelle," *Revue d'Economie Industrielle*, numéro spécial sur "Le dynamisme des services aux entreprises," no. 43 (1988).

7. "Deregulation: Is It Working?" *Business Week*, March 1988, pp. 21-24.

8. Thomas G. Gunn, *Manufacturing for Competitive Advantage: Becoming a World Class Manufacturer* (Cambridge, Mass.: Ballinger, 1987).

9. Giorgio Spriano, "Odette: Normes télématiques dans l'industrie automobile européenne," PROMETHEE Working Paper no. 9, Paris, March 1986. See also EDI, "Putting the Muscle in Commerce and Industry," *Datamation* (March 1988): 56-64.

10. Giorgio Spriano, "The ESPRIT Program: The Management of R&D in European Information," PROMETHEE Working Paper no. 8, Paris, March 1986.

11. We refer here to Oliver Williamson's seminal work, *Markets and Hierarchies: Analysis and Antitrust Implications* (The Free Press: London, 1975).

2 SERVICES AND THOUGHTWARE
New Dimensions in Service Business Development

Leif Edvinsson
John Richardson

A NEW MENTAL DAWN

A new realization is dawning that our economic thoughts may not reflect the very different behavior of markets.[1] A new power structure is emerging with implications for academicians, businesspeople, and politicians.

Eurostat, the statistical office of the European Community, cannot present figures for the EC's external trade in services in more detail than 13 subcategories, a level of detail that only became available for the first time in 1984. The NIMEXE, the external trade classification of the Community, contains 9,000 different items. Exports of services in 1984 totaled 112 billion ECU (356 billion for goods), and the aggregated volume of each service category was almost 9 billion ECU as compared to 39 million ECU for goods. A detailed map for goods but a rough map for services!

The imbalance evident in the availability of statistics is mirrored in the structure of administrations. Again the EC provides an example. Its executive commission has long had a whole directorate-general concerned with "industrial affairs," including three administrative units dealing with steel. But it was not until early in 1987 that a small, new unit was created within that directorate-general to develop a policy for services in general.

THE CHANGING BUSINESS ENVIRONMENT

The driving force of change is identified to be the diffusion of information technologies in the economy. Certain easily identified, separate functions in companies have now begun to pervade the whole business world. It is revolutionizing market structures, changing the way inputs are brought together in production, and rearranging the way companies relate to their customers and their suppliers.

This technology-driven change has resulted in the development of new skills. These skills are associated with information-related functions such as computer-aided design or manufacturing (CAD/CAM), or they deal with the increasing complexity of the production system, as in ergonomics, or they are loaded into products as in the safety design in a Volvo car. This has led to rapid growth of separate and often external companies providing software services, communications services, distribution services, consulting services, and the like, to companies that used to provide them in-house.

Such trends are evident with respect in particular to employment and establishment statistics. In France UNEDIC statistics demonstrate that from 1976 to 1983 the proportion of salaried employees working in large companies employing more than 500 people fell from 20.6 to 16.5 percent. At the same time the proportion employed in small companies with fewer than 50 employees rose from 43.1 to 49.1 percent.[2] In the United States approximately 600,000 new companies are started every year, a large proportion within the services sector.

This growth of external service functions has led some to suggest that "hollow companies" emerge, which concentrate on their main operation and buy in specialized services. One example of a hollow company is the largest furniture company in the world, IKEA, which concentrates on research and development, functional design and distribution systems with no factory outlets of its own but approximately 1 million square meters show space at almost eighty retail outlets in nineteen countries.

On the other hand, many companies have taken the opposite road, developing internal information-related capabilities, and have grown through the exploitation of internal economies of scale.

Another phenomenon is the development of the services functions needed to handle the increasing technical complexity of the production system. It is a highly specialized job coping with complexity, as described by Quinn and Gagnon:

Within companies, the effects of complexity reinforce economies of both scope and scale. Companies can deliver better and more varied services with no significant cost penalties. They can simultaneously achieve a high degree of segmentation in their activities and lower their costs. Computerized reservation systems allow airlines to analyze their costs and their customers' buying behavior in such detail that they can optimize margins on each type of demand and meet each competitor's response. The resulting crazy quilt of prices leads customers to concentrate more on services provided, which offers the major carriers further opportunities to segment with services like specialized meals, wheelchairs, committed seat assignments, luggage verification, and even counseling for nervous passengers.[3]

The interlinking of different services to provide a consumer with a complex package, or "compack," has been explored in detail by Bressand.[4] Increasing complexity is thus not only a characteristic of production technologies but also of the package offered to the consumer and thereby of the relationship between producer and consumer, and of consumer demand itself.

This process does not represent just a shift from manufacturing to services functions in the economy but a reordering of the input-output relations in economies, where "soft" functions are increasingly provided by separate companies. It is for this reason that policymakers with an understanding of the phenomenon call for governments not to institute a "services policy" but rather an integrated structural business environment policy and climate that would emphasize neglected service functions.[5]

STRATEGIC DETERMINANTS OF SERVICE VALUE-ADDING

Increasingly, successful companies focus on what can be called *service value-adding* and do so around the three interlinked dimensions shown in Figure 2–1, information networks, customer relationships, and "thoughtware."

Efficient production is increasingly dependent on the skillful use of information networks. The increased complexity of consumer products and their increasing differentiation requires a new emphasis on the interface between producer and user. Customer focus and

Figure 2-1. Service Value-Adding.

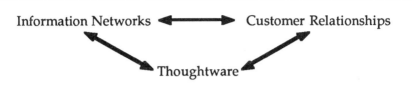

relationships have again become, as in preindustrial times, a key determinant of success. Third, the handling of this new complexity of production and relationships is dependent on the company's ability to develop its "thoughtware"—the knowledge content in its business, which needs constant maintenance and improvement.

Information networks increasingly pervade the relations between companies, their suppliers and customers, and the external infrastructure upon which they rely. The links between local, national, and international networks are multiplying fast. The futuristic idea of an integrated global network of networks, as described by Bressand and Distler,[6] begins to look less like a vision and more like a forecast. The crucial determinant of profitability for many companies has now become the ability to use these networks to maximize the value added by their "soft" assets, or thoughtware[7] and create a delivery with a recognizably higher application and use value for the consumer, a process referred to as "smartening the delivery."

One example of such a creative exploitation of networks is given by Japan's biggest trucking company, Yamato Transport.[8] Modern information technology was introduced into the company in the late 1960s to handle traditional functions such as accounting, finance, and personnel administration. When on-line data processing became available, internal networks could at last handle the tracking of goods in transit. The next development, in the early 1980s was the ability to offer a new, "smart" door-to-door delivery service. This, however, required a nationwide delivery network, which was only possible by integrating the company's subsidiaries and affiliates into the system, which thereby had to be registered with the Ministry of Posts and Telecommunications as a "small business value-added network." Yamato was the first Japanese company to set up such a system (in December 1982).

In this way a new intangible competitive intercompany asset was created. The latest development is to use this soft asset to generate more value-added through the exploitation of new economies of scope. Japanese truckers are beginning to provide other complementary services, such as cargo storage, pricing of merchandise, quality control, packaging, inventory control and the writing of shipping instructions. All are based on the exploitation of their information networks. Some truckers have now gone into mail order retailing with the objective of creating even more demand for their door-to-door delivery services. The combination of new information technology and of creative response to it by dynamic companies has thus led both to the restructuring of an old service industry and to the creation of a new one whose motto might be "from truck transportation to computerized mail order retailing."

The customer relationship itself is the asset upon which economies of scope can be based. Confronted with a new product, whether it be a new financial service such as swaps, a computerized hotel reservation service, a mail order opportunity, a new form of consultancy, or a software system, consumers may simply be unable to judge its usefulness or value. Hence, a company that has established a relationship based on trust with its customers possesses a priceless asset and can build on this asset by offering new packages to the same customers.

Finally the thoughtware dimension is reinforced by information technology. The modern company is replacing muscle power by "thought power." Employees are working more and more with processing information in knowledge-intensive functions, such as maintenance of a digitalized welding robot, supervision of CAD/CAM lines, or development of customizing service concepts.[9]

THE NEW INFRASTRUCTURE: INFORMATION NETWORKS

Twenty years ago a young Venetian shop assistant and his sister, a garment factory worker, set up their own business. By 1986 Benetton clothes were being sold through a network of 4,000 shops in 62 countries with a turnover of about $1,000 billion, 1,500 employees of Benetton's own and 25,000 within the external network.[10] The forecasted turnover for 1988 is $1,300 billion.

The key to this success story is the information system and information logistics. Not only does the company's computer system handle CAD, automatic production, and merchandising, and the traditional functions. It also allows a daily update on sales, a quick identification of trends in consumer taste, rapid replenishment of the appropriate stocks, and delivery around the world within a matter of weeks. Mainly because its ability to react quickly to changing consumer trends, Benetton is allowed to incorporate or load an extra service into its product. In reality, it is the customer's fresh feeling of "being in the fashion" that differentiates its products and allows their sale at a premium. The key to this ability is the maintenance of close contact with the consumer's tastes through the advanced information system. A daily market intelligence from 4,000 outlets with a computerized interface from 57 countries, allows quick reaction. At the headquarters 85 information specialists twirl the business kaleidoscope every day. The company is thus able to develop new seasonal packages within 25–30 days. Instead of committing itself to a production schedule for a whole summer or winter season, it can offer its outlets three or four customer-oriented packages each season, closely following consumer trends. In 1987 they produced 52 million Benetton items.

Recently Intelsat gave approval for a new high-speed telecommunications facility on the north coast of Jamaica.[11] The reasoning behind this investment is that Caribbean countries have the potential for a major expansion of their data processing industries (data input, preparation of manuscripts, airline and hotel ticket processing), based on low labor costs, proximity to the United States and reduced costs for transmission by satellite. Such "teleports" are now on the drawing board in many countries as a major new source of export earnings. Indeed the most thoroughgoing attempt to exploit such opportunities is being made by Singapore, the teleport of Asia. In December 1986, its national information technology (IT) plan was officially launched.[12] It embraces the development of IT manpower skills, promotion of IT applications, the coordination of research, but also "the promotion of an IT culture," appearing as nothing less than an attempt to remodel Singapore's entrepreneurial culture to exploit the commercial possibilities offered by international information networks.

SWIFT (Security for Worldwide Interbank Financial Telecommunication) provides standardized clearing services for over 2,000 banks in sixty countries. The Scandinavian Info Link is a network set up by Volvo, Ericsson, SAS, and Verimation to handle data communication among forty or so major Scandinavian companies. Transpotel, set up by four companies from the Netherlands, Germany, United Kingdom, and Switzerland provides an information service to the whole of the freight transport world. All these networks have one thing in common: they provide on a private, usually cooperative basis an essential infrastructure for the operation of other companies. The traditional cleavage between public provision of infrastructure and private use of infrastructure no longer holds. Territories as well as business sectors blur into new competitive infrastructures, and infrastructures that are costly to build need creative financial approaches, such as cooperative alliances.

An understanding of the phenomenon requires rejection of traditional concepts and willingness to see the network as the essential structural characteristic of the system. Such a change in focus has important public policy implications. As pointed out by PROMETHEE researchers, "antitrust and competition laws will therefore have to be reassessed in the light of the changing nature of scarcity and monopoly in a world of networks rather than territories."[13] In a world of international networks, a service company can operate worldwide as a single, decentralized, complex operational entity with comparative advantage no longer tied to a specific country. A striking example is that of Honda Motor Company which recently switched from a value-added network (VAN) into a local area network (LAN) on an international scale, with a triangular configuration. Thus, any Honda terminal in Japan is able to communicate with a Honda terminal in Europe via the Tokyo and Belgium "gateways." The predicted annual increase in data transfer of 12–13 percent was greatly underestimated, actual growth registering 830 percent over a two-year period. The total investment of 1 billion yen was soon recovered.[14]

Another already classic example of networks is Citicorp. The company's aim is to provide a worldwide package of financial services to its customers, many of whom themselves have major international operations. Some of these services, such as worldwide cash management, are only possible thanks to Citicorp's network of leased lines, linking IBM mainframes in New York and Lewisham in London—through over 60 minicomputers in regional offices around the world—to personal computers on the desks of the corporate treasurers of all the bank's customers. It must be noted here that the value-added accrues and the employment is generated wherever Citicorp has establishments.[15]

BUILDING ON CUSTOMER RELATIONSHIPS

The second strategic dimension characterizing profitable companies in the new soft economy is consumer relationships. This asset is seldom registered in national or company accounting but is a strong driving force for service business development. Increasingly, successful long-term relationships in the fields of advertising, accountancy, management consultancy, and other business services depend on the creative interaction between suppliers and customers raising the functional quality, use-value, of an increasingly complex delivery.

The mass holiday market in Europe is dominated by the provision of airline packages using "identikit" hotels with relatively homogeneous leisure packages. Competition concentrates on price, and margins are correspondingly slim. How is it then that the Club Méditerranée can apparently offer a similar product at a premium price that still leaves enough profit to make it one of the fastest growing leisure industry companies?

Club Med's founder and chief executive, Gilbert Trigano, stresses the customer orientation of his staff, a traditional recipe for success in the hotel business. But this orientation also manifests itself in the delivery. What "Le Club" has succeeded in doing is to tailor make a package whose use-value to its customers bears little relation to the operational costs, with increasingly diversified services. The introduction of computer-learning courses in its holiday centers was one such diversification that has been so successful that Club Méditerranée is now the biggest provider of such education in France. Diversification was based on more intensive use of an existing asset: the customer relationship.

A similar philosophy lies behind the development of differentiated services for loyal customers by airlines, hotel chains, and other service providers. The most obvious example of this phenomenon is the expansion of plastic card-based systems such as Diners Club and American Express. But the interactive nature of these customer relationships is less marked than those exhibited by packages of travel services now being offered by airlines such as SAS. In this sense American Express Travel Service, as a comprehensive package for the traveler, is a more illustrative example of customer focus than the American Express credit card as a payment system.

One of the most important implications of the focusing on pleasing customers is that diversification is based not so much on which new offering fits best into the operational structure of a company but on which package customers would most like to add to those they already buy from the producer. Sometimes this simply means that a new facet is added to an already existing multifaceted package (compack), which can thus be sold at an even higher price, as in the above example of software training by Club Méditerranée. The alternative is that it is sold separately, using existing consumer relationships, and existing networks, to achieve lower marginal costs.

THOUGHTWARE: THE NEW MANAGEMENT CHALLENGE

Industrial management has traditionally focused on physical activities such as technical research, production, or distribution—that is, on the manipulation of hardware and activities. The new management focus needs to be on "soft" entities, revealing a new approach, which the Japanese call "softnomics." Since the key element in a world of knowledge-intensive companies is in fact human thought, it is helpful to think of the vital aspects in service-linked business as "thoughtware."

This new concept of thoughtware symbolizes the new management trend, which concentrates on the indirect functions of the company, the invisible, immaterial assets and the information flows, the social engineering of relationships and networking, and the commercial application of soft assets to maximize value. Thought processing will be the core of service input and output. The management challenge for the 1990s lies in the identification of these intangible assets, the analysis of the soft-business environment, the development of a new value business map, and the search for new management approaches to unbundle thoughtware assets.

A new management culture is evolving, one personified by such companies as Apple, Club Méditerrannée, or Benetton. The flavor of this vision can perhaps be illustrated by the metaphysics often used to describe products from such companies.[16] It might also be possible to elaborate on a new management mix based on the "soul" of Apple, the "aura" of the compacks produced by Yves St. Laurent, the "personality" of Club Med, the "charisma" of Ferrari, the "warmth" of Disney. Human values are suddenly once again an important element of competitiveness.

This management approach requires a company to ask itself strategic questions, focused on soft dimensions: Why do our customers stay with us? Where does our value-adding occur, and how do we measure it? Can we upgrade the thoughtware content of our offerings (staff, services, and compacks)? Do we take full advantage of our soft competitive assets? How can our information technology literacy be improved? Do our management approaches create the right climate for the exploitation of thoughtware?

THOUGHTWARE DIMENSIONS

Thoughtware incorporates three major dimensions: professional skill to solve the customer's problem, organizational skill to handle the complexities of networking, and commercial skill to package the final solution.

The concept of thoughtware is based on the notion that the modern company has to be organized to perceive and receive information and transform it systematically into tradeable compacks that embrace more than the obvious product. Thoughtware can be looked at as the ultimate item in a complex evolutionary process that transforms raw data into information, extracts knowledge from it, applies this knowledge on the basis of experience, and incorporates it as an integral element of a compack. In providing the glue for compacks, thoughtware reveals itself as a major competitive tool.

SKF, the world's leading manufacturer of ball and roller bearings, is a good example of a company exploiting this tool. It has launched a thoughtware complement to the sales force, called CADalog. It has made its application know-how of bearing technology, based on 75 years of experience, available on PCs through information technology as CAD program packages. SKF's CADalog creates efficient communication between SKF and designers, is used as a graphic aid by the engineers, and provides on-line access to information on SKF delivery readiness and the company's internal standards and priorities. SKF will be among the first companies in the world to make such a product catalogue easily accessible to its customers—in the customers' computers—allowing for international on-line communication between suppliers, design engineers, and purchasers.

MAPPING OF THOUGHTWARE FLOWS

In the search for a methodology to grasp the soft intangible flows within a company's operations and to identify their key determinants, we should distinguish between three major categories: input services associated with thoughtware such as market intelligence and R&D; services in the core process such as CAM and LAN; and interface services such as distribution, consumer advice, and applications development. (See Figure 2-2.[17])

Usually one finds that the traditional supervisory system in a firm focuses only on the core process. Critical management tools such as quality control and in-house training have very much been oriented to hardware dimensions and neglected the soft components of the

Figure 2-2. Thoughtware Flows.

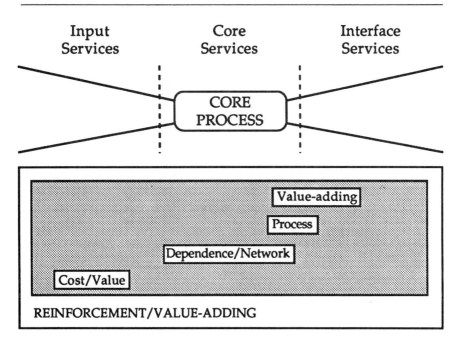

overall process. In spite of interest in these soft flows (which represent 50 to 75 percent of the cost structure in a country like Sweden), cost-centered (rationalizing costs) approaches prevail, rather than the profit-centered (maximizing value) approach of thoughtware.

Input services and interface services contribute on average, respectively, 40 and 50 percent of the value-added of companies. This is because the value of services and thoughtware does not originate at the production center but rather at the application center. The mapping of soft flows must also take into account the increased externalization of service operations through the various networks in which a company participates. Think of the value-adding taking place at the 125,000 terminals distributed around the world in the Reuter system network.

It thereby becomes essential that the service company construct an "infogram" to map the business aspects of the information landscape in which it operates, to identify not just flows but also interconnections and interdependencies. The mapping process, as an instrument for value accounting rather than just efficiency and cost accounting is far from the traditional linear thinking based on the idea of a physical production process being carried out within a factory. Such infograms have already led some companies to adopt a new organizational terminology. Rank Xerox in the United Kingdom distinguishes actively between core workers, who perform primarily internal functions, and networkers, who work mainly at the interface with the outside business environment.

NETWORK MANAGEMENT AS
SOCIAL ENGINEERING

Having identified its thoughtware assets and mapped their flows, a company needs to create the environment in which the value it adds can be maximized. Much of this will depend on the evolution of long-term customer relationships.[18] Therefore it is essential to develop a cycle for application networking and learning over a two- or three-year period. Major steps in this process are as depicted in Figure 2–3.

The management of this type of interaction and networking can be thought of as a kind of social engineering, in which customer partiticipation becomes an essential tool. Illustrating this participation are the so-called user clubs offered by certain software suppliers. Other illustrations are social engineering activities such as VIP pro-

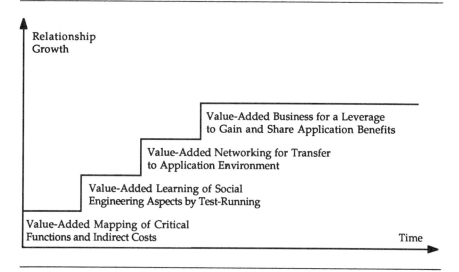

Figure 2-3. Steps for Maximizing Value-Added.

Relationship
Growth

Value-Added Business for a Leverage
to Gain and Share Application Benefits

Value-Added Networking for Transfer
to Application Environment

Value-Added Learning of Social
Engineering Aspects by Test-Running

Value-Added Mapping of Critical
Functions and Indirect Costs

Time

grams, networking through plastic cards, or alliances such as business schools' alumni clubs or the Coalition of Service Industries.

To develop such interaction on a systematic basis, "service laboratories" can be created as initiated to date by TRW, AT&T, Holiday Inn, the Stockholm School of Economics, and Volvo. TRW considers the essential elements of a service laboratory to be a multidisciplinary team, a process that is creative rather than analytical or reductionist, the simulation of user applications in order to test prototypes and concepts, and a system for managing the user interface.

Volvo has recently developed a so-called computer-aided everything (CAE) application center, which is a kind of thoughtware and information laboratory. A basic concept is that information technology must be oriented toward the user—in other words, information ergonomics. A comprehensive meeting place for information-technology-related experiences, CAE was designed to marry technology and human expertise and has been given the appearance of a space center. Intended to be a hotbed of ideas for the future, the center is run in collaboration with IBM, Digital Equipment, Hewlett-Packard, and the Swedish Telecommunications Authority. It is a "metacorporate network" (see Chapter 1) devoted to the search for new communication systems between the corporation and the outside world.

THOUGHTWARE ACCOUNTING

The human skills that are a main component of thoughtware are covert assets, with a clear acquisition value (cost) but an unclear application value. They are not reflected in traditional accounting techniques, which tend to measure visible capital, the hard assets of a company. These invisible assets are often revealed for the first time in the premium paid for "goodwill," when the company is taken over. Except on such an occasion no systematic attempt is made to use accounting techniques to maximize the return on soft assets.

Studies on this subject demonstrate the difficulties of making an assessment of thoughtware assets and the service capital by using a company's annual report.[19] A new form of accounting is needed to show in addition to financial capital, customer capital, organizational or skill capital, and image capital. In practice it may be difficult to perform such accounting for lack of the necessary data and practice, but the very attempt to do so is useful in raising a company's awareness of its thoughtware assets.

The first step is to move away from accounting concepts centered on the basic production unit. "Thoughtware accounting" must be more horizontal, using ratios such as accumulated human skill assets (which may exceed $100,000 for a professional), depreciation ratios for thoughtware, customer benefits per contact, return on human skills, annual investment in skills, annual maintenance of thoughtware, annual investment in customer relationships, technological enhancement of skills (usually through the application of information technologies), and so forth. Such concepts lead to the structuring of new thoughtware accounting ratios into four major categories:

1. Input index—number of training days per employee or number of Ph.Ds in the work force.
2. Output index—number of different services delivered or thoughtware packaged or indirect activities.
3. Relations index—number of different relationships or contacts or networks.
4. Applications index—number of created customer benefits or user values.

These aspects usually account for more than 50 percent of the outlays of the modern company, but are seldom found in annual

Figure 2-4. Value Triangle for Services and Thoughtware.

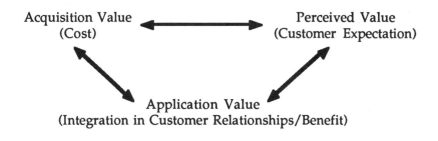

Acquisition Value
(Cost)

Perceived Value
(Customer Expectation)

Application Value
(Integration in Customer Relationships/Benefit)

business statements. The commercial challenge is to build values out of these soft but costly assets. The key to successful thoughtware accounting and pricing is probably the ability to distinguish the different types of value involved (see Figure 2-4).

The acquisition value is based on the cost of the delivered service. It is usually subject to negotiations and often the only dimension in a commercial service contract. The perceived value is covert for the purchaser, but of strategic importance. This value is based on the expectations of the buyer and subject to influences by more or less "golden" packaging (for example, Ambassador Class versus Economy Class). Finally, from a commercial viewpoint, it is essential to relate the price of a service to the application value revealed at the moment of use. Traditional pricing and accounting procedures therefore need to be broadened to integrate the perception and application dimensions.

Franchising companies represent an example of how the soft assets of goodwill, image, systematic skills (in terms of relationship management techniques spelled out in detail in the franchising contract) are turned into value-added through an expanding network of relationships with the franchiser.

CONCLUDING REMARKS

The Mental Management Function

The concept of thoughtware, like the word itself, is relatively new. Trying to define it and illustrate how it can be applied in a practical business environment is like groping toward a distant goal through thick fog. Recent experience suggests that attempts to grapple with its implications can lead to major increases in profitability.[20] And as more experience is gained, the fog will gradually clear, allowing a clearer understanding of the essential value elements of the emerging soft economy.

NOTES

1. For a discussion of this subject in the field of international trade theory, see J.B. Richardson, "A Sub-Sectoral Approach to Services' Trade Theory," in *The Emerging Service Economy*, edited by Orio Giarini (Oxford: Pergamon Press, 1987), pp. 54–82.
2. *Le Monde*, October 16, 1984.
3. J.B. Quinn and C.E. Gagnon, "Will Services Follow Manufacturing into Decline?" *Harvard Business Review* (November–December 1986): 95–103.
4. Program of the European Commission, Albert Bressand, ed., "Europe in the New International Division of Labor in the Field of Services," PROMETHEE Report Prepared for FAST (Forecasting and Assessment in the Field of Science and Technology), 1986.
5. R. Shelp and G. Hart, "Understanding a New Economy," *Wall Street Journal*, December 23, 1986.
6. Albert Bressand and Catherine Distler, "Le Prochain Monde," *Le Seuil*, 1985.
7. Leif Edvinsson, "Services and Thoughtware Go International," *Services Marketing in a Changing Environment*, American Marketing Association Services Conference Proceedings, 1985.
8. Monthly Economic Review of the Long-Term Credit Bank of Japan, no. 84, February 1986.
9. One illustration of the thoughtware dimension is the diagnosing of malfunctions on a modern teleswitch board by means of an expert system (artificial intelligence).
10. *Financial Times*, May 24, 1986.
11. *Financial Times*, May 19, 1987.
12. *Singapore Economic Bulletin*, January 1987.
13. "Global Networks," *Project PROMETHEE Perspectives*, no. 2 (April (1987), Paris.
14. *Tokyo Business Today*, May 1987.
15. Recruit Company, which was founded in 1960 in Tokyo to provide employment information to graduating college students and which went on to provide general buyers information, gave birth to Recruit's Remote

Computing Service (RCS) in 1984, another successful example of world-wide use of VANs. RCS is a case to follow in the near future.

16. Lars Peder Hedberg, "Marketing Metaphysical Cars," *Scanorama, SAS Magazine* (October 1987): 124–31.
17. Leif Edvinsson, "The New Business Function," *The Services Industries Journal* (Spring 1987).
18. Leif Edvinsson, "The Export Sales Life Cycle: International Relationship Marketing of Services," from Proceedings of the Nordic Workshop of Marketing of Services, Helsinki, Finland, 1983. Published in E. Gronroc and E. Eummesson, *Service Marketing: The Nordic School Perspectives* (University of Stockholm: Stockholm, 1985).
19. See Consultus Intenational AB et al., "Service Systems in Industries," Stockholm, 1986.
20. Leif Edvinsson, "A New Approach to Value-Added in Service Industries," paper presented at The Conference Board Strategic Planning Conference, New York, 1986.

3 COMPUTER RESERVATION SYSTEMS
Networks Shaping Markets

Albert Bressand

The market is a network. In the field of air transportation, this motto is finding a concrete expression in the emergence of computerized networks not just as a management tool but as the locus of competition in which airlines as well as service providers have to position themselves. Yesterday's marketplace has become a networked market.

INFORMATION MOVING PEOPLE

Providing air transportation services involves networks and networking in more than one way. The first network at stake is obviously the route system of each individual airline. Yet the value of individual airlines operations critically depends on the broader transportation network of which it is part and notably on efficient and timely connections with other airlines. The trend toward "hub and spokes" operations in the postderegulation era in the United States illustrates the impact of overall network architecture on the profitability of individual routes. The conditions under which an airline can plug into the broader network of airline networks has emerged as a commanding aspect of its competitive position.

But there are other networks on which an airline's operation has come to depend. Intercorporate network, to use the terminology introduced in the first chapter of this book, include not only "hub

51

and spoke" agreements but also a complex web of maintenance, repair, and equipment-sharing agreements. In this chapter, we focus on transcorporate networks, which are becoming increasingly important to the air travel industry. Thinking of airlines' relationship with customers in the traditional framework of a market where supply and demand simply meet fails to reflect the depth and complexity of the networked market in which today's air transportation services are provided.

Selling and buying air transportation services are increasingly sophisticated activities involving relationship management by real-world service providers rather than reliance on a mythical invisible hand. Travel agents are becoming indispensable partners to the airline industry. Whereas for instance they accounted for only 38 percent of tickets sold in the United States in 1978, the proportion had risen to 80 percent in 1986 for domestic flight and to as much as 90 percent for international flights.[1]

Air transportation services therefore should be seen in the context of packages that include the information management services now needed to make efficient use of the airline system. Such packages or "compacks" in turn open new strategic opportunities for service providers, notably through the use of bundling and unbundling.[2] The success of low cost, no frills companies like People's Express directed attention to the unbundling of the primary service—flying the passengers—from such services as in-flight hospitality and luggage handling. Another profound change has been the unbundling of information-intensive services.

Once a natural and almost unnoticed aspect of airlines' services, the provision of information about schedules, prices, and connections has become an indispensable aspect of operating a transportation service in a period when price changes number in the thousands per day and when the same ticket can be purchased at vastly different prices depending on specific conditions of use and payment. Reservations and ticketing since deregulation have become a massive data processing operation calling for expertise and large capacity. Providing such services is no longer necessarily best done by airlines as a growing number of service providers now specialize in information management activities as a separate line of business. Companies like American Express have been able to apply the data processing expertise developed for other services (such as credit card operations) to airline reservations. Similarly, an affiliate of the Times Mirror group has been very successful in providing airlines with on-line flight-plan services.

The unbundling of information-intensive services from the actual operation of airlines is thus a major aspect of the restructuring of air transportation services. Yet, to state directly conclusions reached in previous analysis, bundling and unbundling must not be analyzed in traditional combinatorial terms but rather as part of an innovation process. Indeed, once unbundled, services can be rebundled in innovative ways within as well as outside of their sector of origin. Flight and price information services can be integrated with other information services in the field of air transportation itself (for example, helping customers identify the most cost effective routing), in the broader field of travel and entertainment (railway, car rental, and hotel services), as well as in very different fields as illustrated by integrated service packages that combine the traditional travel agent's role with corporate accounting and management services. Recent initiatives by British Telecom to provide travel services through its Prestel videotex network as well as Rupert Murdoch's innovative Jaguar hotel booking and video brochure service are also clear indications that new entrants are knocking at the door.

Rather than being merely agents of the airlines, travel agents have a critical role to play in helping customers find their way amid a bewildering array of routes, fares, discounts, and packages. Yet travel agents have no other source on which to rely to discharge this greatly expanded role than the airlines themselves. Hence the strategic importance of the systems through which airlines and travel agents interact, namely computer reservation systems (CRS).

CRS already play a critical role in bringing together passengers, travel agents, and airlines. The relative market power of these various actors is now in large part a function of the ways in which CRS are designed, used, and, to some extent, regulated.

Because they are actual providers of most of the critical information concerning their operations, airlines are in a position to strongly influence the architecture and rules presiding over the use of these networks. Yet the costs involved in setting up such systems (which can be the equivalent of a fleet of five Boeing 747s), as well as the need for a critical mass of route and connection coverage, exceed the resources of small and medium companies.

By the end of 1987, more than $1.5 billion had been spent on the five major American systems, namely TWA-Northwest's Pars, Delta's

Data II, Texas Air's System One, United Airlines' Apollo, and American Airlines' Sabre. American Airlines' Sabre system connects 10,600 travel or booking agents through about 60,000 terminals, while United Airlines' Apollo has 7,400 agents connected through 50,000 terminals. Together these two systems account for more than three-quarters of the tickets sold by U.S. travel agents.

Airlines have to pay fees (ranging from $1.50-2.00) for each reservation on their own flights made through another company's network. In addition to these direct financial revenues, CRS can help a company present its own flights in the best possible ways—a critical factor in light of a U.S. Department of Transportation finding that travel agents make reservations 80 percent of the time from the first screen called up and two-thirds of the time from the first or second line that appears before their eyes.[3]

A vivid illustration of the changing nature of competition within the air transportation industry is provided by the importance of CRS services in the overall profitability of those airlines that have moved most aggressively toward the information intensive services. Thirty to forty percent of American Airlines' profit (as opposed to about 8 percent of its total revenues) stem from the Sabre system. No wonder then that Robert Crandall, president of American Airlines, remarked in 1986 that he would rather divest from the airline than from its computer operation.[4]

THE TALE OF THE CHARTER AND OF THE COMPUTER

The role of CRS goes much beyond expediting in a cost effective way the traditional tasks in the airlines "back office." Seen as strategic rather than as logistical tools, they allow the air transportation industry to live with an astonishing variety and number of changes of prices and schedules and can be used by companies as a basis for competitive advantage through the fine tuning of customer relations. The number of discount seats of various types can for instance be adjusted to fit the patterns of customer demand almost on a flight-to-flight basis so as to optimize load factors and individual flight profitability.

The ultimate failure of People's Express, a company once held as a model of new strategies before its eventual acquisition by Continental Airlines in 1987, can be seen as an illustration of this move from the era of mass production and consumption to that of mass customization. While many factors (including notably the ill-advised acquisition of Frontier Airlines) have accounted for the People's Express failure, one critical element was that companies with a higher cost structure were nevertheless able to match People's Express's very low prices. Obviously, they could not do so across the board, but instead they put their CRS to work to target the customer groups for which rock-bottom prices were the key incentive, while continuing to receive higher payments for a substantial portion of their seats.[5] Discount airlines relied on strategic concepts developed by the charter companies that had helped move the industry toward mass consumption but that were vulnerable to the customized strategies made possible by computerized networks.

Obviously, the customization process made possible by the CRS applies only to some aspects of airline activities, such as pricing and the organization of more individualized travel packages. As air travelers know, many other aspects of the flying experience lack in such customer-oriented sophistication. . .

AMADEUS VERSUS GALILEO: SOFTWARE AS A FORM OF STRATEGIC ALLIANCE

The mid-1980s might be remembered in the airlines' world as the time when attention gradually moved from the turmoils created by U.S. deregulation to the potentially greater changes that might come from global competition. Once sheltered by an impressive combination of national monopolies, government ownership, and unrestricted cartelization, European companies are now under pressure to prepare for the 1992 unified European market. Modest measures have already been implemented at the invitation of the EEC Commission such as allowing 40–60 percent traffic sharing instead of the 50–50 formula in favor with bilateral "pools."[6] It takes little imagination to realize that competition in Europe will probably not be restricted to the relatively well-behaved European Club but that American (and at some point East Asian) companies will increasingly make their pressure felt on the Continent itself.

Global competition however need not begin, as traditionally envisioned, with American companies carrying European passengers within Europe and vice versa. The delivery of services on a global basis can be just as significant. In this sense, American CRS are as much of a threat for European airlines as American planes.

Each of the major European airlines had already developed a CRS of its own: Air France relies on Esterel, Swissair on Traviswiss, Lufthansa on Start, KLM on Corda, British Airways on BABS, and SAS on its 6,000-terminal-strong Smart network. Yet, in general, the national booking systems in Europe lack a number of the add-on functions (back-office accounting, word processing) developed in the United States. They are also heavily tilted in favor of the operating company, to the point of making the more "neutral" U.S. systems very attractive for independent travel agents. Hence, around 1980, it was becoming clear that the American CRS—at least Sabre and Apollo—would spearhead the U.S. offensive toward Europe.

A number of European national airlines became worried not only about losing the electronic reservation business but also about seeing nonnational airlines use these electronic systems to challenge their dominance in highly protected markets.

CRS therefore came to be seen as a central aspect of the counteroffensive that European companies had to mount in preparation for intensified worldwide competition. At first, the European reaction was to look for a umbrella under which to bring all national computer systems. Discussions within the twenty-one-member Association of European Airlines for the creation of a "global distribution system," however, quickly broke down into two smaller competing groups, with a number of companies undecided.

A first group initially consisted of Air France, Lufthansa, Iberia, and SAS. Capitalizing on large domestic markets, these four companies accounted for 60 percent of the scheduled intra-European market in 1986 and represented 90–100 million bookings. One of the factors that brought them together was that they were all using Unisys (previously Sperry) systems in combination with IBM systems for their existing CRS. Ironically though, one of their first decisions was to turn to IBM for the software and hardware on which their future joint system would depend. The decision was based on superior IBM transactional capacities as well as on the need to design a system to which as many other airlines could connect (Unisys, however, will provide the Fare Quote part of the software). Together these four companies decided to launch Amadeus, an advanced computer reservation system designed to handle 1,750 reservations per second (10–20 times today's rates) through 40,000 terminals.

Setting for themselves a July 1989 deadline, the Amadeus group has agreed to commit about $270 million dollars to the system, with $140 million going to IBM alone.[7] Cost overruns at the national level are likely to bring the total closer to $400 million. Chairman Kurt Ekstroen, formerly in charge of Data Processing at SAS, will preside over a 550-person operation with headquarters in Madrid, software development in Nice, and operation staff in Munich.

A second group, around British Airways, brought together a number of companies that had already sided together on other European air transportation issues (being in general more open to deregulation) and that were looking for ways to go on line without a complete overhaul of their existing systems. Consisting, in addition to British Airways, of Swissair and KLM, the group announced the creation of a system code named Galileo heralded by Colin Marshall, British Airway's CEO as, quite simply, "the most important development in airline information and reservations systems that Europe will see this century."[8] The budget initially envisioned for the Galileo system is $120 million for a 140-person operation. While Amadeus's four founding members share equally in the equity of the Amadeus holding company, 52 percent of the Galileo holding company's equity is in the hands of British Airways and its American ally Covia, the CRS subsidiary of United Airlines.

Competition between the two rival European alliances has already translated into efforts to sign in new members for each of the systems. Air Inter (the French domestic airline), Linjeflyg (Sweden), Finnair (Finland), Icelandair, Jat (Yugoslavia), as well as the French national railway company (SNCF) and four hotel groups, have joined the Amadeus group, while British Caledonian (now part of British Airways), Alitalia, and Austrian Airlines (which already had technical cooperation agreement with Swissair) opted for Galileo. Claiming to have secured links with over 15,000 travel agencies in Europe, Africa, and the western hemisphere and bringing together companies that had carried 80 million passengers in 1987 against 46 million for the Galileo group, Amadeus felt in a position (obviously open to challenge) to look at itself as "the major travel distribution system in the European market."[9] Its objectives are to connect to 20,000 agencies worldwide to expedite over 150 million reservations a year for an annual turnover of $300 million and to make a profit by 1992.[10]

In the meanwhile, Galileo scored a major success by enlisting Sabena, the Belgian carrier. Sabena's move does illustrate the strategic implications now associated with choosing a CRS as it was widely interpreted[11] as a preliminary step toward a cooperation agreement with KLM, Swissair, and the Luxembourg state airline Luxair. The move was obviously a blow to the efforts of Amadeus member SAS of establishing some form of permanent cooperation or even merger with Sabena.

While competing in principle with the leading American CRS, whose inroads into Europe had triggered their creation, the European systems may also be seen as a first step toward the wave of global strategic alliances that is likely to result from the globalization of competition. A transatlantic alliance may already be detected behind the decision of the Galileo group to accept Covia, the subsidiary of United Airlines responsible for the Apollo system, as a major shareholder in the project and a key software supplier. The Amadeus group rejected a similar offer from Sabre's owner American Airline, choosing instead to purchase a license from System One. The decision was based on the fact that Texas Air was the only vendor willing to give Amadeus a worldwide license without asking for an equity position. The decision also reflected what was seen as superior connectivity to other systems. A licensing agreement was signed in July 1987.

While European and American systems were making the headlines, East Asian airlines were also taking steps to become major players in the global networked market now emerging. In December 1987, Cathay Pacific Airlines, Singapore Airlines, and Thai International agreed to set up a joint CRS, called Abacus. The group's objective is to have a 10,000-strong terminal network throughout East Asia and Southeast Asia by the end of 1989, with a capacity to handle some 300 reservations per second and, as in the European case, a number of smaller regional companies plugged into the system. Figure 3–1 illustrates the 1988 CRS landscape.

A view often taken within the industry is that over a period of time, no more than three to five systems will be able to remain in the market. Hence the frantic search for connections and alliances among American, European, and Asian CRS, as illustrated by the talks in progress between Amadeus and Abacus.

Figure 3-1. The Computer Reservation Systems Landscape (*1988*).

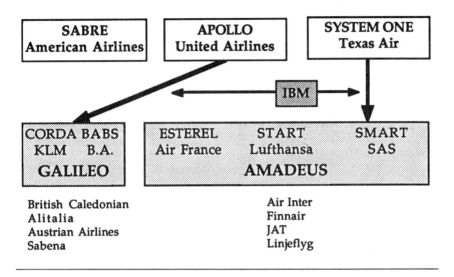

| SABRE American Airlines | APOLLO United Airlines | SYSTEM ONE Texas Air |

IBM

CORDA BABS KLM   B.A. **GALILEO**

ESTEREL   START   SMART Air France   Lufthansa   SAS **AMADEUS**

British Caledonian
Alitalia
Austrian Airlines
Sabena

Air Inter
Finnair
JAT
Linjeflyg

STRATEGIC POSITIONING IN THE O-S-U TRIANGLE

CRS should not be seen only in the framework of airline competition but also as part of an effort by airlines in general to regain the upper hand from travel agents, especially from large agencies such as Wagon Lits and American Express, for the provision of the information services that have become one of the most lucrative parts of a deregulated air transportation market. Markets are traditionally analyzed in terms of interactions among buyers (or customers) and sellers (suppliers):

Suppliers ◄────► Market ◄────► Customers

The development of CRS is yet another illustration of the emergence of the networked markets that are taking us beyond this traditional paradigm. The air transportation market is better analyzed in the framework associated with networks and notably the O-S-U triangle put forward by PROMETHEE (Figure 3-2).

A first implication of looking at CRS in this analytical context is to draw attention to the flexibility of roles characteristic of the

Figure 3-2. The O-S-U Triangle Model for Analyzing Strategic Positioning within Networks.

O-S-U dynamics. The general trend is for operators increasingly to look at themselves as service providers as they seek to provide more value-added services. In the meantime, service providers as well as users have, at least potentially, some capacity to influence network architecture to the point of sometimes becoming network operators themselves. In the air transportation case (unlike the telecommunications one), users (the passengers) have little capacity to bypass and compete with operators and service providers. Nevertheless, the services developed by the International Airline Passengers Association illustrate the ways in which users can play a role in, and extract benefits from, the operation of networked markets. On-line reservations services developed by user groups can compete with airline and travel agents' services. But the most active aspect of O-S-U dynamics in this case involves a complex form of competition cum cooperation in which airlines end up providing new services (car rentals, credit cards) through the CRS that they operate, while such large service providers as American Express would like to preserve or extend the role of their own networks (in this case the American Express card) as the backbone of this networked market.

Competition takes place, however, within a cooperative framework: operators, service providers, and users can be seen cooperating for network operation while at the same time competing over network architecture. Computer reservation systems illustrate not only how powerful networks have become strategic tools but also the growing convergence and interconnection among previously very different types of networks. In this case, CRSs play a critical role in the development of synergies among at least three types of networks:

1. The network of *airline routes* for which connection and pricing issues have become so complex as to require massive information-processing capacities.

2. The network of formal or unformal *airlines alliances*. Sharing a CRS is a major step toward, and an instrument of, cooperation among airlines. By contrast, preserving an airline's independence is probably not compatible with the pooling of critical information and decisionmaking tools. This sensitivity was clearly illustrated by the failure of the European "umbrella" agreement and by the creation in the United States of the Neutral Industry Booking System (NIBS), a consortium formed in June 1985 by thirty U.S. airlines without a CRS of their own.

3. The *networked market* bringing together airlines, other service providers, and air transportation users into an integrated electronic marketplace. Within it, competition develops not so much in terms of traditional market shares as in terms of strategic positioning.

In the past, these three types of networks would have been considered as of a totally different nature, namely physical (route interconnection), strategic (corporate alliances), and informational (customer/provider interface services). By providing a common strategic tool for their management, CRS have a major impact in structuring the broader, integrated market in which air transportation is now merging with a wide range of other value-added services.

ELECTRONIC CARTELS?

So important have the strategic implications of CRS become that they need to be carefully taken into account in any analysis of trade liberalization and antitrust perspectives. As we have just suggested, such analysis should not be restricted to the air transportation market as traditionally defined but should rather be seen in the broader context of trade in services so as to take into account the variety of services—such as insurance, credit card, and accounting services—that can be bundled with transportation services and sold through CRSs.

On July 26, 1988, the European Community Commission put forward a computer reservation code, to be approved by the member governments, covering all reservations systems operating in the EC as well as the related scheduled and charter traffic. Technically, the code is part of an antitrust exemption decision under article 85 of the Treaty of Rome without which airlines would not be allowed to pool resources in the Amadeus and Galileo projects. The code bans all forms of discrimination in the presentation of flight information on computer screens as well as in speed of access and quality of information. It also guarantees the right of any carrier to gain access, at fair fees, to a given CRS and bans exclusive terms that would prevent a new participant in a CRS from joining another reservation system. The EC Commission's code follows quite closely the guidelines set up in June of the same year by the European Civil Aviation Conference, a private body representing European airlines.

Providing a "neutral" reservation service is, however, only one aspect of competition in the air travel services field. Another important aspect involves the conditions under which competition can develop among different computerized distribution systems. So far, U.S. airlines have been the most vocal in trying to establish such rights for their CRS. After failing to enter into some cooperative agreement with Amadeus or Galileo, American Airlines has been at the forefront of a legal battle with European airlines. Such activism is easily understood in light of the fact that only 250 of the more than 30,000 travel agents in Europe have signed up with Sabre, a far cry from the situation in the United States, where it ranks first. Because Sabre was denied the right to issue British Airways tickets in the UK, American Airlines took British Airways before England's High Court as well as before the European Court of Justice. An out of court settlement was reached at the end of June 1988, whereby British Airways agreed to allow its tickets to be issued through Sabre in exchange for greater prominence of its own flights on Sabre, especially in the United States. A similar conflict developed with Japan Airlines at the end of 1988 and prompted the U.S. Trade Representative to threaten restriction of JAL's ticketing rights in the U.S.

But airlines are not the only possible operators of CRS or similar computerized systems, and present codes and rulings offer very little protection against a monopoly by the airlines as a group over the sophisticated reservation and information services now developing around air travel services. While it looks natural for airlines to consider such services as integral parts of their core activities, the potential contribution of new entrants must not be overlooked. CRS are likely to emerge gradually as global distribution channels not simply for the airlines but for an increasing variety of services ranging from hotels to insurance, and it is not clear that a monopoly by airlines over such delivery networks is in the best interest of the customer. Some consideration has been given in the United States to a possible divestiture of airline-owned CRS, probably an extreme approach. But the possibility of offering air-travel-related, information-intensive services should be open to as many types of actors as possible.

Another key dimension vying for attention is the link between what PROMETHEE calls the "transcorporate" and "intercorporate" networks—in this case, the CRS and the (implicit or explicit) alliances entered into by airlines within Europe as well as overseas. It is not a coincidence that alliances, such as that announced in October 1988 between the Scandinavian Airlines (SAS) and Texas Air tend to take place among CRS partners.

Analysts should notably raise the question of the potential conflicts between the objective of airline deregulation in Europe and of the creation of the two powerful coalitions into which European companies are entering at the very moment when they prepare for what is supposed to be a more competitive market. European airlines are used to the cozy world of national monopolies, bilateral quotas, and price fixing. It will take more than a few speeches on the merits of competition and on the challenge of the European 1992 internal market objective to change such habits. CRSs will play an essential role in this strategic change (or lack thereof) because, they are not simply a tool but, rather, they are becoming the (electronic) marketplace itself. Prices that used to be set in the proverbial smoke-filled rooms are now set electronically. Critical decisions on the true extent of price competition (among airlines as well as between them and other service providers) are now embedded into CRS software and esoteric programming procedures. It is a little worrisome, therefore, to see that airlines have become so keen on sharing these critical strategic and pricing tools at the time when they are expected to behave more competitively.

At the global level, the links forged between the mammoth American systems and the emerging European CRS duopoly would also deserve some critical analysis. One can only regret that the anticompetitive practices that might develop in the electronic shadow of such agreements are, at best, at the periphery of the field of vision of the small number of regulatory or judicial institutions with a mandate for free competition.

While deregulation of air transportation has lost much of its initial appeal, largely because of the failure to develop the new infrastructures called for by a greatly expanded traffic, it remains an essential dimension of economic dynamism. Movement of people is even more important to a service- and information-intensive world economy than to a traditional industrial one. The rapid development of a billion-dollar CRS market can be a powerful force in facilitating higher levels of individual movement, as long as its darker potential for electronic cartelization is kept in check, at the national as well as international level.

NOTES

1. *The Economist*, November 7, 1987, and *Libération*, January 29, 1988.
2. For a detailed presentation of the analytical framework applicable to bundling, unbundling, and innovation in a service economy, see Albert Bressand and Kalypso Nicolaïdis, "Les services au coeur de l'économie technorelationelle," *Revue d'Economie Industrielle*, special services issue (January 1988).
3. "The Other Reason Frank Lorenzo Wants TWA," *Business Week*, December 1985.
4. Quoted in *The Economist*, "Sabre Rattling," November 7, 1987, pp. 74–77.
5. Donald C. Burr, founder of People's Express, was quoted in the *Business Week* cover story on "The Frenzied Skies" as saying: "in 1983 and 1984, you heard [American's] Crandall talk about a high-tech airline. I didn't understand he was talking about his computer system. But he knew he would be able to underprice us. And the minute they took our price point away, we were defenseless." *Business Week*, December 19, 1988, p. 72.
6. *Europolitique* 50/50.
7. Sam Webb, "Four European Airlines Agree Joint Computer System," *The Financial Times*, June 23, 1987.
8. Michael Donne, "Airlines Agree Reservation Link-Up," *The Financial Times*, July 11, 1987.
9. Kevin Done, "Amadeus Expands Booking Network," *The Financial Times*, September 2, 1987.
10. Jean-Didier Blanchet, Directeur-Général d'Air-France, in *La Lettre Service Plus*, no. 2, January 1988, p. 2.
11. See for instance Susan Carey, "Sabena's Plans to Join Galileo May Herald Joint Ventures with Other European Carriers," *Wall Street Journal*, February 17, 1988.

4 R&D NETWORKS
The Emerging Market for Technological and Scientific Services

Giorgio Spriano

Research and development (R&D), one of the most typical industrial corporate functions, has become a strategic factor for modern industrial systems. At the same time, however, it has gained a certain autonomy from traditional manufacturing phases. This does not mean that it can be considered independent, but, together with other technological services, it follows new organizational patterns and market criteria. This chapter is based on the belief that the traditional tripartition of economic activities in agriculture, manufacturing, and services, is increasingly meaningless, and that many fast-growing activities have in fact developed on or across the border between industrial and tertiary sectors. These structural modifications are detectable in the changing nature of several corporate functions regardless of the original sector of the company. This is particularly true for R&D since it is a knowledge-intensive activity that is becoming increasingly autonomous from downstream production phases. Although the largest part of R&D activities is still internalized by large industrial companies, it is legitimate to speak of an R&D industry and of an R&D market.

In a study on the service sector, there are several interests in looking at the development of R&D activities. First, the growth of R&D activities, together with other corporate functions such as finance and marketing, is an indication of the increasing "tertiarization" of industrial corporations. The same manufacturing companies are becoming more and more knowledge- and information-intensive; in production processes the software component is at least as important as the hardware; and the sale of products needs to be accompanied by adequate services. Second, together with the internalized R&D, there is also the growth of a market for science- and technology-oriented services and the development of new R&D suppliers, which include not only large corporations but also universities, public and private research centers, and small high-technology firms. Finally, the organization of R&D activities is developing toward new patterns—collaborative networks, "tele-travail," and international information flows, using new communication means such as electronic mail, file transfers, or CAD networks—which could in the future be extended to other tertiary activities.

THE STRATEGIC ROLE OF R&D

R&D capacity, both internally and externally acquired, is becoming more and more important to determine the competitiveness of a firm, not only in the so-called high-tech sectors but also in more traditional industries. In the struggle for the world market between American, Japanese, and European companies, success is in great part determined by the capacity to transform R&D results into marketable products. In many sectors, given the reduction of technical scale economies brought about by new production techniques and forms of automation, the real entry barrier is the investment in R&D and the access to technologies and know-how. Furthermore, global competition has shortened the life-cycle of many products, which has meant an increase of R&D cost per single product because these costs must be distributed in a shorter period.

This has brought about an apparently contradictory situation. On the one hand, given the rising costs of R&D, only very large companies, with considerable world market share, can afford large R&D projects. On the other hand, R&D investment is becoming indispensable also for smaller firms, if they want to remain competitive at international level. It is therefore easy to understand why R&D has become a crucial factor both in corporate strategies and in public policies, and why many public and private initiatives have sprung up in this area, together with new organizational attempts. Japan, the United States, and, more recently, European governments have launched several initiatives to support industrial and university R&D

activities and, indirectly, to foster the competitiveness of their national industries (for a complete analysis of such policy initiatives see Arnold and Guy, English and Brown, and Spriano).[1] Most of these initiatives are based on the interfirm collaborative and cost-sharing concept.

Given the increasing costs of R&D, several companies started to look for some sort of out-sourcing, either in the form of contracting out entire projects or subcontracting only parts of it to specialized units. This is gradually creating a proper market for R&D products, technological services, and scientific consultancies. This market can offer new opportunities for university departments, public and private research centers, technologically specialized service companies (software houses, design and engineering companies, private laboratories), and stimulate the creation of science-based small firms.

International collaborative research projects have a long history in the academic and scientific field, as well as in industries dominated by the public sector, such as research in nuclear energy in Europe, or defense projects in the United States. In recent years this way of organizing R&D activities has been extended to market-oriented sectors and to a wider participation of private firms. Many projects of this kind have sprung up in the microelectronics and information technology areas in the United States, Japan, and Europe; similar initiatives have begun to appear also in other high-technology sectors and in more traditional industries.

The Japanese initiatives, some of which, like the very large scale integration (VLSI) and so-called fifth generation computer programs, have had a considerable international impact, are primarily government-led programs and most of them are coordinated by the Ministry of International Trade and Industry (MITI). On the other hand, U.S. collaborative R&D ventures are usually private sector initiatives, while in Europe both types of collaboration occur. The objective of these initiatives is the same: to lower R&D costs per firm by reducing duplications and by focusing research efforts so that larger scale economies (or critical mass) can be achieved more quickly. These objectives can be obtained in different ways. The organizational form of these R&D projects varies considerably. While in the United States and Japan they tend to be organized in a concentrated form and to be nationally limited, in Europe projects tend to involve firms and R&D centers of several countries and to be organized as international networks.

NEW ORGANIZATIONAL PATTERNS
FOR R&D ACTIVITIES

The Japanese Model

In the economic and industrial development of Japan MITI has certainly played a major role. Several programs were launched in the 1950s and 1960s to catch up with Western technology but, starting from the late 1970s and throughout the 1980s, MITI launched industrial R&D programs aimed at developing leading-edge technologies, particularly in the fields of microelectronics and information. Characteristic of all these programs is the close collaboration of all the main Japanese manufacturers together with MITI technicians in the R&D work.

The VLSI program (1976–79), for example, involved the five main Japanese semiconductor chip manufacturers, Nippon Telegraph and Telephone (NTT), and the MITI. A joint association was created (the VLSI Technology Research Association) together with a central laboratory located in Tokyo in facilities borrowed from one of the partners (NEC). More than 100 researchers from the different partners worked together in the same site, and for the same project for three years.

The most ambitious of the Japanese R&D projects is the Fifth Generation Computer (5G) Program (1981–91). The 5G research work is sponsored and coordinated by MITI and is undertaken at the Institute for New Generation Computer Technology (ICOT). The central ICOT laboratories employ 50 permanent full-time researchers, while 350 other researchers from the industrial partners work part-time at ICOT and at their respective companies' laboratories (where another 1,000 technicians also work on the 5G project); they serve as *trait d'union* (the link) between the basic research conducted in ICOT and the applied research undertaken by the partners. Technology, as well as an application feedback, is therefore transferred by face-to-face cooperation.

In the Japanese collaborative R&D model synergies and scale economies are probably maximized, but the access to these projects seems to be restricted to a limited number of large corporations. The eleven collaborative R&D projects launched by MITI since 1962 have involved only eleven companies. Small companies, universities, and private research centers are usually excluded.

Private Sector R&D Joint Ventures

Large U.S. corporations also find it increasingly difficult to cope with rising R&D costs. In 1983, as a response to the success of the Japanese VLSI program and to the ambitious plan of the 5G projects, and partially inspired by the Japanese model, 21 large U.S. information technology and aerospace companies decided to set up a joint research center, the Microelectronics and Computer Technology Corporation (MCC). MCC is completely funded by its industrial shareholders, which also contribute most of its technical personnel. Located in Austin, Texas, MCC employs around 300 top-level researchers selected among the parent companies and other research institutions. Some 60 percent of the research staff is employed directly by MCC; a further 20 percent is on full-time secondment from corporate members but will return to their companies; and the remaining 20 percent work only part-time at MCC and function as liaison with the corporate members' laboratories. Thus technology transfer occurs primarily through people. MCC's R&D activities are subdivided into five projects narrowly focused on specific aspects of information technology (IT); the industrial partners can choose to fund two or more projects among them and can benefit from monopoly of rights resulting from the funded projects for three years.

A similar initiative has been undertaken by some European computer manufacturers. In 1984 Bull, ICL, and Siemens founded a common research center in Munich, the European Computer-Industry Research Center (ECRC), which focuses mainly on advanced information-processing technology for the next-generation computers. The personnel is totally provided by corporate members, and the research results are shared by all partners.

The European Approach: R&D Networking

If R&D collaborations are important for U.S. and Japanese IT large corporations, they are even more essential in Europe, whose industry is characterized by smaller firm size and narrower markets. After the failure of some cooperative attempts in the 1970s, such as the computer joint-venture Unidata, several pan-European initiatives were launched in the early 1980s in the information technology field. Most of them have been promoted by the European Community (EC); the best known, and so far the most important, of these R&D collaborative initiatives has been the European Strategic Program on R&D in Information Technology (ESPRIT). The pilot phase of this program was launched in 1983; the first five-year plan started in 1984 with a budget of 1.5 billion ECU.

The organizational formula chosen for ESPRIT and for other EC sponsored R&D programs differs considerably from the Japanese and U.S. ventures and is based on the concept of networking. The program is subdivided in a large number of projects (around 200). A key requisite is that each project must involve at least two industrial partners from different member countries (the average project size is four to five partners, but there are projects involving more than ten participants from different nations). ESPRIT does not envisage the creation of new R&D facilities or the concentration of researchers in central laboratories. The R&D activity, which is 50 percent funded by the EC and the rest by the participants, has to be carried out in the premises of each single participant. The idea is to create the same synergies of joint R&D centers and to reduce research duplications without the concentration of researchers in a single site.

By contrast with the ESPRIT networking approach, a concentrated approach offers the advantage of easier human contacts and face-to-face information exchanges, but it has the disadvantage of considerable fixed costs in setting up the new facility. A central laboratory seems therefore more suitable for very-long-term projects or for very expensive scientific equipment which each single partner could not afford.

Furthermore, in the European case, the choice of a geographically distributed organization seems particularly suitable given the fragmentation of the European IT industry and of the research community. In Europe the industrial R&D potential in IT is not restricted to 10–12 companies as in Japan; similarly many university centers have important scientific capabilities, and the creation of a limited number of joint research centers would have discriminated against both the units of smaller size and those peripherally located. To maximize the R&D resources in Europe it therefore appeared necessary to

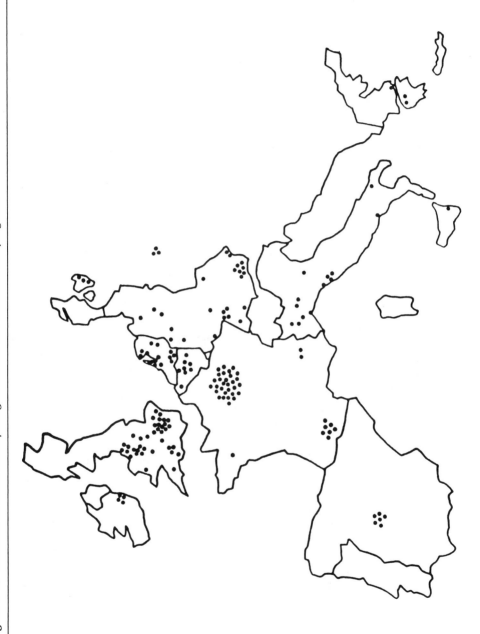

Figure 4-1. Location of Units Participating in the ESPRIT Software Subprogram.

mobilize the largest possible number of units, which meant making the initiative accessible not only to large corporations, but also to medium-sized and small firms, university departments, and private research centers.

At the conclusion of ESPRIT Phase 1, more than 400 units had taken part in at least one project (Figure 4–1 gives an idea of the extensive participation in the ESPRIT software subprogram). Other EC R&D programs have followed in different sectors (RACE [Research and Development in Advanced Communication Technology in Europe] in telecommunications, BRITE [Basic Research in Industrial Technologies for Europe] in manufacturing technologies), and they all share the same organizational philosophy, namely interfirm networking. However, this complex web of interfirm collaborations calls for frequent and reliable communications, both in the form of personnel exchange and meeting, and of data transfer and other computerized information transfer. Telecommunication services are therefore vital for the success of decentralized R&D collaborations. To this purpose, the Commission of the EC has launched a Europe-wide Information Exchange System (IES), based on several services, which include electronic mailing, data bases, and a newsletter. At the beginning of 1987 the electronic mail network EuroKon had more than 1,500 users and was used as communication means by 40 percent of the ESPRIT teams.

The Growth of a European Market for Scientific and Technological Services

The flexibility and the lower fixed costs of such type of R&D collaborations give larger margins to corporate strategies. Each firm can in fact have a plurality of joint projects, with different partners according to the specialization of the project; or the same team project can be modified during its execution. The objective is to create a more transparent R&D market and a more collaborative environment in Europe. Thus, many joint projects of "variable geometry" could be set at the initiative of individual firms. These conditions should enable large corporations to diversify their collaborations, to share their R&D costs, and to find more easily external sources for specialized research and know-how. However, small and medium-sized science-oriented firms or R&D centers should also benefit from

the opening up of a Europe-wide market for scientific and technological services (research contracts, consultancies, software, or sub-
components development).

Large companies have often made use of small subcontractors or
research centers in their R&D activity, but in the past these relationships tended to be one-way dominated and of local type. In other
words, for a science- or technology-oriented small firm it was very
difficult to enter the international market and to go beyond the privileged relationship with a few national companies.

The multiplication of R&D collaborative projects in Europe gives
new opportunities to these small companies. The first opportunity is
clearly to diversify their customers, by getting in touch with foreign
companies. In high-tech sectors it is not easy for a small company to
get a sound reputation, to prove its technological expertise, and to
gain the customers' confidence. Participation in a joint project, eventually in a first phase as subcontractor of a large national company,
is the best way to start establishing both scientific and personal contacts. The second opportunity for small and medium-sized enterprises (SMEs) is to link up with other SMEs so as to achieve larger
scale economies, greater financial and managerial capabilities, and
become competitive in the international market.

In the ESPRIT projects one might find both types of collaborations: relationships between large and small firms as well as collaborative networks of SMEs.

Large-Small Firms Collaboration:
R&D Subcontracting

The collaboration between large and small companies assumes particular importance in R&D projects when manufacturing and service
expertise have to be brought together, or when users' needs have to
be matched with the available technologies. Software houses, in particular, play a very important role in ESPRIT, by linking together IT
manufacturers and IT end users. These service companies are often
inserted in quite complex collaborative networks.

Cap Sogeti, one of the largest European software houses, for example, participates in 7 ESPRIT projects and has established links
with 29 companies and 9 universities. Only 6 of the 38 collaborations this French company established are with national partners.

Figure 4-2. Collaborative Networks Established by Christiaan Rovsing
International (DK).

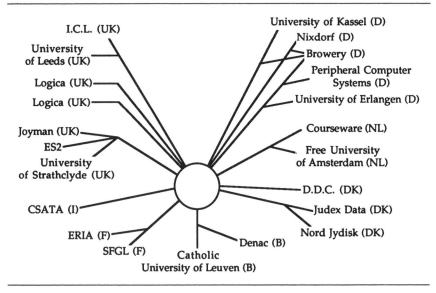

However, smaller software companies also have exploited ESPRIT
to find international partners and to create collaborative R&D networks. Illustrative collaborative networks have been created within
ESPRIT by three software houses: Christiaan Rovsing International
(Denmark), Logica (United Kingdom), and System and Management
(Italy). Despite the relatively small size of these companies, their
technological and commercial horizon is certainly international: the
collaborations with foreign partners are much more important than
those with domestic companies. Christiaan Rovsing International participates in 7 ESPRIT projects with 22 other partners (15 companies
and 7 universities), of which only 3 are Danish (see Figure 4-2).
Logica is involved in 4 ESPRIT projects and has established R&D collaborations with 12 companies and 5 universities and respectively 11
and 3 of them are foreign.

The collaborative networks established by these software houses
are diversified both in nationality and in type of partners. From a
first analysis it appears that several of these links are with large
computer manufacturers or with large IT industrial users. In several
ESPRIT projects there seems to be a clear division of labor between
computer manufacturers, software houses, and industrial users, both

in research work and in future commercial interests. In between the IT manufacturers' interest, which is primarily to develop and sell computers and other equipment, and that of users, which is to adapt the best technology available to their own specific needs, there is enough space and scope for a software houses' role. European software houses, having chosen a custom software strategy (as opposed to the U.S. standard software packages approach) have developed very close ties with final users. However, in many cases this strategy, closer to service demand than to hardware development and supply, has limited the market of these companies within national boundaries. Moreover, the involvement of such companies in the R&D for new hardware and software architectures has been quite limited. In many cases their strategy was restricted to the IT application phase and to the specific requests of users.

The R&D collaborative links established by these companies in ESPRIT therefore represent a considerable change and a decisive step to respond to U.S. competition in this area. ESPRIT projects are an occasion for closer collaboration between software houses and computer manufacturers of several different countries. This means a greater involvement of software houses in basic and applied research (development of computer architectures and joint software and hardware design) which should enable them to pursue longer-term technological strategies and to enlarge their own market geographically.

This longer term and more international strategy is now pursued by relative large software houses such as those previously analyzed (Cap Sogeti, Logica), but smaller software companies find it more difficult to follow. Some medium-sized and small software houses show different aggregation patterns. System and Management (Italy), for example, is a medium-sized software house, but its market is primarily a domestic one. System and Management participates in three ESPRIT projects and has established collaboration links with thirteen companies and five universities. In this case, however, the domestic links are more important: in all the projects the participation of System and Management is accompanied by that of a large Italian IT manufacturers (Olivetti and Italtel) or users (Sipe Optimation is the information services branch of a large Italian bank). It seems, therefore, that for this company a privileged relationship with a large domestic company is still very important. One might argue that its technological and commercial horizon is still nationally restricted and that its participation in ESPRIT is somehow conditioned by that of its domestic partner. Several other cases can be found of joint participation in ESPRIT of medium or small software companies and national large manufacturers and for which these considerations might be repeated. However, even if this assumption (SMEs participation conditioned on a link with a large firm) is true it must not be interpreted in a totally negative way. System and Management, for example, thanks to ESPRIT and the traditional relation with domestic companies, has now established links with ten foreign IT manufacturers which, apart from the R&D collaboration, might help the company to internationalize its market.

Programs like ESPRIT and, more generally, international collaborative ventures can be very useful to SMEs, even if these firms have a relatively dependent position in them. They are in fact an instrument to get access to international technological and commercial circuits and, moreover, to make themselves known abroad and to establish the formal and informal contacts with new potential customers.

Inter-SMEs Collaborations

A subordinate position of small and medium enterprises is not always the rule in the ESPRIT projects. If it is true that in many projects SMEs only perform research subcontracting, in other cases SMEs have started establishing collaborative ties among themselves. In the software and artificial intelligence areas it is possible to find several ESPRIT projects managed entirely by SMEs, eventually in collaboration with university centers.

It is the case, for example, of project 1033 aimed at the provision of a formal framework and a suitable tool set for the development of asynchronous embedded micro and distributed systems. It is led by Advanced System Architecture (UK) and the consortium includes another SME, Erno (Germany), and two university centers, the Imperial College of London and the University of Kaiserslautern. One can also mention project 1256, led by Imperial Software Technology, a spin-off of the Imperial College of London and which includes also two other SMEs, DELPHI (Italy) and Non Standard Logics (France); or project 1252, where three SMEs—the Belgian Institute of Management (BIM), HITEC (Greece), and Interprogram (Netherlands)—work together with Telefonica (Spain) and the University of Manchester. In project 1258 three small software houses—John Bell

Systems (UK), Liverpool Data Research Associates (UK), and Software Engineering Services (Germany)—cooperate with the City University of London and the University of Liverpool.

Still in the ESPRIT software subprogram, two other projects (892 and 928) are carried out by consortia of SME. Project 892 (Advanced Interactive Development of Data-Intensive Applications) is led by BIM, a Belgian SME specialized in software and artificial intelligence applications, and also includes the Cretan Research Centre (Greece), Scientific Control Systems (Germany), and the University of Frankfurt. Project 928 (A Rule-Based Approach to Information Systems Development) is carried out by James Martin Associates, a small Dutch software house, together with BIM (Belgium), Micro Focus (UK), and the University of Manchester.

In the area of artificial intelligence (AI) several important ESPRIT projects are carried out without the involvement of large IT manufacturers. It is the case of project 107 (A Logic-Oriented Approach to Knowledge Data Systems Supporting Natural Users Interaction) which is led again by BIM (Belgium) and includes the Fraunhofer Institute (Germany), Scicon (UK), the University of Creta, and Scientific Control Systems (Germany) as partners, and INCA (Germany), the Cranfield Institute of Technology (UK), and the University of Munich as subcontractors. Another important AI project (440) is carried out by DELPHI, an SME based in Viareggio, Italy, together with Bell Telephone Manufacture (Belgium) and the Free University of Brussels. Project 599 does not include any large IT manufacturer: it is led by Logica (UK) and includes Christiaan Rovsing International, Judex Datasystemer, Nord JYDK Udviklings Centre (all of Denmark), and the University of London.

Even in the ESPRIT-Computer Integrated Manufacture, which is generally dominated by large IT manufacturers or large IT industrial users, it is possible to find examples of SME-led projects. Project 850, for instance, is carried out by CSEA, a small Italian company specialized in electronics for industrial automation, together with ERIA (Spain) and Eurosoft Systems (France).

Some SMEs, therefore, start to build their network of international collaborations. For many of them this process still passes through a privileged link with a large partner but for others this network already has its own autonomy. A company like the Belgian Institute of Management (BIM), for example, through the four projects in which it participates, has established links with eight companies and six university and research centers, all of them located outside Belgium. In two of these projects then BIM is the prime contractor. The technological but also commercial horizon of this company is certainly international (at least European), and in its relationships with the several foreign partners, one cannot identify any symptom of subordination or dependency. Eventual collaborations with larger companies would certainly be balanced partnerships and not traditional relationships dominated by the larger firms.

Extending this network analysis to other SMEs participating in ESPRIT, one can identify a certain number of firms that, despite their small size, operate both in technological and commercial terms at the international level. It is the case of Generics (Ireland) and DELPHI (Italy): even if they participated in only two ESPRIT projects each, these SMEs have clearly gone beyond national borders. They established several international research collaborations, often assuming the leading role. The technological and commercial strategies of these companies can therefore be considered independent from large corporations.

These examples show that, despite the increasing R&D costs and the oligopolistic concentration of several segments of the IT industry, there is a place for autonomous strategies of independent small companies, particularly if they can establish forms of collaboration with other SMEs.

CONCLUSIONS

The pace of technological change and the growing costs of R&D have increased the need to rationalize the use of scientific resources and maximize the results from R&D investment. In such a light, the development of an international and transparent market for technological services and scientific research activity is a very important step forward. This market is particularly important for Europe because its scientific resources are extremely fragmented and, therefore, they could be efficiently mobilized only reducing the transactional costs of R&D out-sourcing and of interfirm collaboration. The development of this science-oriented service sector has already occurred in the United States, where "spin-offs" from universities and private companies are frequent and contributed to the development of new technologies, such as microelectronics and biotechnologies. In

Europe labor market rigidities, institutional constraints, but also corporate investment practices, have long inhibited the development of such science- or technology-oriented small firms. The new collaborative environment established in Europe by programs like ESPRIT can probably create the conditions for the development of such activities, but this must be accompanied by initiative aimed at reducing the rigid institutional barriers between university and industry, increasing the mobility of labor, and making sources of finance more accessible to SMEs.

NOTES

1. E. Arnold and K. Guy, *Parallel Convergence: National Strategies in Information Technology* (London: Frances Pinter, 1986). M. English and A. Watson Brown, "National Policies in Information Technology: Challenges and Responses," *Oxford Survey in Information Technology*, 1 (1984): 55–128. G. Spriano, "ESPRIT: An Attempt at Policy Evaluation," PROMETHEE Working Paper no. 8, 1987.

II DEVELOPMENT, TRADE, AND ECONOMIC POLICIES

INTRODUCTION, BY BRUNO LANVIN AND MURRAY GIBBS

Services are now recognized as a major dimension of the emerging international division of labor. Whether they currently are or not exporters of services, all countries have high stakes in this reshaping of international economic relations. For developing countries, new possibilities could arise to break away from the vicious circle in which debt and an excessive dependence on commodity exports have locked most of them for the last decade. Yet, with regard to growth and development processes, the key services are increasingly dependent on the availability of advanced information technologies and related knowledge. For developing countries, this means that the sources of wealth creation are being moved farther away from their own factor endowments. They fear being kept at the periphery of the information revolution. This part attempts to analyze and illustrate these two sides of the coin, both from an analytical point of view (Chapters 5-7) and by drawing on the experiences of a developing country (Chapter 8).

Murray Gibbs, in Chapter 5, stresses the importance of so-called producer services (as opposed to final services) for the development process of developing countries. He underlines the fact that, when a developing country attempts to build new comparative advantages, its strategy will be more or less constrained, depending on that country's ability to develop domestic capacity in such intermediate (especially information-intensive) services. Gibbs then examines how this objective could be pursued in the context of the Uruguay Round of Multilateral Trade Negotiations and concludes on the need to foster multilateral cooperation in the area of services and development. Bruno Lanvin, in Chapter 6, looks at the same issue from a slightly more analytical point of view. He argues that information intensity is becoming a major dividing line in international trade specialization, and he suggests that negotiators and decisionmakers will have to deal ex ante with this "horizontal" issue before they can move productively to sectoral services negotiations. Lanvin also suggests that some major services-related issues will not be tackled properly by analysts until an intellectual revolution takes place, which will acknowledge the "reversal of logic" implied by the services revolution. Pascal Petit comes to a similar conclusion in Chapter 7 after examining the impact of the growing international service economy on production structures and trade (specialization) patterns. Petit looks in detail at the different trade-offs that major service companies have to face in terms of their international investment strategies. He suggests that, in an increasingly uncertain economic environment, national deregulation strategies may require an overall (that is, international) regulatory framework.

Fernando De Mateo and Françoise Carner (Chapter 8) underline the difficulty that any developing country will face when trying to assess the importance of services in its own development process. Using the example of Mexico, De Mateo and Carner make the case for developing countries to first challenge "dominant theories" if they want to identify objectively their own interests in the context of the services revolution. They stress the crucial importance of information-technology-based services, as well as the fact that a certain degree of openness of the Mexican economy to foreign direct investment will have to be carefully considered. Like all the other authors in this part, De Mateo and Carner take as a starting point criticism of the traditional Heckscher-Ohlin-Samuelson explanation of trade patterns and exploration of various alternatives or at least complements to this theory.

5 TRADE IN SERVICES
A Challenge for Development

Murray Gibbs

> Showing a greater fondness for their own opinions than for truth, they
> sought to deny and disprove the new things which, if they had cared to
> look for themselves, their own senses would have demonstrated to them.
>
> —Galileo, *Letter to the Grand Duchess Christina*

Services have always been crucial to the development process.[1] The
contribution of health, transportation, educational, financial, and
communications services to the development process has been almost universally recognized. The articulation of economic activities
through the efficient operation of such services to overcome bottlenecks and ensure the smooth flow of goods, services, and persons is
one of the characteristics of a developed economy. Such infrastruc-
tural services have been the prerequisite for, and not the result of,
development.[2] The role of services in the economy is not new, however, it has been enhanced by dramatic changes in information and
communication technology to the extent that a rethinking of economic theories and development strategies may be called for.

THE SERVICE ECONOMY

The phenomenon of the service economy has been the subject of
analysis and debate in the economic and political context at the in-

The author is a staff member of the UNCTAD secretariat. The views expressed in this
chapter are those of the author and do not reflect those of UNCTAD.

ternational and national level. This has often led to conflicting diagnoses, which may reflect different political perspectives but may also arise from the inadequacy of traditional economic theory and terminology to describe and analyze the major changes taking place in the world economy.[3] The growth of the service sector in the industrialized countries seems to be the result of a variety of often opposing tendencies operating in parallel. Among these tendencies are the differing rates of application of new technologies and management techniques in the industrial, agricultural, and service sectors, the externalization of service production, and appearance of new services, and the enhanced supply of more traditional services.

Analysis of the new role of the service sector has been somewhat hindered by two related factors. First, "trade in services" was invented for negotiating purposes and has become a category ex post facto. This involved the intellectual basis for multilateral negotiations on services constructing arguments in favor of reciprocal negotiations in which access to markets for goods could be exchanged for concessions by developing countries with respect to services (and by implication, investment and technology policies).[4] By extracting certain elements of conventional economic theory, the aim was to convince all participants that they had something to gain from such reciprocal liberalization. These arguments have largely been based upon comparative advantage principles and tend to suggest that the shift to services within developed market economies is taking place as a result of resources being forced out of the manufacturing sector by imports from developing countries. From this perspective, developing countries have a comparative advantage in goods, while the industrialized countries possess a comparative advantage in services, and hence increased exports of services are required to provide jobs for employees displaced from the manufacturing sector by imports from developing countries.[5] Other analysts have focused on what is seen as the inherent fallacies of this approach demonstrating 1) that the shift to services (in the United States at least) is not trade induced[6]; 2) that most income from services is acquired through return on investments rather than exports of services as such and therefore is not creating alternative employment opportunities in the United States[7]; and 3) that, in any case, the penetration of world markets for goods is closely related to international service activities, and vice versa. Liberalization of trade in services would not have much effect on employment and only marginal impact on the balance of payments. It would, however, strengthen the knowledge-based service industries on which manufacturing competitiveness depends.[8] In other words, the U.S. objectives in the multilateral negotiations on trade in services were basically of a strategic nature. Some studies have also shown that the growth in trade in services has been in those services sectors most closely linked to the production and export of goods.[9] In other words, a strong competitive position for the export of goods is not an alternative to, but dependent upon a strong domestic service sector.

The comparative advantage approach implies an acceptance of the so-called three-stage theory of development by which the process of development was said to move from the agricultural and extractive stage, to the industrial stage and only later to the postindustrial stage or the service economy. This theory derives from proccupation with the differing demand elasticities for goods and services as well as comparative figures relating to production and employment in services for countries at different levels of development. The most serious fault in this theory is simply historical, since most of the countries now considered developed or industrialized have always been service economies and the development of services has usually been as much a prerequisite for as a result of industrialization and development. Statistical comparisons do not take account of such phenomena as the large informal service sector in developing countries, the externalization of service production in the developed market economy countries, and the different application rates of new technologies and management techniques to the agricultural, manufacturing, and service sector.

Proponents of the three-stage theory derive support from overall balance-of-payments statistics showing that developed countries as a whole have a surplus in trade in services and account for 85 percent of such trade, owing to the fact that developed countries have become service economies.

This theory and its implications can be contested in many ways. Within the overall group trade figures there exist great differences among countries—developed countries with large deficits and developing countries with surpluses. More onerous barriers face services linked to the movement of persons than of capital or information. Most important, the theory does not take account of the link between export of goods and export of services: services are vital to maintaining a competitive position in the production of goods and their sale on the world market. In fact, as will be discussed below, the ability to integrate services and goods may be the key to export performance in the future, and, furthermore, that ability may be much more the result of concerted strategies than of the allocation of resources.[10]

The third theory is that because services, especially producer services, constitute an input into the productive process and a key to competitiveness on the world market, developing countries' interests would be best served by policies giving their producers access to the most efficient and advanced services available in the most advanced countries. This argument is obviously valid at the short-term microeconomic level. When seen in the context of the greater "service content" of goods, however, its flaws become apparent.

COMPARATIVE ADVANTAGE IN GOODS AND SERVICES AND THE INFORMATION REVOLUTION

Statements to the effect that developed countries possess a comparative advantage in services while developing countries possess such an advantage in goods, drawn from a superficial perusal of balance-of-payments data, are not well founded in fact.[11] Rather, information-rich countries have a comparative advantage in both knowledge-intensive goods and services, while information-poor countries have an advantage in information-poor and, usually, labor intensive goods and services. (For an analysis of information as a factor of production, see the next chapter, by Bruno Lanvin.) The problem facing the latter countries is that world demand for labor-intensive goods is stagnant and subject to protective measures, the new technologies have eroded the labor cost advantages of developing countries in the production of goods as well as that formerly provided by plentiful raw materials. Furthermore, the ability to export labor-intensive services is hampered by a variety of regulations that impede cross-border movement of labor to a much greater extent than the movement of capital, goods, or information.

Knowledge-based services provide a critical part of the foundation for the production of high-value-added manufactured goods. Exports of high-technology services stimulate the export of knowledge-intensive services and vice versa.[12] The same relationship does not apply between labor-intensive goods and services.

Information wealth is not a natural resource endowment, but rather a product of history, culture, and level of development. It is only relatively recently, with the so-called information revolution that countries have recognized the crucial importance of this resource and that national strategies have been adopted to develop it and protect it from competitors. Developing countries finding themselves in a knowledge-poor situation should find little comfort in arguments based on comparative advantage. The only viable solution for these countries would appear that of becoming both knowledge rich and labor rich (low cost/high skill) while taking advantage of the possibilities offered by the new technologies to develop the related services, and while adopting external policies and strategies designed to eliminate or overcome barriers to entry into foreign markets for labor- or information-rich goods and services.

Several studies have emphasized that one major difference between trade in goods and trade in services is that for goods movement of capital is usually an alternative to trade, while for services, movements of capital are complementary to trade. However, depending on the service sector concerned, the same complementary relationship can be said to exist among all four factors of production, or as have been described by UNCTAD, four "modes" of delivery (see discussion under Different Concept of Barriers in this chapter), capital, labor, goods, and information. Thus, in designing strategies for the export of services an important consideration relevant for the negotiations in this area is that various combinations of the four factors can be used to penetrate foreign service markets. For example, the export of consultancy services can take the form of pure information flows, through some form of transborder data flow, but can also involve the travel of a person (the consultant) to the importing country. The definition of whether such cross-border movement of a physical person represents movement of the labor as a factor of production or the export of a service depends on the rather arbitrary criterion of the time spent on the foreign country, and the rather subjective criterion of the "information content" of the person, raising the question of the extent to which a person acquires enough information to qualify as a consultant rather than a worker.

Similarly, the growth of franchising represents an increase in the information content of the capital information mix. Banking service can be provided by various combinations of goods, capital, information, and persons. Restrictions on the cross-border movement of one factor will encourage new combinations. Where entry of people is restricted, goods will be sent abroad for repair or assembly; trucks will cross frontiers but their drivers will change. Restrictions on direct foreign investment can result in an relative increase in information or person flows. In some cases restrictions on one of these factors effectively blocks trade. For example, leasing service can be precluded by restrictions on the entry of the goods being leased. The effect of the advances in information and communications technology is that flows of pure information are providing an alternative means of transmitting a widening variety of services across borders.[13]

An additional consideration affecting the ability to compete in service markets is that services are sold without a change in ownership. Although services are incorporated into the production of other goods and services, generally one cannot purchase a service and resell it to someone else.[14] This characteristic contributes to "first in" advantage in many service sectors, in which barriers to entry to latecomers become progressively more formidable.[15] These barriers to entry can be created through the proprietary ownership of information and the establishment of private information networks.

From the point of view of development, the situation described above could lead to a further strengthening of the dominant position of the service transnational corporations, an exacerbation of the dependent position of the developing countries, and a consequent decline in their international competitive position for both goods and services. On the other hand, it could permit developing countries to leapfrog in the technological sense, allow them to overcome traditional barriers such as distance from markets and make use of advantages previously undetected. The outcome will be a result of policy decisions taken by individual developing countries at the national and regional levels and by the international community as a whole.[16]

As was true of energy in the past, information is rapidly becoming the key element in the productive process. The leaders in the development of knowledge and information are obviously tempted to restrict its diffusion with a view to both increasing its market value and affecting their competitive positions vis-à-vis foreign competitors. In other words, there will be a tendency for governments to adopt strategic trade policies aimed not simply at liberalization but at securing a larger share of the rent on the production and export of information.[17] Such strategic policies could involve actions aimed at achieving an improved and secure access to world markets for knowledge-intensive services, particularly through the investment mechanism, while restricting the bargaining leverage of host country governments in negotiating with foreign investors, particularly in negotiations aimed at transfer of technology.

Advances in information and communications technology have created both opportunities and challenges for developing countries. While access to more sophisticated services from developed countries is facilitated, overreliance on such services could undermine possibilities for development of a strong domestic producer services sector. This is not a matter of infant industry protection, rather, it is the need to develop a national capacity and infrastructure for the production of higher value-added manufacturing goods, which 1) permits the manufacturing, agricultural, and other service sectors to adapt to changes in technology, improvements in infrastructures, and intensified international competition, and 2) serves to retain the value-added derived from the increased service content in production. Terms derived from more traditional economic theory may not be sufficient to accurately describe these phenomena.[18] Transnational corporations have become leaders in the development of new technologies and processes. The ability of governments to ensure a transfer of these resources to the domestic producer service sector will be a crucial factor in future development strategies.

PRODUCER SERVICES

Future development strategy will have to take account of the role of what has been defined as producer or business services, those services purchased by enterprises as inputs into the production and sale of goods or other services.[19] Developed market-economy countries appear to be witnessing a phenomenal growth in the producer service sector. Producer services are becoming more varied, more specialized, more efficient, and more available, thanks to the process of externalization of services production—that is, services previously provided within large enterprises are now subcontracted to independent firms or subsidiaries established for this purpose.[20] Thus the services associated with the operation of an enterprise are available on the open market, the amount of initial capital required to establish a small or medium-size business is reduced, and the adaptability and competitiveness of such enterprises once established are reinforced. Producer services thus enter directly into the structural adjustment process, facilitate firms' ability to adapt to new market conditions, to apply new technologies, to improve their products, and to penetrate new markets. They constitute a dynamic factor in the national economy.[21] Producer services make an important contribution to the development:

1. They permit enterprises in other sectors, including other service sectors, to increase their productivity, to adopt new technologies, and to adjust to world market demands.
2. They stimulate new investment in small and medium enterprises.
3. They create an environment conducive to innovation and creativity.
4. They overcome bottlenecks in the production and distribution process.
5. They provide employment and business opportunities, given that the demand for such services is a function of the needs of other sectors to adapt to increasingly competitive situations and therefore is not easily saturated.

Information technology has contributed to the expansion of the producer service sector. First, many producer services are, in themselves, information or data services, which are a direct product of advances in information and communication technology. These include, for example, software development, telecommunications value-added services, data entry, and data processing. However, a much wider range of traditional services have been rendered more efficient by the application of these technologies.[22] Often this enhancement contributes to the externalization process,[23] as it facilitates the successful operation of smaller, more dynamic, specialized firms. Information technology has also increased the "tradability" by government policies with respect to services and thus the facility in obtaining such services from abroad.

Seven Yardsticks for Producer Services

Following the comparative advantage argument, improved access to the most efficient producer services supplied on the world market should constitute a major contribution to international competitiveness. There is obviously some validity in this position with respect to short-run goals. However, it must be qualified with respect to the given objectives of developing countries. The importance of the producer service sector to the economy, and the question as to the extent to which it should be provided domestically, is related to its contribution to the following goals:

Innovation. The service sector, particularly the enhanced producer service sector, is the key to adapting to new technologies and the process of continuous innovation crucial to maintaining international competitiveness in the modern world. Although foreign producer service inputs may be required to maintain productivity levels, a loss of control of these services or their absence could lead to dependence on foreign innovations and a lower level of domestic innovative activity and thus could undermine the ability to compete internationally in the longer term.

Interface. Producer services can also be envisioned as being located on the interface between infrastructure services and production. For example, producer services show producers how to make effective use of modern telecommunications infrastructure for the purpose of improving their productivity. They permit producers to adapt to new technological advantages and intensified competition as well as to take advantage of new opportunities.[24] There is a question as to whether this strategic function of interface management can be monopolized by a foreign firm.

Value-Added. The increasing service content of goods implies that more of the value-added of any manufacture or semimanufacture is attributable to services. In practical terms this means that each product (or service) produced or exported contains a greater input of services at various levels of production, from design through production and quality control, to advertising, distribution and market analysis. The success of the product on the world market will depend much upon the efficiency and quality of the ever-increasing percentage of services incorporated. To the extent, therefore, that these services are supplied by foreigners, there is a danger of a structural imbalance occurring in which ever-increasing exports of goods will be required to obtain the same level of retained income for the developing exporting country.[25]

Feedback. Enhanced producer services contribute to international competitiveness in both goods and services, particularly if organized in an "integrated system."[26] They assist producers in conceiving and designing products (or services) to meet the exigencies of foreign market demand, and in improving efficiency and maintaining the quality of their products; marketing and order processing services provide continuous "feel" for the needs of the world market. Linkages between "upstream" services (design and engineering), "onstream" services (inventory management and quality production control), and "downstream" services (Marketing, market research, distribution, order processing) permits the continuous adaptation of both market demand and new technologies. The ability to maintain such a continuous feedback process may be the key to the export successes of certain countries and an important factor in "created" or "dynamic" comparative advantage. As a result of continuous and rapid technological advance, uncertainty has become the general rule and comparative advantage can now be seen as the "ability to adapt." The producer service sector is the key to that ability.

Employment. Producer services generally provide the higher quality jobs in the service sector, and increasing the size of the producer service sector has the effect of upgrading the service sector as a whole. Dependence on foreign suppliers could block such opportunities, creating a bias in the service sector toward low-paying, low-skill jobs. The development of the necessary domestic skills and the subsequent incorporation of the informal service sector into producer services would thus seem to constitute a priority objective for many developing countries.

Balance of Payments. The demand for producer services tends to increase as the economy develops and becomes more complex, reflecting the increased service content in value-added. Thus, although access to foreign supplied of sophisticated services, particularly those involving high technologies, may be inevitable, reliance on foreign sources can lead to a growing drain on foreign exchange, thus leading to a structural balance-of-payments disequilibrium.

Management of the Economy. In effect the overall role of the producer service sector is that of managing the national economy, to organize resources, factors of production, and information in such a way as to maximize the attainment of national goals, whichever they may be.[27] If incentives were not created to channel benefits appropriately, control of the producer service sector by foreigners could undermine the ability of governments to implement coherent development strategies.

SERVICE EXPORT STRATEGIES

Services can provide developing countries with an opportunity to increase their foreign exchange earnings. A lucrative world market for services exists for those able to penetrate it and TNCs find themselves well placed in this respect. If liberalization is to provide any meaningful gains for developing countries beyond those of inputs cheaper than immediately available locally, they will have to improve their capacity to penetrate foreign markets.[28] Acquiring a competitive position in services would seem to depend, in the long run, upon the development of human capital and of technological capabilities. However, the adoption of specific service export strategies can also increase service earnings in the short run.

Variations on Traditional Approaches

Many developing countries are in the process of exploring, and some actually applying specific export strategies. These can be applied to service sectors of traditional interest to developing countries such as tourism, where new markets can be pursued successfully (other sectors include business, cultural, health, and education).[29] Others have maintained international competitiveness in transportation (airlines, shipping facilities, and so forth), often with high reliance upon producer services, such as advertising. Advantage can be taken of special geographic and cultural characteristics, although these can also work to their disadvantage.

Labor Cost Advantages

An obvious strategy for expanding the foreign service earnings of many developing countries is to build upon their traditional advantage of low labor costs. The essential problem is how to deliver the labor-intensive service to the foreign markets or to foreign consumers. This can be achieved through the direct export of manpower (construction workers, for example), or through the export of a services package that incorporates labor (construction services). On the other hand, the purchasers of such services can be attracted to the developing country concerned. Apart from more traditional types of tourism, the growing costs of various personal services in developed countries can provide new opportunities for foreign service earnings, for example, by attracting patients for health services or receiving goods for repairs.

The advantage of low labor costs is also relevant in service sectors associated with higher technologies. The successful entry of a number of developing countries into the international market for data services[30] (data entry, data processing, software) has been make possible by the same advances in communication and information technology combined with improved education in developing countries; the possibility of obtaining niches in the "labor-intensive high-tech" sector warrants further examination by more developing countries. These niches can be related to cultural advantages, for example in the area of translation (including of software) or of assistance with respect to the interface between different legal systems.

Exporting Service Content

Certain developing countries have been able to export the service content (chemical engineering, oilfield services) of manufacturing and extractive industries (phosphoric acid, petroleum), thus gaining foreign exchange from both goods and services from the same productive process. This has been accomplished through externalization by modifying the corporate structure in existing industries, so that the services associated with primary and secondary production are transferred to national enterprises, which concentrate on the development of human capital. Many sectors, extractive, industrial, agricultural processing, would seem to lend themselves to this approach.

Service Centers

As the competitive position of a firm can be increased by its ability to offer a package of services,[31] so can that of a geographical locality. In the past, services have sprung up around transportation centers such as ports and airports, as well as around financial and trading centers that have reached the necessary critical mass. Such service centers have become the nucleus of regional or national growth and of service export earnings. At present, countries are experimenting with the creation of service centers as a stimulus to domestic growth and the development of a foreign service earnings capacity. The determinant factors for the success of such ventures would appear to be the existence of a modern communications and information infrastructure, effective links to more traditional activities in the national and regional economy (such as transportation, trading, petroleum extraction, and agricultural processing), a comprehensive package of services, appropriate geographic location, and supportive institutional arrangements.

DIFFERENT CONCEPT OF BARRIERS

The progressive liberalization of trade in services (as stated in the Uruguay Declaration) implies that action will be taken to reduce or remove barriers to trade in services, or as stated in the agreed negotiating plan, perceived barriers to such trade. The use of the word *perceived* in the relevant GATT text is quite appropriate, as there exists no clear agreement as to what measures constitute *barriers* to trade in services, a term that itself has not been adequately defined. Much of the work on barriers to trade in services has been to identify those government regulations that impede the freedom of operations of the TNCs, which in any case are best able to identify such barriers from their own experience.

It is fair to state that the service sector is subject to more extensive regulations than the goods sector and that a variety of reasons can justify such regulations, including those applied differently against foreign and domestic suppliers. The high cultural and strategic context of services has made it difficult to identify which regulations are primarily designed to protect the economic position of domestic producers.[32]

The debate has focused on the need to define trade in services and barriers to such trade. Regardless of the outcome of the more esoteric aspects of this debate, it would seem quite clear that in order to penetrate a foreign market for services at least one of the four factors, capital, labor, information, or goods, has to cross the frontier.[33]

These have been described as *modes of delivery* a term coined in UNCTAD documentation. Therefore, any measure that restricts such movements could act as a barrier. However, the very fact that cross-border movements of these factors take place does not in itself mean that trade has taken place, as trade also requires that the service is produced by a resident of one country and consumed by the resident of another.[34] The extent to which regulations dealing with investment, migration, transborder data flows, or entry of service-related goods can be considered as barriers to trade in services would seem to be a subject for international negotiation.

The barriers to the flow of these "modes" are usually prompted by their peculiar characteristics: movement of capital, has obvious implications for national sovereignty, while movement of labor have important social impact. The implications of information flows are less well understood, particularly by the population as a whole, but it is clear that as governments gain a clearer understanding of the crucial role of information in production, policies are likely to emerge that will treat information as a resource in itself rather than simply a medium.

In most cases protection in favor of national service industries can be provided by either restricting the entry of foreign corporations or individuals or by limiting their activities in the domestic market. The move toward negotiating on the basis of "appropriate" regulations would imply that all regulations on services would have to be justified against multilaterally set criteria with little room for reciprocal bargaining. Under such an approach, the GATT negotiations of the overall multilateral framework of rules and principles take on paramount importance.

In this respect some promising developments have been taking place in the international debate around service negotiations. First, most countries appear to be opposed to any link between the GATT obligations of trade in goods and the Uruguay round negotiations on services. Second, it appears that strictly investment issues will not be taken up, and priority will be given to trade aspects. This may largely be due to the recent initiatives by the European Community to provide direction to the service negotiations. Furthermore, Mexico has stressed that the parameters around the "obstacles" to trade in services should first be defined by identifying which measures should *not* be considered as obstacles to such trade (such as regulations related to foreign investment).

Barriers are somewhat in the eye of the beholder. Developing countries face a variety of obstacles to entry in the world market for services, going beyond government regulations, including dominance by established suppliers, lack of access to technologies or to an adequate services infrastructure, restrictive business practices, and the like.

DEFINITIONS AND THEIR
NEGOTIATING IMPLICATIONS

The work on defining trade in services has begun relatively recently. Thus the very concept that services could be traded has largely been developed by protagonists of including services in GATT negotiations, and thus the whole conceptual debate is somewhat an ex post facto exercise. While some authors have claimed that the same laws of comparative advantage apply to both goods and services, certain reputable economists have challenged this view, going so far as to question whether one can speak of trade in services or simply movement of factors of production. The term *trade in services* did not appear in commonly used economic language before the end of the 1970s, after political decisions had been taken to negotiate service issues in GATT. Classical economic textbooks up to most recently still did not mention any topic such as trade in services.[35] The debate in the Uruguay Round has largely focused on drawing the line between trade and investment in services, although some developing countries, notably Mexico, have introduced the labor and goods factors, claiming that temporary migration of labor as well as the value-added in outward processing (*maquiladoras*) should be considered as trade in services rather than goods. Regardless of the intellectual arguments, the definition of trade in services has become a matter of international negotiation in the GNS (Group of Negotiations on Services).

Whatever the definitions finally negotiated, it is evident that for a service producer to penetrate a foreign market, combinations of at least one of capital, persons, information, and goods must cross borders. (Examples of capital are banking offices, of persons are consultants, of information are transborder data flows, and of goods are repairs to ships.) On the other hand, all such movements do not constitute "trade" in services, and the question is where to draw the line. A definition of "services" designed for the purposes of negotiation, if not necessarily intellectually satisfying, will at least have to be equitable, so that all countries will gain from any liberalization. For many developing countries, temporary migration of labor is the only means at their disposal for penetrating foreign markets for services, so a definition favoring capital-intensive, information-based services would certainly not meet the test of equity, which is a sine qua non for any meaningful multilateral agreement. In other words, if "trade" in services is to be defined narrowly, then it would have to exclude all movements of factors of production, if a wider interpretation were to permit some degree of investment-related activities, labor movements should logically be included as well. It may be necessary to have a separate definition of trade for each mode of delivery and possibly concentrate on defining what is *not* trade (that is, investment, migration, import of goods).

Definitions developed for statistical purposes may be quite different from those elaborated to define the scope of legal commitments (as in other sectors). It is necessary, however, that such definitions be compatible and not contradictory. In other words, the work on statistic and legal definitions should not be conducted in mutual isolation, but it should be kept in mind that one does not substitute for the other.

MULTILATERAL COOPERATION ON SERVICES

Multilateral trade negotiations on both goods and services will undoubtedly be complicated by the growing perception that the underlying economic assumptions seem to have changed. According to the theories of comparative advantage, all parties were assumed to benefit from the efficiency effects of international specialization. Under the new technological paradigm, however, there may well be a zero-sum negotiation, where those retaining an advantage is knowledge-based production (goods and services) will "win" while the others will "lose." This does not mean that liberalization of trade in services cannot be beneficial to all. It does imply, however, that efforts at liberalization cannot be undertaken according to those principles and concepts applied in past decades to multilateral negotiations on goods. For example, they must concentrate on achieving balanced results rather than reciprocity. The redistributional and strategic aspects of the liberalization will have to be taken into account so that no country or group of countries is required to incur an inordinate degree of loss and that no country's future ability to compete in international trade should be crippled by such results. Part II of the Uruguay round ministerial declaration, which identifies expansion of trade in services as a means to achieve the economic growth of all trading partners and the development of developing countries, does implicitly recognize this fact.

An optimum package to emerge from the Uruguay round negotiations on services should include solutions to the problems that developing countries face in exporting or delivering their services to world markets. Liberalization measures primarily directed to solve the problems of developed country service transnationals might not effectively accomplish this. The package should also ensure that developing countries' efforts to develop crucial service sectors, particularly those directly related to the production process, are not only unhindered but also actively stimulated by the results of the negotiations. Developing countries, in particular, would seem to have a major interest in arriving at the multilateral framework rules and principles for trade in services envisaged in the Uruguay Round Declaration at an early date. Their prime interest would be to firmly establish the legitimacy of measures taken to stimulate the contribution of services to the development process, shielding them from the coercive approach suggested by certain developed countries' trade legislation. The Uruguay Round Declaration implies that the development objective must be incorporated as an integral component of the framework and not be in the form of "special" or "differential" treatment applied in favor of developing countries as an exception to the general rules. This development objective could contain the following elements:

1. Recognition of the sovereign right of developing countries to apply measures in the service sector to increase the contribution of services to their development process, to improve their competitive position in world trade, and to pursue other economic and social objectives through the development of their indigenous technological capacities. Measures taken in this respect would not be considered as barriers to trade.

2. Such framework would include a definition of trade in services that excludes foreign direct investment, access to markets would be that necessary to provide or receive a specific service.

3. Unconditional most favored nation treatment.

4. Equitable access to developed countries' markets for services for developing countries, including movement of persons and participation in information networks; actions to liberalize trade in services would be taken consistently with development objectives and lead to the expansion of trade of developing countries, in conformity with the Declaration on the Uruguay Round; in such liberalization, preference would be given to the modes of delivery of services most accessible to developing countries.

5. Provisions to ensure entry for developing countries to the world market for services when impeded by nonregulatory barriers (for example, domination by transnational corporations, lack of access to information and information networks, low technological levels (RBPs).

6. Recognition of rights of developing countries to condition liberalization of access to their markets upon contribution of the foreign service supplier to the development of a competitive national service sector, including access to their information and distribution networks; any improvements in access to markets for services would be matched by improved access to knowledge and information.

7. The multilateral framework would provide the guidelines for subsequent sectoral negotiation, the sectors would be selected so as to give priority to those where developing countries have demonstrated competitive strengths.

8. The provisions in support of the development process would be an inherent element of the multilateral framework and translated into specific measures at the sectoral level; special or differential treatment in favor of developing countries would not be applied as an exceptional treatment but could be an integral and organic part of the framework.

9. It would be recognized that in certain service sectors developing countries may not have attained a sufficient level of technological development to compete internationally, where apropriate

future access to world markets would be reserved for developing countries.

10. The negotiations would address the nonregulatory barriers facing the service exports of developing countries. The aim would be to establish guidelines for multilateral cooperation touching upon a variety of areas and falling within the competence of various organizations. Governments would assume responsibilities to take various forms of action supportive of the expansion of the service sector and service trade of developing countries.

NOTES

1. See UNCTAD document TD/B/1100 on the role of services in the development process. Under TDB Decision 309(XXX), the secretariat concentrated on three specific areas 1) the role of services in economic growth, 2) services and the external sector, and 3) proposals for multilateral cooperation, and more recently TD/B/1162.
2. See, for example, M.C. Monnoyer and J. Philippe, "Facteurs de localisation et stratégies de developpement des entreprises des services," unpublished paper presented at Dynamique des Services et Théories Economiques, colloque, Université de Lille, 1987.
3. These phenomena were discussed in UNCTAD documents TD/B/1039 Part II, and TD/B/1081. See also Daniel Bell, *The Coming of the Post-Industrial Society: a Venture in Social Forecasting* (New York: Basic Books, 1973).
4. See, for example, G. Feketekuty, "Negotiating Strategies for Liberalizing Trade in Services," unpublished paper presented to the Third Annual Workshop on U.S./Canadian Relations, Ann Arbor, Michigan, October 1984.
5. A paper prepared by PROMETHEE under the FAST Program of the European Communities to analyze the extent to which the principle of comparative advantage applied to trade in services compared this to a reply to a question put to actor Woody Allen, who said, "I'm not sure that I understand the question, but the answer is yes."
6. See Robert Z. Lawrence, "Can America Compete?" The Brookings Institution, Washington, D.C., 1984.
7. The ratio for U.S. service exports to sales by U.S. affiliates abroad increased from 1:3 in 1974 to 1:5 in 1982. See K. Sauvant, *International Transactions in Services: The Politics of Transborder Data Flows* (London: Westview Press, 1986).
8. See U.S. International Trade Commission, "The Relationship of Exports in Selected U.S. Service Industries to U.S. Merchandise Exports," Wash-

ington, D.C., September 1983, and more recently the Office of Technology Assessment, *International Competition in Services* (Washington, D.C.: U.S. Congress, 1987).

9. Notably by the Paris-based CEPII (Centre d'Etudes de Prospectives et d'Information Internationales).

10. The Office of Technology Assessment of the U.S. Congress states, "Domestically as well as internationally, services and manufacturing depend on one another. . . . There is no choice to be made between a manufacturing economy and a service economy. The choices concern the pace of change and the kinds of skills that America will need to work productively in emerging industries," *International Competition in Services* (Washington, D.C.: U.S. Congress, 1987).

11. For an excellent critique of the application of comparative advantage to trade in services, see Jacques Nusbaumer, *Services in the Global Market*, Bostsa/Dordrecht/Lancaster, Kluwer, 1987.

12. The export of consultancy services can lead to the export of capital goods, the export of aircraft to training and maintenance contracts (Office of Technology Assessment, *International Competition in Services*, p. 34). Exports of clothing do not similarly lead to exports of tailoring or dry-cleaning services; however, the value-added can be increased through increasing the service content, i.e., adapting to or even setting fashions through "feedback," quality control, and advertising.

13. J. Rada, "Information Technology and Services," International Management Institute, Geneva, 1986.

14. Refer also to T. P. Hill, "The Economic Significance of the Distinction between Goods and Services," unpublished paper presented at the International Association for Research in Income and Wealth, Twentieth General Conference, Rocca di Papa, Italy, August 23–29, 1987, for a more detailed argument on the fact that trade in services cannot occur without movement of factors of production.

15. Rada, "Information Technology and Services."

16. Studies by the FAST Program of the European Communities have demonstrated that the expected benefits to more peripheral regions arising from the increased "tradeability" of services can be frustrated by corporate policies. See J. Howells, "Technological Innovation, Industrial Organization and Location Services in the European Community. Regional Development Prospects and the Role of Information Services." FAST Occasional Paper 142, Commission of the European Communities, Brussels, April 1987.

17. For a discussion of the concept of strategic sectors and policies see Paul Krugman, *Strategic Trade Policy and the New International Economics* (Cambridge, Mass.: MIT Press, 1986).

18. Thierry J. Noyelle, "Services and the World Economy: Towards a New International Division of Labour," unpublished paper presented to Economic and Social Research Council Workshop on Localities in an International Economy, University of Wales Institute of Science and Technology, Cardiff, September 11-12, 1986.

19. Producer or business services (the terms are often used interchangeably) can include such services as software, data processing, research, engineering and design, management, legal, and other consulting, training, import-export trading services, advertising, market studies, and public relations, insurance, banks and financial services, testing and chemical and physical analysis, leasing, accountancy, investigation and security, distribution, maintenance, and quality control.

20. See discussion in UNCTAD document TD/B/1100, paragraphs 4-7.

21. See O. Ruyssen, "Les Services a Maree Montante," in *La fin des habitudes* (Paris: Editions Seghers, 1985).

22. Accountancy, advertising, tourism, shipping, storage, and handling, to name but a few, see Rada, "Information Technology and Services."

23. For example, office services can be more easily subcontracted, even to foreign suppliers.

24. For example, the U.S. Office of Technology Assessment describes computer software as "sitting between the system and the people who use it," *International Competition in Services.*

25. Many developing countries already find themselves in this situation. See Trade and Development Report 1988, Geneva, UNCTAD.

26. See UNCTAD document TD/B/1100.

27. See Ruyssen, "Les Services a Maree Montante."

28. Liberalization could benefit in the form of cheaper inputs; however, developing countries could adopt such policies autonomously. It is one thing to liberalize as part of an economic development strategy; it is quite another to be obliged to do so by international obligations and the threat of retaliation.

29. See D. Riddle, "The Service Audit: A Key to National Competitive Positioning," unpublished paper presented at the annual meeting of the Academy of International Business in London, November 1986, as well as *Service-Led Growth,* by the same author (New York: Praeger, 1986).

30. See discussion in UNCTAD document TD/B/1100 paragraphs 48-55, and in TD/B/1162.

31. TD/B/1100, paragraphs 53-54 (footnote 86).

32. See discussion in Services and the Development Process, TD/B/1108/Rev. 1, as well as Chapter 11, by Geza Feketekuty.

33. See UNCTAD documentation TD/B/1162 and the Trade and Development Report 1988. In his most recent book, G. Feketekuty has modified the

UNCTAD terms by referring to *money* rather than *capital*, which is perhaps an improvement. See G. Feketekuty, *International Trade in Services: An Overview and Blueprint for Negotiations* (Cambridge, Mass.: Ballinger, 1988).

34. See discussion in Services and the Development Process, TD/B/1008, Rev. 1.

35. See discussion in Kalypso Nicolaïdis, "Trade in Services: The Issue of a Definition," UNCTAD Working Paper, November 1987; and Kalypso Nicolaïdis, "Contactors versus Contractors: Towards an Integrated Approach to Defining Trade in Services," Working Paper 39, PROMETHEE 1988, Paris.

6 INFORMATION, SERVICES, AND DEVELOPMENT
Some Conceptual and Analytical Issues

Bruno Lanvin

The present chapter argues that, contrary to the implicit assumptions of a large body of recent service literature,[1] international trade specialization in services tends to take place in a *horizontal* fashion (according to corporate structures, production, and delivery systems), rather than in a *vertical* or *sectoral* manner (by service activities). In other terms, in the emerging international division of labor, countries will tend to specialize, for instance, in labor-intensive services, or network-type services, rather than in, say, travel or catering services.

Starting from a traditional vision of international specialization strategies, an attempt is made to consider information as a separate (disembodied) production factor, and to reexamine specialization strategies from this particular angle. This exercise proves useful, and preliminary conclusions drawn from it suggest that the current trend toward increased information intensity in the production and delivery of internationally traded services will reinforce the tendency toward horizontal specialization strategies. Such a phenomenon is bound to bear important consequences for 1) the pace, structure, and even purpose of ongoing trade negotiations on services (the Uruguay round), and 2) all countries involved in international services transactions, and especially developing countries.

The views expressed here should be considered as those of the author. They do not necessarily reflect the positions of UNCTAD, where the author is an economist. This article benefited from the useful comments made by Kalypso Nicolaïdis.

It has been argued that the ongoing multilateral trade negotiations would make or break the General Agreement on Tariffs and Trade.[2] To many observers, analysts, and negotiators, it seems indeed that GATT is now faced with authentically new challenges. This is particularly obvious in the area of services.

It has been suggested quite convincingly[3] that a negotiation on services held under the auspices of GATT needed to be of a sectoral, or even subsectoral nature. The implicit analytical assumption lying behind this proposal is that countries (and firms) specialize in service activities (that is, vertically). However, one of the implicit driving forces behind the pressure exerted by some countries for freer trade in services relates to *information*, rather than to services per se.[4] As a matter of fact, one could reasonably see the information factor as the common denominator to most of the services sectors that fall under the ambit of ongoing multilateral trade negotiations.

Although information is of different importance depending on the sectors considered, it constitutes a common basis for the whole service economy. In particular, it is a key factor in the ability of service-producing companies to maintain their ability to easily switch from trade to investment and vice-versa. As such, it is key to the relevance of the current GATT exercise (Figure 6–1).

It therefore seems logical to reexamine specialization strategies in light of certain tendencies such as the increasing information content of output, the implied reversal of logic in international trade, and the resulting technological possibilities available to firms and countries alike.

Figure 6–1. Information and Service Sectors.

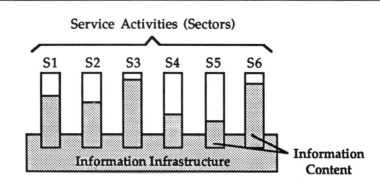

A DRAMATIC INCREASE IN THE
INFORMATION CONTENT OF OUTPUT

In early 1986 fears were expressed in different circles of the possible hollowing out of some advanced economies. What was meant at the time was that, through a chain of individually logical decisions, some major industrial companies were progressively selling their souls in a truly Faustian process, where short-term competitiveness was being restored by getting rid of the aging part of the production process (that is, mainly physical production), while retaining (and expanding) the profit-making part of that process (namely services).[5] This reflection triggered a quasi-unanimous call to investors and decision-makers to "come back to realities."[6]

One interpretation of the October 1987 stock market crash is precisely that the market had to come back to reality. The eighties have been characterized by a widening hiatus between a persistently depressed world demand (with remarkably low levels of investment in particular) on the one hand, and buoyant financial markets on the other hand. In such a contrasted context, it was therefore no surprise that 1) investment in physical assets would remain low, thus further weakening prospects for a rapid recovery in major economies, and 2) the performance of stock exchanges would be both increasingly spectacular and increasingly artificial, until the necessary adjustment (the crash) took place.[7]

As far as physical production is concerned, however, the increase in the nonmaterial component of the end product appears as an irreversible phenomenon. Beyond the often-quoted example of the automobile industry (whose end product now costs much less in material components than in services, including design, sales, marketing, advertising, and financial services[8]), some figures are worth keeping in mind: for the average microelectronic chip produced in the United States in 1985, the total cost of the rather expensive raw materials used does not exceed 3 percent of the total final cost of the product; 50 kilograms of optical fiber can carry, over the same distance, as many telephone conversations as one ton of copper cable, and their production requires twenty times less energy.[9] At an economywide level, a recent study by the International Monetary Fund has shown that, since 1900 (with the exception of the two world wars), the quantity of raw materials necessary to produce one unit of product has decreased on average by 1.25 percent per year. The figure is even more spectacular in the case of Japan: for the same quantity of product, the necessary raw material input diminished by 60 percent between 1973 and 1984.[10]

In the emerging networked economy, the battle for competitiveness is to be fought on a twenty-four hours a day. In most markets excellence will be determined by the capacity to innovate continuously. The shortening of the product cycle (with a productive life sometimes very close to the product's development time) represents a major threat for those who had anticipated following imitating strategies. It is also a Damocles' sword above the heads of those innovating companies that will make the wrong bet. It is therefore most likely that the more advanced companies will 1) multiply their strategic alliances (with their suppliers, consumers, and competitors) in order to increase their flexibility and ability to respond to market signals, and 2) deepen their information infrastructures (notably networks) in order to better manage the risks associated with increasingly innovation-intensive strategies.

A CONCEPTUAL ISSUE: THE REVERSAL OF LOGIC

Efforts to initiate a multilateral trade negotiation on services have triggered a refreshing phenomenon in which substantial parts of textbook economics are being revisited. Faced with a growing demand from services negotiators to come up with a conceptual framework, the analyst finds himself surprisingly underarmed. Indeed, when it comes to explaining services, existing economic theory presents several obvious shortcomings. One is the astonishing lack of links between microeconomics and macroeconomics. Another stems from the blatant inadequacy of the ways in which evidence is collected and processed, that is, the absence of a proper statistical framework for services.

However, the services (and more precisely the information-intensive services) phenomenon challenges more than existing theories: indeed, it shakes the very bases of such theories by suggesting *a reversal of their underlying logics.*[11] At least three examples of such a reversal immediately come to mind. They refer, respectively, to the logics of organizations (logistics), to the logics of wealth creation, and to the logics of complexity.

Organizational Networks versus Information Networks

One way of differentiating a transnational corporation from a global corporation is to ponder the relative weights of their respective organizational networks (localization/hierarchy) and of their respective information networks. In the seventies, the usual logics and logistics would lead TNCs to locate themselves in various countries in order to minimize costs.[12] After such decisions have been made and implemented, the companies would establish the information networks required to manage such complex organizations. With the eighties, and the growing involvement of TNCs in information-intensive services,[13] the existence of information networks and facilities (including that of an "adequate" legal framework) became a prerequisite to the decision of global corporations to establish in new locations.[14] The way in which this "infostructure" prerequisite is met if of relatively little importance here. However, it should be kept in mind that this can happen in two main ways, namely 1) through the provision by the host country of adequate facilities, public (government owned and operated) or private, and 2) through the existence of sufficient legal leeway (openness to the activities of foreign companies) for the TNCs involved to set up their own facilities or bring in their usual providers of information-intensive services.

In any case, the conclusion is the same, and the first pillar of the temple has thus been upset: information is now emerging as a genuine production factor and, as such, it is reinforcing the new hierarchy where information networks tend to preempt and shape organizational structures.

Wealth Creation and the Mutations in International Trade

In the context of the so-called pure theory of international trade—the Hecksher-Ohlin-Samuelson (HOS) model—the validity of the notion of comparative advantage (which happens to be one of the conceptual foundations of GATT) relies on a number of hypotheses. One of these stipulates that factors of production are supposed to be immobile, whereas products are supposed to be perfectly mobile across borders.

There is no need to recall here how the second part of this particular hypothesis has been challenged by protectionist realities. More interesting (and challenging) is the fact that its first part is also being challenged by reality. By becoming increasingly information-intensive, services have proved increasingly transportable (if not tradeable): the expansion and deepening of international information networks (telematics) has helped to turn information into an almost infinitely mobile production factor. This phenomenon, in turn, has triggered a true reversal of the HOS logics since, in many cases, the factors have become at least as mobile as the end products. One immediate consequence of this evolution was that, as could be expected, ongoing multilateral trade negotiations on services have had a tendency to shift away from pure trade issues toward "presence" issues (rights of establishment plus national treatment).

As far as developing countries (and more generally capital-scarce and information-scarce economies) are concerned, this change in emphasis among the "sources of wealth of nations" is both good news and bad news. The good news is that, in the new dynamics of comparative advantages, natural factor endowments will be less binding than before and comparative advantages will more often be built than inherited. The bad news is that all networks are not created equal and that first-comers have a tendency to occupy natural monopoly sectors; once the initial network has reached its critical mass, it will tend to process *risk* as a commodity, that is, to select acceptable risk and to export bad risk. While volatility and flexibility combine in sulfurous nuptials, the peripheries of the networked economy will become a target for such exports. The reversal of the Prebischian paradigm (the periphery being chiefly a source of cheap *imports* for the center) is one of the most striking achievements of services in upsetting the basis of current economic thinking.

FROM INFRASTRUCTURES
TO METASTRUCTURES

When attempting to describe the evolution of societies, most organization theories will offer complexity as a measurement of societal advancement. The more complex an organization, the more advanced it is supposed to be, and vice-versa. By analogy, it has often been assumed that, in complex organizations, the latest (freshest) layer, the superstructure, has to be more complex than its predecessors, lower levels of organization.

For this reason, services (especially information-intensive services) have often been seen as the freshest organizational layer of our modern economies, and thus exclusively as a superstructure of such economies. The point made earlier about global corporations' strategies shows that services (and information) superstructures, once established, have a tendency to become a necessary infrastructure for competitive modern organizations like global corporations. The way in which this phenomenon takes place is one of pervasion of the organization from its highest level (superstructure) down to its very roots. By transcending the organizations they emanated from, information networks have thus become a *metastructure* of modern corporations.[15]

AN ANALYTICAL ISSUE: TECHNOLOGY AND COMPARATIVE ADVANTAGE

One of the positive aspects that many developing countries have identified in the current services revolution is related to these countries' increased ability to break away from their dependence on natural factor endowments (especially commodities) and to adopt leapfrogging strategies in order to rapidly build up competitive services sectors. The emergence of information as a central element of this revolution suggests that analysts should take a somewhat rejuvenated look at so-called specialization strategies when such strategies are to focus on information-intensive services activities.

Specialization in Goods versus Specialization in Services

According to the pure theory of international trade (HOS), the optimum specialization strategy for any country consists in exporting the items whose production requires a combination of factors that are as close as possible to the combination in which these factors exist in the country's natural factor endowment. From a technologi-

Figure 6-2. The Traditional Technological Paradigm.

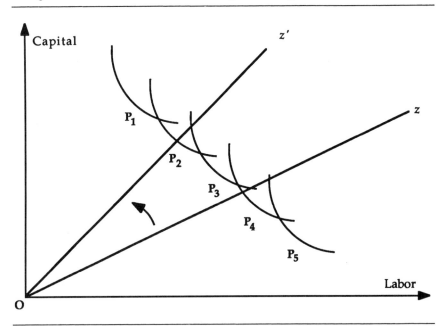

cal point of view, this means that national specialization should change as the country's typical capital/labor ratio increases.[16] Figure 6-2 is a traditional graphic representation of this, where only a few isoquants (indifference curves in terms of provision of production factors by the national economy) will intersect with line Oz (which represents the capital/labor ratio of the economy at time t). When the country acquires the necessary technology for this capital/labor ratio to move from Oz to Oz', its specialization can switch from product P_4 to product P_2.[17]

In the case of services, however, one may reasonably think that the span of capital/labor ratios that are adequate to produce a given service is substantially wider than in the case of goods. Actually, many services (banking, insurance, government, tourism) can be produced in a very capitalistic, generally information-intensive way, but also (and quite competitively) in a much more traditional, generally labor-intensive, fashion. Using the terminology mentioned above, this means that service isoquants will be flatter than goods isoquants.[18] (See Figure 6-3, where S_1 and S_2 are the isoquants of two distinct service activities.)

Figure 6-3. The Service Technological Paradigm.

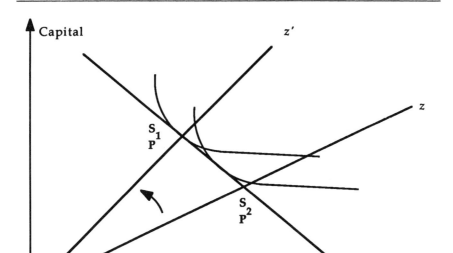

A typical developing country could choose the following specialization strategy: first, it will specialize in the production of a service
(or set of services) requiring a relatively low input in capital; then,
as the country's capital/labor ratio increases, rather than switching to
another, more capital-intensive type of service specialization, it will
switch to a more capital-intensive way of producing *the same service.*
This new possibility may appear as of crucial importance for many
developing countries, since the barriers faced by newcomers on many
international services markets are currently very high.

Information-Based Specialization versus
Capital/Labor "Pure" Mix

In this technology-oriented specialization model, several elements
point at information as a discriminant factor. For instance, a more
capital-intensive way of producing banking services could be to offer
more advanced financial services through existing branches, or to
extend the usual service hours by installing automatic teller ma-

chines (ATMs), or to speed up interbranch operations through electronic fund transfers (EFTs). By and large, the higher capital-intensity of the service seems to go hand in hand with its higher information intensity.

However, this is not necessarily the case. As a matter of fact, many information-intensive activities happen to be labor-intensive ones: computer programming, data base building (collecting and encoding information in computer-readable format), checking and verification of information, for example, are all labor-intensive high-tech activities in which many countries with labor-abundant economies could successfully specialize.

In analytical terms, this means that, in an information-intensive world economy, international specialization strategies could ill afford to be based on the sole consideration of a "pure" capital-labor mix. Information has to be individualized (disembodied) as a genuine production factor if countries (developing countries in particular) are to be able to identify the strategic possibilities available to them.

Figure 6–4 uses a three-dimensional representation of the technology-based model described earlier in order to show that, for any

Figure 6–4. Service Production and Technological Development.

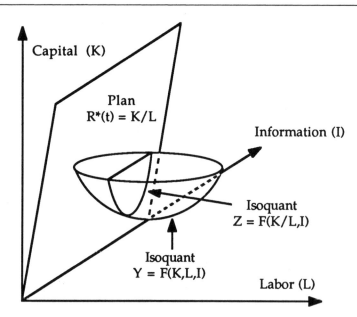

given (or chosen) capital/labor ratio (for any given level of techno-logical development), there exists a continuum of information-based specializations that a country may wish to adopt. The different points on this continuum (actually a two-dimensional isoquant) reflect different degrees of information intensity in producing the service considered.

On any given isoquant, and for any given capital/labor ratio (for example, $R^*(t)$, the optimal capital/labor ratio for the economy at time t), the same service $S(i)$ can be produced in several different (more or less information-intensive) ways. These different levels of information intensity correspond to the different points of the two-dimensional isoquant $Z = F(K/L, I)$, constituted by the intersection of the three-dimensional isoquant $Y = F(K, L, I)$ on the one hand, and of the plan $R^*(t) = L/K$ on the other.

It must be noted here that there is a clear difference between microeconomic behaviors (corporate strategies) and macroeconomic policies (national trade specialization choices). In the first case, it will be the information intensity of its productions that will partly determine a corporation's choice in terms of capital/labor ratio. On the contrary, in the second case, the economic authorities of a coun-try will often take the capital/labor ratio as an exogenous charac-teristic of their economy. It is in this context that one can see information-based specialization strategies as a way for an economy of moving away from the "HOS curse," and the dictatorship of natural factor endowments.

CONCLUSION: STRATEGIC CONSEQUENCES
FOR DEVELOPING COUNTRIES

The conceptual and analytical remarks made here suggest that devel-oping countries have to respond quickly to the challenges of the emerging information/service economy in order to stand a chance to escape their current peripheral condition. In particular, it seems that, given the level of uncertainty that still plagues future prospects for international trade and the world economy as a whole in terms of international division of labor, a relatively safe course for developing countries would be to imitate the leaders. In the absence of clearly identifiable niches, their specialization strategies should initially repeat those currently followed by dominant actors, i.e., horizontal ones. A horizontal specialization strategy (as opposed to a vertical or sectoral one) consists of adopting a way of doing rather than a type of product. In other words, a horizontal specialization is one that gives priority to the *how* to produce, over the *what* to produce. Such a specialization strategy is particularly obvious when a company (or a country) identifies information as the main source of its competitive (comparative) advantage.

Only then, depending on the evolution of supply and demand factors, could these countries adopt fall-back strategies based on vertical (sectoral or subsectoral) specialization lines (either traditional or new). Depending on their course of action, developing countries should then negotiate accordingly.

In practical terms, this suggests that developing countries grant immediate priority to those efforts that are most likely to reinforce their capacities to do two things:

1. Acquire information capacities in ways that reflect the current (or desired) capital/labor ratio of the economy. Such ways may include

   a. Using domestic resources (financial and human) to generate a national capacity to produce, collect, process, and use information;
   b. Dealing with foreign investors likely to bring part of their information know-how to the host country;
   c. Importing the locally lacking components of such information-intensive resources (hardware, software, expertise, information services, and information itself).

Most probably, countries will adopt a mix of such possibilities, depending on their own economic constraints (in terms of resources available, trade structure, existing trade relations) and political choices (in particular vis-à-vis so-called sensitive sectors like telecommunications or defence).

2. Efficiently negotiate by contributing to a mutually beneficial trade agreement. This will necessitate developing countries, like many developed countries, to envisage the ongoing process as a two-layered one.[19] Information-related issues will first have to be dealt with (either in GATT or in a different, more specialized, forum) before the negotiators can move to a productive multi-

lateral discussion of individual services sectors. This will be a delicate process in which developing countries will have to prevent two types of failures from happening: that the first stage (dealing with information) involve only a few advanced countries, and that this first stage be shortcut through bilateral trade agreements.

NOTES

1. See, for instance, J. Bhagwati, "International Trade in Services and Its Relevance for Economic Development," in O. Giarini, ed., *The Emerging Service Economy*, Services World Forum, Geneva (New York: Pergamon Press, 1987).

2. Murray Gibbs, "The Uruguay Round and the International Trading System," *Journal of World Trade Law* 21, no. 5 (October 1987): 199–218.

3. See John Richardson, "A Sub-Sectoral Approach to Services Trade Theory," in O. Giarini, ed., *The Emerging Service Economy*, Services World Forum, Geneva (New York: Pergamon Press, 1987).

4. Rather than "information," most negotiators generally use term "transborder data flows" (TDF). See Karl P. Sauvant, "Transborder Data Flows: Importance, Impact, Policies," *Information Services and Use* 4 (1984): 3–30.

5. In March 1986, both *Business Week* and *Fortune* magazines published special surveys on "the hollow corporation." See also J. Lempérière, "Quand les Etats-Unis achètent à l'étranger leur matériel de production," *Le Monde Diplomatique*, September 1986, pp. 8–9.

6. The basic message was: "Services cannot be a basis for national competitiveness *in isolation*: they need an industrial basis to be a genuine source of wealth creation." See for instance Ron Shelp and Gary Hart, "Facing the Challenge of a New Economy," *Wall Street Journal*, December 28, 1986, p. 1.

7. Every catastrophe (in René Thom's sense, a break) always brings its cohort of brilliant ex-post predictions. A self-quotation is thus here in order. See B. Lanvin, "Réseaux et Compétitivité," *Bulletin de l'IDATE* 25 (November 1986): 615–25.

8. One response of U.S. automobile manufacturers to imports competition has been to shift the battleground from the good (the automobile) to the services. At some point, some U.S. banks have even considered General Motors and Chrysler as unfair competitors. See "The Market Share Fight over Auto Loans," *Fortune*, October 27, 1986, p. 66.

9. These examples are quoted from E. Larson, M. Ross, and R. Williams, "Beyond the Era of Materials," *Scientific American*, June 1986.

10. "Real Primary Commodity Prices: An Analysis of Long Run Movements," D. Sapsford, internal memorandum dated May 17, 1985, International Monetary Fund, Washington, D.C.

11. The difference between challenging the theory and questioning its underlying logics may be compared with the difference between the Einsteinian revolutionary concept of relativity (which challenged Newtonian mechanics without significantly altering everyday physics) on the one hand, and the Copernican revolution (which, by reversing the Ptolemaic hierarchy, triggered a complete intellectual renewal in Western civilization).

12. As far as the strategies of service TNCs are concerned, Dunning's "eclectic theory" has a somewhat greater explanatory power than Vernon's "product cycle" approach. Both, however, rely extensively on HOS hypotheses. See R. Vernon, "International Investment and International Trade in the Product Cycle," *Quarterly Journal of Economics* (May 1966): 190–207; and J. Dunning, *International Production and the Multinational Enterprise* (London: G. Allen and Unwin, 1981).

13. One explanation of this increasing involvement is of course the generation of externalities: in those TNCs that had built efficient and sophisticated information networks, information (and risk) became a marketable commodity.

14. Or to "access" new locations through strategic alliances: the notion of internetwork complementarity (both functional and geographical) has emerged as a key element in recent cross-investment and merger agreements between global corporations, especially in financial and insurance services.

15. The prefix *meta* is used here in the sense "of a higher or second-order kind." as in "metalanguage."

16. Which could be considered a simplified way of describing Hicksian labor-saving technical progress.

17. It is likely that, in the occurrence of Hicksian labor-intensive technical progress, the isocost (the unrepresented common tangent to the isoquants in Figure 6–1) would also change slope (otherwise, one would be in a Rybczynski-theorem type of situation). This aspect is neglected here, for the sake of clarity. It can be easily proved, however, that the point made remains valid in spite of this simplification.

18. An interesting analytical point would probably deserve further exploration in this respect: the combination of isoquants of different curvatures is typical of situations in which factor-intensity reversal may occur (Leontief paradox). In such situations, it can be argued that a relatively labor-abundant country may reasonably specialize in information-intensive productions. For reference, see M. Michaely, "Factor Proportions in International Trade: Comment on the State of the Theory," *Kyklos* (June 1964).

19. It has been argued that the December 1987 U.S. proposal in the context of the GATT negotiation was precisely an attempt to skip the first of these two layers by offering negotiators the possibility of discussing the adoption of the presence principles (right of establishment and national treatment) before moving to sectorial discussions.

7 THE ORGANIZATIONAL APPROACH TO INTERNATIONALIZATION OF SERVICES

Pascal Petit

DISPARATE TRENDS IN TRADE SERVICES

Since the 1960s trade in services has expanded more quickly than national gross domestic products. But in contrast with what happened at the domestic sectoral level, trade in services did not grow faster than trade in goods once factor services (returns on investment, representing half of the trade in services)[1] are set apart (see Table 7-1).

Within nonfactor services, trends appear more diverse: some trades have been expanding during the last decade more quickly than trade in goods (like the miscellaneous services in Table 7-1) and some other have relatively stagnated (like transport and travel).

Two main theses can be called upon to analyze this development in international trade. According to the standard thesis on trade specialization, industrialized economies tend to specialize in areas of services, where they still have some comparative advantages. Alternatively the other thesis, labeled hereafter the organizational thesis, underlines changes in production and exchange processes due to technical changes and market integration, which has led to an important internal development in producer services and to an even larger external development in service trade linked with the internationalization of productions and markets. The comparative advantage explanation has given way to various estimates, which mainly support

121

Table 7-1. The Relative Growth of Trade in Nonfactor Services (1973–84).

	Europe				United States			
	Export		Import		Export		Import	
	a	b	a	b	a	b	a	b
Nonfactor services	173,817	417	159,195	390	52,299	546	52,039	562
Transports	57,520	340	59,163	337	21,412	578	26,925	608
Travel	43,350	437	42,510	360	14,479	620	20,396	544
Miscellaneous services	72,947	493	57,522	503	16,408	462	4,718	437
Goods	711,277	435	703,706	437	279,674	576	425,011	886

a. 1984 value in millions of ECUS.
b. Growth rate 1984/1973.
Source: Balance-of-payments statistics from the Statistical Office of the European Community (SOEC), Luxembourg.

it in the case of slowly growing service transactions such as transport or tourism. By contrast the organizational thesis often remained loosely specified but was mainly directed toward the rapidly growing producer services.

Market perspectives for industrialized countries will be very different whether or not the specialization or the organizational thesis hold.

The breakdown in the seventies of the postwar international regime has increased the general level of competition. In terms of expansion in trade in services this implies two types of evolution: either a move toward more advantageous specializations or a general reorganization of production and exchange norms.

THE COMPARATIVE ADVANTAGE THESIS APPLIES TO SLOWLY GROWING SERVICE TRADES

Let us, first, sum up the main arguments and empirical work that explain the structure and dynamics of trade in services through the comparative advantage thesis. The Heckscher-Ohlin-Samuelson (HOS) model tries to explain comparative cost advantage in terms of relative abundance of factor inputs. The main difficulty is to clearly define the proper inputs. If input factors are not theoretically predefined and limited in number, the HOS theory leaves way to adhocery when output is not itself clearly defined in volume and quality. This shortcoming is most prominent in the case of services as reflected in empirical works, either the HOS theory is too crude or it fails to explain trade structure.[2] For the industrialized countries, none of the indicators of factor endowment appear to be correlated with a credit or deficit balance for trade in services. There is such a correlation for developing countries as far as trade in transport services, tourist expenditure, and insurance services are concerned, but none in the case of specialized services. HOS theory only gives a rough picture when comparing highly differentiated cases. It fails when developed economies or when more elaborated services are considered.

Is there any theoretical ground to account for this deficiency? According to Richardson, there is not.[3] The question of properly defined inputs and outputs is not a tractable issue, which suggests that the HOS theory cannot be refuted. Another way to look at this question is to stress that most of the shortcomings of the HOS approach are reinforced in the case of service transactions:

- Markets are not competitive: the localization of services in transport, tourism, the intrinsic regulation in banking and insurance, the cultural and legal practices in specialized services, all converge in fragmenting the markets.

- Products are not homogeneous: the tailor-made dimension of many services blurs the perception of output, of production efficiency, and therefore of unit-costs of production.

- Economies of scale: both internal and external economies of scale in service activities (with traditional reference to transport and telecommunications, but also relevance with producer services) can foster "new" advantages.

- Joint productions: dominant positions in other trades pave the way to set up service networks and to link services with trade flows currently practiced in transport and insurance.

The limitations of the HOS thesis are especially stringent in the case of the fast growing trade of producer services, where the organizational thesis may be more in accordance with observed trade flows.

REORGANIZING FIRMS AND MARKETS IN TIMES OF STAGNATION

As an alternative to the HOS thesis, we shall develop an approach that mainly focuses on shifts in firms' organizational forms. The organizational thesis states that increased competition in world trade, new information technologies, search for economies of scale, and search for economies of scope within big firms and between small firms all concur in stimulating internal growth in producer services and in developing services trade flows.

Let us recall the characteristics under which some producer services have developed. Transport, communication, and finance networks were set up independently; separate organizations of these industries were effectively achieved at the turn of this century. The rate of expansion and the forms of producer services depend on large firms' internal organization and on small firms' external organization. The organization of large firms into departments by function:

finance, marketing, manufacturing, engineering (the U-form, for unitary structure, in Chandler's terminology) constituted, at the end of the nineteenth century, a major step, allowing for internal economies of scale. A shift from these U-forms to what Williamson called M-form firms (multidivisional structure in which profit centers organized along product, brand, or geographic lines are operating semiautonomously) took place in the United States in the thirties, in response to greater market pressure and internal organizational deadlocks. These changes only occurred in the fifties and the sixties in Europe.[4] The M-form was seen as an intermediate optimum form between the U-form, largely unmanageable over a certain size if confronted with market hazards, and the H-form, or holding form, where production management expertise was overlooked and financial concerns were overwhelming. Therefore the M-form specifically concentrated in one place the strategic part in management and control. This new organization of firms is more prone to develop and to use producer services, for the center to define and to control the implementation of strategies, and for the divisions to take advantage of external expertise and scale economies in tertiary tasks. The fact that big firms either set up these services or directly back their development is decisive, as this offers a market, from which service can expand toward other firms, large, medium, or small.

The following five points specify the present stage of this organizational change.

1. The M-form tends to be dominant, as it concerned 78 percent of large U.S. firms in the 1970s. (Pousette has discussed the diffusion stage of the M-form in some European countries.)[5] There are limits nevertheless to this diffusion[6] and there is a large variety of quasi–M-forms where decision power is more or less deconcentrated. One can assume that the more decentralized, the more prone the firms will be to use external services.

2. Multinational firms have a need for coordination that leads them to be particularly active in setting up international networks of services.[7]

3. Banking and insurance firms are also especially liable to support development of producer services. Lots of these service activities can help them in certifying, controlling, auditing, or more generally in processing information concerning or interesting their clients.

4. The trends in organization do not erase national specificities in sectoral division labor, nor does it suppress national biases toward more vertical or more horizontal information structure within firms.[8] These persisting national differences explain the discrepancies between service classifications. Proper tests of the organizational thesis are therefore difficult to implement using standard statistical surveys.

5. The rise in producer services allows for a greater vertical disintegration within firms, but it also facilitates a greater (horizontal) concentration in all industries including services. Oligopolistic structures are thus quickly developing in such services as auditing and advertising.

Can such transformation of firms and markets organization be detected in the case of the expansion of the trade in "miscellaneous services"? A first global indicator is given by a specialization index. According to the organizational thesis exports and imports of producer services should expand simultaneously and trade exhibit a despecialization trend, as it effectively does in Table 7–2.

A second important supporting evidence should stem from the growth of service exchanges between parent firms and foreign affiliates. Transactions between affiliates and parents either give way to income transfers and are then registered as factor services or they remunerate the links with parent firms as a royalty or fee or as professional or managerial services. But trade data of the U.S. Department of Commerce show that most of affiliate-parent transactions are still channeled through factor incomes.[9] A third type of indicators could be found in the way services can effectively be traded. Affiliation—the need to invest and to produce locally—is a central issue in all service trades. The choice for the firm is to balance the respective share of local and home productions. Often transaction cannot take place without some local affiliate (or assimilated). Reciprocally, some kind of linkage has to be maintained between decision centers and local production sites. Dunning gives three general reasons for direct investments:

1. Direct investment retains all the advantages of the parent company: brand image, organizational and technological capabilities, and supply network.

Table 7-2. Specializations in Trades of Nonfactor Services.

$$Index = \frac{Exports - Imports}{Exports + Imports}, \%, 1973, 1984$$

	West Germany		France		United Kingdom		Italy		United States	
	1973	1984	1973	1984	1973	1984	1973	1984	1973	1984
Nonfactor services	-27	-17	13	16	11	12	5	14	2	0
Miscellaneous services	-20	-0.5	38	27	40	37	-16	-4	188	37

Source: Balance-of-payments statistics, SOEC, Luxembourg.

2. It enables firms to benefit from the particular conditions of access to local markets, whether this involves avoiding customs restrictions or tailoring their products more closely to the local market.

3. Finally, it enables firms to reduce production costs by using cheaper labor and inputs and more convenient transport arrangements.[10]

In the last decade, however, the balance may have shifted toward more direct exports of services. Liberalization of trade, reductions in factor prices differences among developed economies, greater integration of worldwide markets, especially financial markets, all concur in facilitating this new balance. But the key issue in that respect lies with changes in information technology and telecommunications. Computerized communications technology has provided new possibilities for transborder exchanges, with reduced local ties. Producer services has taken advantage of this opportunity in order to extend their activities worldwide, setting up affiliates in close touch with the main decision center. Better and cheaper connection with home decision centers has lessened the size of initial investment and therefore reduced barriers to entry. Foreign markets have thus become within reach of medium-size service firms.

Similarly, internal reorganization and emergence of information technology have pressed already existing multinational firms to make a more extensive use of external service network, if only to harmonize management. Caves (quoting studies by Dyas and Thanheiser and by Franko) mentions the role played by American consulting firms in reorganizing multinational firms.

This set of arguments leads us to expect more services (especialiy producer and finance services) to be exchanged, due to changes in production norms and exchange conditions. Yet while supporting the organizational thesis, they do not predetermine the macroeconomic outcome.

MACROECONOMIC AND POLICY PERSPECTIVES

In fact the supply-side effect of services did lead to a build up of country specialization but at a level of more precisely defined and diverse service trades. Thenault and Olivry have listed dominant positions of national industries in a survey on prospects for trade liberalization that concerned twelve service sectors.[11] Table 7-3 gives a summary of this information that shows the widespread range of these specializations.

Two polar cases may correspond to this intraindustry specialization process.[12] One polar case refers to an international division of labor, where intrabranch specializations, evenly distributed, induce interdependence between any pair of trade partner-countries. The second polar case corresponds to a division of labor with asymmetric relationships between buyers and sellers. Country B will always buy from A and sell to C. An example of such a triangular trade can be found with A as a dominant economy, B a developed medium-size economy, and C a developing economy. Both cases will display lack of specialization in overall service trade.

Scattered and narrow specializations imply very specific advantages, some of them being tied to available organization forms and network opportunities. Hence, such advantages either can be developed by other economies or can disappear.

Therefore, the past decade may have been a first phase open to widespread narrow specializations and the forthcoming decade may witness a reshuffling of positions. The difficulty[13] for France's software industry to keep its dominant position illustrates one side of this evolution. Similar drawbacks are being experienced in engineering and construction international transactions.

The last decade of service trade expansion did not put an end to the supremacies acquired in finance (by the United States and the United Kingdom) or in technology trade (for the United States). But the trend was toward a marked reduction in these positions (see Table 7-2).[14] The main challenge in these fields has come from the Japanese economy.

We can now summarize the argument. A general shift in firms' organization both facilitated and took advantage of expansion in producer services. This reorganization was accompanied by an increase in service trade and allowed for narrowly defined specializations. In a second phase, wider specializations and new strongholds will tend to emerge, brought about by further standardization of productions. Questions arise on the extent of such cyclical moves in the organization of trade in services. Is there a specific product cycle? What is the role of medium-size developed economies in this process? A macroeconomic perspective on this emerging service trade

Table 7-3. Trade in Services: Market Structures and Prospects of Liberalization (1984).

Branch	Dominant Firms in the Early 1980s	Type of Competition	Prospects of Liberalization
Insurance			
Life	National firms dominant on their home market	Strong competition, need of long-term confident relationships	Bounded
Transport	U.K. firms	Segmented markets	Joint services insurance/transport
Reinsurance	Importance of German firms Among the first 15[a]: 1 FR, 1 U.K., 5 U.S. 6 W.G.	Free access to market, Bankruptcies in the mid-70s	Free market Mobility of capital
Banking	Among the first 20[a]: 3 FR, 8 JA, 4 U.K., 3 U.S., 1 W.G.	Networks regulations, dominance of some financial places	Exchange control Rights of investments
Engineering and construction	Among the first 50[a]: 22 EEC (36%)[b], 8 FR (13%), 3 JA (5%), 7 Korea (8%) 4 U.K. (7%), 14 U.S. (48%), 6 W.G. (9%)	High specializations Export subsidies Financing conditions Public markets	Subsidies Open public market Firms joint venture Mobility of factors
Computer services	Among the first 20[a]: 10 FR, 1 U.K., 3 U.S., 1 W.G. U.S. hegemony on data bank[a]	Highly diversified Segmented markets Dependance relationships with communication networks	Mobility of professionals Fiscal harmonization Access to telecommunications

	Market shares		Constraints on local affiliates
Technical engineering	Market shares FR (9%), JA (3%), U.K. (14%), U.S. (34%), W.G. (6%)	Exports toward the developing countries Lack of home market	Problems of norms and fiscal harmonization
Trading houses	Over one-third of transactions in Italy, Japan, U.S., W.G.	Working at national level	Exchange controls, rights of investment
Audit	Market shares CA (12%), U.K. (10%), U.S. (37%)	Local affiliates	Rights of investment, qualified workers
Advertising	Market shares EEC (10%), JA (14%), U.S. (75%)	Open market Agreements between firms' local affiliates	

a. Markets include home sales.
b. Figures in parentheses show market shares.
Source: A survey by J.P. Thenault and D. Olivry, "La perception du secteur privé des services des intérêts communautaires, pour une libéralisation du commerce international des services," Document CEE, SEMA METRA, 1984.

will bring part of the answers and set the main challenges in economic policy.

The focus in the previous sections has been on producer services, which constitute only 10 percent of service trade but nevertheless are at the core of the present debate on trade liberalization in service industries. What is at stake is actually more important than the modest share in transactions may suggest. First, the value of these transactions is increasing more quickly than average, and more important, it tends to set the standards of competitiveness and profitability. This strategic aspect derives partly from the kind of entrepreneurship externalization, which they allow[15] and from the new capacities to adjust production and to screen demand that they provide. In a world of competition these new capacities making an extensive use of new information technology, tend to become norms—necessary conditions.

Changes in production norms, linked with the use of producer services, can be seen as increasing the flexibility of supply, while changes in exchange norms can be seen as a drive toward prediction or stabilization of demand. Lots of marketing activities, sales of packages or compounded products (goods/services "compacks"[16]), customization, fostering client loyalty, credit facilities, all tend to remedy intrinsic demand uncertainty and instability for a given firm.

We are, therefore, back to the traditional opposition between rigidity of supply (implying that entrepreneurs have to take a long-term view of the economy so as to organize production) and genuine volatility of demand. Changes in firms' organization are a means to cope with this discrepancy. The present move combines a trend toward vertical disintegration—that is, more market forces as compared with fully integrated big corporation—with a trend to monitor markets, so as to reduce the unpredictability of competition.

The key question as far as liberalization policies are concerned is to know how far can market forces achieve such an objective at the international level. A first paradox comes from the fact that externalization of services, which originates from deadlocks in channeling information within large firms, is rapidly confronted with specific other information problems, such as those referred to in the literature on asymmetric information. Cases of moral hazards or of adverse selection illustrate transactions where producers have all the information and buyers have not. Institutional solutions to the previous problem have to be found. Holmstrom lists four types of market responses to quality assurance in service activities:

- Contingent contracts, depending on observable variables relevant to the delivery of the service
- Reputation, which performs as an implicit contracts, enforced by the seller's concern about future demand for his service
- Signaling, of which educational credits constitute a standard example
- Certification and monitoring, directly oriented to attest service qualifications; this certification sometimes itself being a service[17]

Aside from contingent contracts, these recognition processes are highly conservative. They will play in favor of dominant firms in case of trade liberalization measure, size being the most readily available criteria. The same dynamics will also promote merging or cooperation of firms, even of slightly related trades. Therefore, liberalization moves may lead to accelerated concentration in services industries. The shortcomings of such a trend are two-sided:

- At a micro level, large service firms will themselves face the same difficulties as all large organizations in keeping up with market trends and innovations.

- At a macro level, similar strategic advices or procedures will be given to firms in order to render their production more flexible or to consumers to stabilize demand. This may result in a very unstable system, where all responses to external stimulus converge and amplify initial shocks.

One way to avoid such problems is for liberalization to be accompanied by new certification schemes. Countries with well-institutionalized certification schemes will be more willing to liberalize service trade. Therefore the requirements for trade liberalization not to run into difficulties are stringent. Complex fabrics of institutions are involved in national certification processes. This accounts for the difficulty of suppressing "invisible" obstacles. Setting up a new free transaction zone, as intended with the EC Internal Market (or Project 1992), there requires not only the suppression of obstacles but also the re-creation of harmonized certification procedures.

NOTES

1. Income from direct productive investment abroad and profits from financial investment account for nearly half of the trade in services (46 percent of service exports in the ten European countries of the common market, 62 percent in the United States in 1984). Other factor services—earning from work and government transactions—represent one-tenth of the investment incomes (5 percent of service trade in EEC countries in 1984).
2. A. Sapir and E. Lutz attempted to estimate correlations between distribution of production factors, such as the capital/labor ratio, the size of the country, the extent of the training system, research and development expenditures, with the structure of trade in four nonfactors services (transport, travel, insurance, and specialized services), in 50 countries (including 35 developing countries) during the year 1977.
3. J. Richardson, "A Sub-sectorial Approach to Services," in O. Giarini, ed., *The Emerging Service Economy* (New York: Pergamon Press, 1987).
4. A. D. Chandler and H. Daems, *Managerial Hierarchies* (Cambridge, Mass.: Harvard University Press, 1980).
5. T. Pousette, "Service in Industry: An International Comparison," Working Paper 27p, World Service Forum, Geneva, 1987.
6. R. E. Caves, "Industrial Organization, Corporate Strategy and Structure," *Journal of Economic Literature* 18, no. 1 (1980): 64–92.
7. H. Schwamm and P. Merciai, *Les entreprises multinationales et les services* (Paris: PUF, 1985). F. Clairmonte and J. Cavanagh, "Transnational Corporations and Services: The Final Frontier," *Trade and Development*, UNCTAD, no. 5 (1984).
8. M. Aoki, "Horizontal vs. Vertical Information Structure of the Firm," *American Economic Review* (December 1986): 971–83.
9. In 1977, for instance, income of foreign affiliates of all U.S. service industries parents amounted to $280.2 billion (of which petroleum accounted for 97.2, trade 104.4, banking 23.2, other finance and insurance 17.4, construction 10.1, transportation 3.5, communication 9.9, other services 12.6); to be compared with $19 billion of private nonfactor service exports. Other related data show that U.S. parents in service industries sold $16 billion in 1983 to foreign persons, of which only $4 billion is owed to foreign affiliates. In the meantime, sales of foreign affiliates (majority-owned according to U.S. Department of Commerce statistics) amounted to $68 billion, of which $10 billion belonged to other foreign affiliates and $7 billion to U.S. parents.
10. J. H. Dunning, "Explaining Changing Patterns of International Production: in Defense of the Eclectic Theory," *Oxford Bulletin of Economics and Statistics* 41 (November 1979).

11. J.P. Thenault and D. Olivry, "La perception du secteur privé des services des intérêts communautaires, pour une libéralisation du commerce international des services," Document EEC (European Economic Community, SEMA METRA, Paris, 1984).

12. B. Lassudrie-Duchéne and J.L. Muchielli, "Les Echanges Intra-Branches et la Hiérarchisation des Advantages Comparés dans le Commerce International," *Revue Economique* (May 1979).

13. C. Fontaine, *L'expansion des services*, 3 vols. (Paris: Ronéoté Rexervices, 1987). Office for Technology Assessment, *International Competition in Services* (Washington, D.C.: U.S. Congress Office of Technology Assessment, 1987).

14. OTA, *International Competition in Services.*

15. T.M. Stanback, P.J. Bearse, T. Noyelle, and R. Karasek, *Services: The New Economy* (Totowa, N.J.: Allanheld Osmun, 1981).

16. A. Bressand, "International Division of Labor in the Emerging Global Information Economy: The Need for a New Paradigm," FAST seminar, EEC, Brussels, June 1986.

17. B. Holmstrom, "The Provision of Services in a Market Economy," in R. Inman, ed., *Managing the Service Economy* (Cambridge, England: Cambridge University Press, 1985).

8 SERVICES AND DEVELOPMENT
The Mexican Case

Fernando De Mateo
Françoise Carner

The preparation and launching of the Uruguay Round of the Multi-lateral Trade Negotiations has led to a plethora of studies related to the services sector and trade in services in both the developed and the developing countries. Yet, while developed countries can devote large amounts of resources to such research, developing countries are often painstakingly trying to avoid negotiating in the Uruguay Round actually ignoring their basic strengths and weaknesses.[1] In this chapter an attempt is made to provide an overview of the role of services in the Mexican economy.

THE TRADITIONAL VIEW

The much publicized "three-stage" theory's implicit conclusion is that in the emerging international economic order, developing countries should specialize in agriculture and mining, newly industrializing countries in manufactures, and "deindustrializing" developed countries in services, for this is seen as the natural path toward development.

If the Heckscher-Ohlin-Samuelson theorem applies to trade in services, developed countries should obviously export services, given that they have the capital and human resources lacking in the developing countries. Some of the NICs, however, having reached a stage where they can export "splintered" services, bear a negative services trade balance with developed countries and a positive one with less developed developing countries.

However, theorists have to reconcile the fact that services generally need to be produced and consumed in the same place and at the same time, whereas one of the fundamental assumptions of the HOS theorem is precisely the international immobility of the factors of production.[2] Ultimately, they end up arguing that for comparative advantage dynamics to fully take place it is necessary for foreign direct investment (FDI) to take place.[3] The result is the widespread vision of trade negotiations in which developed countries would grant trade concessions in goods in exchange for concessions in services *and* foreign investment.

This tradeoff might be beneficial for all in the long run if the complementary assumptions of the three-stage theory and the HOS theorem actually applied to services. Yet, we can draw additional lessons from the so-called services revolution most visible in the developed countries, lessons that lead us to question these simplistic conclusions.

THE ACTUAL IMPACT OF THE SERVICES REVOLUTION

The service sector serves to promote and distribute new technologies to the other economic sectors. Generally, speaking, these new technologies are labor-saving, and lead to increasingly "knowledge-intensive" products. Automation and robotization are becoming the new basis of manufacturing in the developed countries, and these and other technological breakthroughs are helping these countries to regain competitive advantage in many of the products exported up to now by the NICs, as in textiles for instance. Thus, the first assumption of the three-stage theory is not fulfilled. Developed countries are not in a stage of deindustrialization and are actually specializing in both services and manufacturing exports.

The second lesson of the service revolution is that the new technologies and service-intensive production techniques conserve raw materials. Plastics, fiber optics, ceramics, silicon, alternative sources of energy, and so forth have been replacing resources such as copper, iron, lead, and oil in the production processes. No wonder that international prices of the traditional primary commodities are today at their lowest levels since the Great Depression of the 1930s.[4] For instance, if the prices of Mexican exports in 1986 had been the same as in 1980, export revenues of that country would have been 66 percent higher. Thus, a second assumption of the three-stage theory is not fulfilled either. Raw-materials-exporting developing countries are in no position to earn the foreign exchange required to foster their economic development (or service their foreign debt).

Under these circumstances, foreign trade multipliers in most of the developing countries have not been able to function adequately during the 1980s. Thus, the so-called locomotive theory has not worked either; this was particularly clear for Latin America during the strong U.S. recovery in the first half of the decade. A more far-reaching conclusion is that the services revolution in the developed countries is reducing developing countries' role both as suppliers and demanders in the world economy to a marginal one.[5]

Moreover, the debt crisis and the contraction of developing countries' growth rates during the early 1980s have led to the concentration of financial and foreign direct investment flows in the developed world. At the same time, the world financial and trade systems have been drifting apart, with an enormous growth of financial flows made possible by new technologies in telematics.[6]

Another characteristic of the services revolution is the dominance of the world market by big transnational services enterprises or, rather, by big "transnational integrated conglomerates,"[7] coexisting with small enterprises sometimes subsidiaries of the former. Among the factors explaining the great dynamism of these TNCs, the most important may precisely be the little tradeability of services, requiring a physical presence in foreign markets. Service TNCs need to follow their goods-producing clients, which internationalized their operations in the sixties and seventies, and hence were bound to develop worldwide operations (see Chapter 6). In this respect, it is worthwhile noting, for instance, that while in 1950 only 32 percent of the U.S. FDI was in the services sector, by 1985 it was 44 percent. In the case of Germany, these percentages were 10 percent in 1966 and 47 percent in 1984.

As mentioned earlier, during the 1980s the developed countries' service sector has served to spread technological advances. The main feature of this phenomenon is what UNCTAD (United Nations Conference on Trade and Development) has called the "externalization process of the producers services," the fact that services that used to be produced in-house by manufacturing enterprises, like accounting, engineering, advertising, and transportation, are now provided by independent services enterprises.

In this respect, the so-called information revolution has played a central role. Analysts in developed countries often stress the fact that data processing is becoming the backbone of the economy, not only as a service in itself but as the infrastructure for producer services. If a manufacturing firm calls for an independent engineering enterprise to provide it with computer-aided design (CAD) and computer-aided manufacturing (CAM) services, its productivity and efficiency might be greatly increased, thanks to indirect benefit from economies of scale, and market access will be made easier through lower levels of necessary upfront investment.[8]

In a nutshell, there is a growing consensus about the fact that the producer services sector has become highly integrated with the other economic sectors, and that this integration is characterized to a great extent by high technologies. A major conclusion is that the industrial foundations of developed countries' economies, far from becoming of secondary importance, have been enhanced by these new intersectorial relations.[9]

Under these circumstances, there is little basis, except for demagogic reasons, for pointing to the deindustrialization of developed countries or the MacDonaldization of these economies. Yet, such clichés are used as the basis for neoprotectionist arguments against allowing for the continued "flood" of imports from newly industrializing countries (NICs), based on an infant-industry type of rationale. The analogy is doomed however, as soon as we recognize that the services sector in the developed countries, through its high-tech interlinkages with other activities, is increasing the efficiency and productivity across the board. In this vein developed countries have regained international competitiveness in textiles but continue to protect this industry, failing to recognize, in effect, that the services revolution is dramatically putting into question traditional visions of specialization patterns.

SERVICES IN DEVELOPING COUNTRIES

There is little information regarding the behavior of the services sector in developing countries. However, we know that while this sector represents a somewhat equivalent share of gross national product in developed and developing countries, the actual participation of the services sector in the overall economy is qualitatively very different.

In the first place, some evidence exists that there has been no externalization process in the developing countries. On the contrary, UNCTAD and SELA (Sistema Economico Latino-Americano) have found that in some countries there might even have been an internalization of producer services within big and transnational corporations, given the low quality of these services when provided by producers in small and, in many cases, artisanal enterprises.

If we assume that the "other services" category of the national accounts mainly represents producer services, we should be able to observe a correlation between economic growth and the growth of other services. However, there has been an inverse correlation for many Latin American countries confirming the view that there has been no externalization process.[10] Thus, it seems that in the developing countries there are no productive linkages between services and the other economic sectors in the way that they are found in the developed countries.

On the other hand, it is indeed possible to observe the impact of the services revolution on developing countries as we note the great increase in imports of other services from developed countries. It is worthwhile noting the high income-elasticity of the demand for imports in periods of growth and the low elasticity in periods of recession. In other words, when national income grows, imports of other services grow relatively faster; when national income diminishes, the reduction of other services imports takes place at a lower pace.

We must admit that these are only working hypotheses, for the truth is that in developing countries this sector has not been studied in depth and that it is regarded, at the most, as a necessary evil, a buffer for the low part of the economic cycle. Most often manufacturing continues to be seen as the only way out of underdevelopment by countries who significantly often prefer to call themselves *indus-*

trializing countries. It is against this background that the Mexican service sector should be analyzed.

THE MEXICAN CASE

For more than 30 years, between 1945 and 1975, Mexico followed an import-substitution model in three stages:

1. Import-substitution of nondurable consumer goods (1945–60).
2. Import-substitution of durable consumer and intermediate goods (1960–70).
3. Import-substitution of sophisticated intermediate and capital goods (1965–75).[11]

During most of these three stages domestic demand grew at a fast rate, while exports fell behind and a chronic trade deficit developed. However, this import-substitution policy permitted the establishment of a broad industrial base.

With the discovery of big oil fields in the mid-1970s, this growth strategy was replaced with a leading sector (oil) model. That model's main assumptions were the following:

- Oil would provide the foreign exchange for the imports required in a high-growth economy.

- The multiplier effects of oil-related investments would provide an ever-increasing domestic demand, which in turn would stimulate domestic and foreign supply.

- Oil would provide the collateral for the foreign credits required to supplement domestic savings.

This growth model functioned quite smoothly in the period between 1977 and 1981, allowing the economy to grow at an average rate of around 8 percent. However, the model collapsed with the 1981 oil price reductions. Unfortunately, then, Mexico's foreign sector was "petrolized," with oil accounting for 75 percent of total goods exports (and a foreign debt of over $85 billion).

Since 1983 a new growth model has been followed, breaking from 40 years of an inward-looking development strategy. As the "leading-sector" model was no longer possible, and the import-substitution model obsolete (given that there were practically no more imports to substitute for), the need to service a gigantic foreign debt determined an export-oriented model.

This strategy, after an uncertain start, seems to be succeeding, with growth rates of nonoil merchandise exports up to 25 percent a year (50 percent for manufactured products) in dollar terms. However, these exports are not yet the engine for growth of the Mexican economy.

While Mexican authorities are very much aware of the country's international competitiveness in tourism and *maquiladora* industry (international subcontracting, mainly in the last stages of the production processes, often located near the U.S. border), the export promotion policy has been directed mainly to manufactured goods. This is only the reflection of the widespread perception that manufacturing is to solve most of Mexico's economic problems.

However, Mexico is among the 15 top service exporters in the world, with services representing more than 20 percent of its total exports.

Tourism and *maquiladoras* account for most of these exports, with "other services" as the third biggest item. This last item is a compensatory or residual one but is known to include reinsurances, engineering, oil exploration and drilling, education (foreign students in Mexico), films, television, and more generally, most producer services exports. In 1985 other services accounted for over $1 billion, almost as much as the *maquiladora* industries ($1.3 billion). Yet, as for most other countries, Mexican figures are not at an adequate level of disaggregation for in-depth analysis. (For an overview of statistical limitations, refer to the chapters by Adrien Lhomme and Claude Fontaine in this book.)

On the import side, services represent 30–40 percent of total imports. The most important items therein are other services (around 10 percent of total imports) and border tourism (also 10 percent).

The other services imports of Mexico may be seen as the link with the services revolution of the developed countries, for this item includes many of the information-related new producer services. As a matter of fact, other services imports grew faster than any other nonfactor import item during the oil boom, and when in 1982 total imports started to fall dramatically, other services imports continued to grow while their contraction after 1983 occurred at a slower pace than that of any other import item.

Table 8-1. Mexico: GDP Structure (*Percent*).

	1970	*1975*	*1980*	*1985*
GDP	100.0	100.0	100.0	100.0
Primary sector	12.2	10.3	9.0	9.6
Secondary sector	27.4	28.0	29.6	29.3
Manufacturing	23.7	24.3	24.9	23.4
Mining	2.5	2.4	3.2	4.1
Electricity	1.2	1.3	1.5	1.8
Construction	5.3	5.4	5.5	4.7
Services sector	55.1	56.3	55.9	57.2
Trade	25.9	25.9	25.7	21.3
Transportation	4.2	5.2	5.9	5.7
Communications	0.6	1.0	1.6	1.9
Other services	24.4	24.2	22.7	28.3

Source: INEGI, *Cuentas Nacionales*; Banco de México, *Informe Anual.*

Table 8-2. Mexico: Share of Service Activities in the GNP (*1985, percent*).

Commerce	21.3
Real estate rental	8.3
Transportation	5.7
Construction	4.7
Public administration and defense	3.7
Other services	3.3
Health services	3.1
Education	2.9
Restaurants and hotels	2.5
Financial services	2.2
Communications	2.0
Professional services	1.5
Amusement services	0.7

Source: INEGI, *Cuentas Nacionales*; Banco de México, *Informe Anual.*

There is actually no doubt that the Mexican economy is a services economy, as may be seen in Table 8-1. With construction included, the services sector represented almost 62 percent of GNP in 1985. At a more disaggregated level, Table 8-2 shows the share of 12 services activities in 1985.[12] Services also represent 60.3 percent of total employment, with a 9 percent increase between 1970 and 1984.

These figures of services share in total GDP and employment are no different from those reported by most developed countries. The question is whether services contribute to growth in the same way as they do in these countries. To examine this question, we have identified the following producers (or business) services: transportation, communications, financial services, and professional services.

In Figures 8-1 through 8-3 the GDP growth in traditional manufacturing, intermediate manufacturing and modern manufacturing are plotted against the GDP growth of producer services.[13]

It may be noted that in each case services and manufacturing growth follow the same trend. However, Figure 8-2 shows that there is a high correlation between intermediate manufacturing and producer services, which is not so clear in the other two cases (the same correlation is found when a lag of one year is introduced).

In order to find out which of manufacturing or services "drags" the other, a number of regressions (by least squares) were carried out, first lagging manufacturing with respect to producer services and then services with respect to manufacturing. In the first place, though most of the correlation coefficients were quite high, the Durbin-Watson statistic showed a high autocorrelation. In the second case, the correlations were high and there was autocorrelation in only a few of the results (see Appendix 8-A).

From the data shown in the appendix a number of analyses may be carried out. However, what is important here is to point out the high correlation between manufacturing and producer services[14] (including transportation and communications) and the high product-elasticity of producer services in relation to three categories of manufacturing.[15] This is not the case in relation to agriculture and mining (except for "other" producer services with respect to mining).[16]

Thus, it may be concluded that it is manufacturing that drags producer services, while growth in agriculture and mining has little impact on services. The relatively high elasticities of other producer services with respect to mining may be attributed mainly to PEMEX, the Mexican oil company, the backbone of the oil boom of 1977–1981.

Another way to determine the importance of services activities for manufacturing is through input-output analysis.[17]

Figure 8-1. GDP Growth in Traditional Manufacturing (*1971–84*).

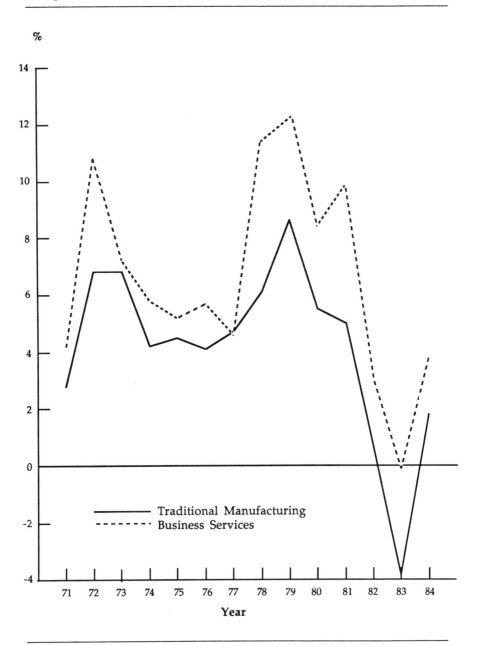

Figure 8-2. GDP Growth in Intermediate Manufacturing (*1971–84*).

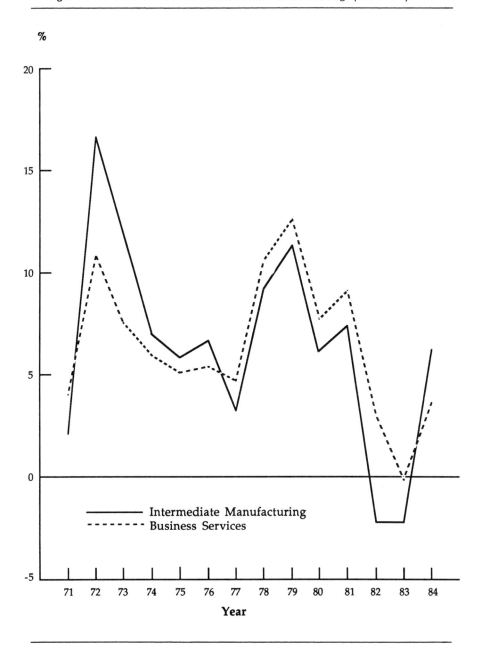

Figure 8-3. GDP Growth in Modern Manufacturing *(1971-84)*.

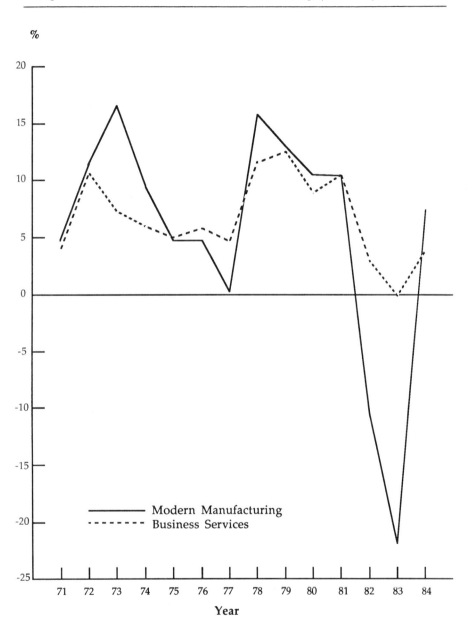

Table 8-3. Mexico: Services Consumption by Destination Sectors (*Percent*).

Destination:	*% of Production Consumed by Manufacturing*		*% of Production Consumed by Other Services Activities*		*% of Production Exported*	
Origin	*1970*	*1980*	*1970*	*1980*	*1970*	*1980*
Transportation	18.4	15.2	13.2	15.5	2.8	4.9
Communication	8.0	3.7	34.1	35.8	—	10.0
Financial services	10.0	7.1	34.1	35.8	—	—
Real estate						
Rentals	4.6	5.9	16.7	20.9	—	—
Professional services	32.5	12.4	59.3	80.8	0.1	—
Other services	8.7	8.6	21.8	24.1	—	2.7

Note: Final consumption is not included in this table, so total does not come up to 100 percent.

Source: Area de Estudios del Secretario de Comercio y Fomento Industrial, *Matrices de insumo-producto de México para 1970 y 1980.*

From Table 8-3 we can note that between 1970 and 1980 the share of the manufacturing sector in total services consumption (including final demand consumption) in the Mexican economy diminished substantially for almost every item, while the share of other service activities registered an important increase, especially in the professional services item. This provides some evidence that during those years there was an important process of services internalization in the manufacturing sector. Moreover, while in the developed countries the service-content of production in manufacturing has increased at a sustained rate, in Mexico service inputs practically did not change in the 1970–1980 period, as may be seen in Table 8–4.

At the same time, the share of services as inputs for the "production" of services has actually declined in two years, as may be seen in Table 8–5.

Also evidence of the lack of externalization process is the fact that though having experienced a high rate of growth in the past few years, the new information services are still in a relatively underdeveloped stage in Mexico when compared with the ones provided in developed countries, which implies that the new producer services

Table 8-4. Mexico: Inputs to Manufacturing (*Percent*).

	1970	1980
Total industrial inputs	78.1	77.9
Total services inputs	21.9	22.1
Total inputs to manufacturing	100.0	100.0

Source: Area de Estudios del Secretario de Comercio y Fomento Industrial, *Matrices de insumo-producto de México para 1970 y 1980.*

Table 8-5. Mexico: Direct Requirements of the Service Sector.

	1970	1980
Total industrial inputs	47.0	48.8
Total services inputs	53.0	51.2
Total inputs for the "production" of services	100.0	100.0

Source: Area de Estudios del Secretario de Comercio y Fomento Industrial, *Matrices de insumo-producto de México para 1970 y 1980.*

infrastructure is correspondingly backward.[18] On the other hand, as already mentioned, there are reasons to assume that the imports included in the other services item of the balance of payments are directly or indirectly related to information services, which implies that the existing externalization has been captured by foreign suppliers.

Finally, while between 1970 and 1984 labor productivity increased by 46 percent in manufacturing, 76 percent in mining, and by 70 percent in electricity, the increase in productivity in services as a whole was only 26.8 percent (that is, even lower than the 30.6 percent registered for agriculture).

Given the difficulties, both technical and practical, of estimating productivity in the services sector, and given also the heterogeneity of the activities concerned, one can only note at a very general level that while in communications, productivity more than doubled in this period, other services registered a reduction of almost 10 percent, including the reduction in productivity in recent years of some important producer services activities, such as banking.

Thus, it seems that, at least until now, Mexico has not embarked on anything near a services revolution. However, it is clear that the lack of adequate statistics calls for further studies on the subject, particularly on the role played by information services and other new producer services in the Mexican economy, which cannot be assessed by national accounts statistics as they actually stand.

The importance of these studies is twofold. On the one hand, the Uruguay round of negotiations calls for a higher level of preparation in order for countries like Mexico to be able to defend their interests. On the other, and more far-reaching, Mexican authorities should be provided with the necessary elements to develop economic policies designed to foster the country's development through the adequate utilization of producer services. This is not to say that there are no policies already followed in Mexico for some specific services activity.[19] However, there is a need for a coordinated policy for all producer services, including services that are imported or provided by transnational corporations.

In this last respect, while in Latin America as a whole more than half of the new FDI flows go to services (including offshore banking) in Mexico that percentage may be as low as 18 percent (24 percent if retail and wholesale trade is included).

There is an apparent inverse tradeoff between FDI in services and what might be called the modernization of the other sectors of the economy. On the one hand, given the relative backwardness of the producer services in countries like Mexico, it could be thought that FDI should be allowed to provide those services at low international prices, which would foster the efficiency and productivity of all economic activities and particularly that of the manufacturing sector. Under this argument, the absence of FDI for most of these activities would perpetuate backwardness for the economy as a whole, in view of the ever-increasing technology gap. To be sure, this situation did not matter so much in a relatively closed economy such as the Mexican one during the import-substitution and leading-sector phases, but the situation is different with an outward-looking development strategy.

It can be argued, however, that because of the strategic character of these services for the economy as a whole, it may be detrimental to let foreign corporations be in a position to control and provide them according to their interests. (For extended argumentation on this point, see Chapter 5, by Murray Gibbs.) Thus, the FDI question is a very tricky and sensitive one, and it seems that the dilemma may be resolved only by a selective approach to FDI and appropriate stimuli to national producers in specific activities and subactivities.

In a country opening its economy after many decades of inward-looking development there is no room for ostrichlike attitudes. Besides liberalizing its foreign trade, Mexico has embarked in a process of industrial restructuring, in the face of the already mentioned perception of the predominance of manufacturing for international competitiveness. However, as stated by the Secretary of Commerce and Industrial Promotion during Mexico's first "National Seminar on the Economy of Services," the more Mexico is able to develop its producer services sector, the more successful this restructuring will be.

The question remains as to the desired level of FDI participation in this process. Of course, all this is relevant to the country's negotiating position in the Uruguay Round, for forecasting the possible effects of the negotiations on the balance of payments, but also for the economy as a whole.[20] In this respect, the Mexican National Study on Services will answer many questions, but it will also pose new ones. Aside from statistical problems and the lack of an economic theory on international trade in services, the absence of a doctrine body about the effects of the services sector on the development process is a severe limitation (notwithstanding the great advances made in this respect by organizations such as ECLA (Economic Commission for Latin America), SELA, and, particularly, UNCTAD, as well as by individual researchers).

To conclude, unless there is a big effort in developing countries like Mexico to develop adequate producer services and promote their tight integration with the root of the economy, these countries will experience the same effects on their development as they did with their incapability of becoming integrated into the first industrial revolution for almost two centuries. The impact is straightforward: economic backwardness.

APPENDIX 8-A

GDP Elasticity of Services with Respect to Other Economic Activities

	GDP Total Services	GDP Commerce	GDP Transports	GDP Communications	GDP Other Producers' Services	GDP Personal Services	GDP Public Services
GDP Agriculture	0.815 (DW = 1.83) (T = 2.48)	-0.557 (DW = 1.82) (T = 3.04)	0.293* (DW = 1.02) (T = 1.11)	0.920* (DW = 2.06) (T = 1.61)	0.373 (DW = 1.80) (T = 1.37)	0.339* (DW = 1.20) (T = 1.18)	0.785* (DW = 1.06) (T = 1.55)
GDP Mining	-0.181 (DW = 1.83) (T = 1.88)	0.197 (DW = 1.82) (T = 3.04)	-0.678 (DW = 1.62) (T = 0.74)	0.360* (DW = 1.06) (T = 1.78)	0.878 (DW = 1.80) (T = 4.22)	0.013* (DW = 1.20) (T = 0.13)	0.315* (DW = 1.06) (T = 1.76)
GDP Traditional Manufacturing	1.102 (DW = 1.58) (T = 27.42)	1.006* (DW = 1.12) (T = 14.96)	1.549* (DW = 0.937) (T = 17.13)	2.639 (DW = 1.66) (T = 38.53)	1.388 (DW = 1.63) (T = 31.89)	0.732* (DW = 1.28) (T = 24.96)	1.469 (DW = 1.39) (T = 35.20)
GDP Intermediate Manufacturing	0.789 (DW = 1.78) (T = 28.78)	7.22* (DW = 1.160) (T = 16.27)	1.116 (DW = 1.34) (T = 13.33)	1.887 (DW = 1.57) (T = 21.30)	0.986* (DW = 1.05) (T = 21.56)	0.525 (DW = 2.22) (T = 30.01)	1.046* (DW = 1.13) (T = 25.34)
GDP Modern Manufacturing	0.724 (DW = 1.36) (T = 13.81)	0.675 (DW = 1.76) (T = 14.39)	1.028 (DW = 1.63) (T = 13.33)	1.717* (DW = 1.06) (T = 12.55)	0.893* (DW = 0.91) (T = 10.79)	0.479* (DW = 1.18) (T = 12.82)	0.943* (DW = .82) (T = 10.61)

Note: DW = Durbin-Watson statistic; T = t-statistic; * = there is autocorrelation in the regression.

NOTES

1. With UNCTAD's assistance a National Seminar was held in Mexico City in 1987, with active participation of the public, private, union, and academic sectors which will greatly encourage new studies. The Secretariat of Commerce and Industrial Development, responsible for the trade negotiations, has already finished a number of studies on the subject and is undertaking many more. The Secretariat of Transport and Communications is also studying transport and telecommunications. The Economic Commission for Latin America and the Caribbean (CEPAL) has recently produced at least four studies on services in Mexico. And with UNCTAD's assistance and United Nations Development Program financing, a national study is to be finalized by the end of 1988.

2. For an adaptation of the "new" trade theories to services refer to the 1987 World Bank *World Development Report*, 1987.

3. This is of course a convenient approach, considering for instance that recorded services sales of American affiliates abroad are five times as big as the U.S. exports of services. (See M. Gibbs, "El debate internacional sobre servicios," paper presented at I Seminario Nacional Sobre la Economía de los Servicios, Mexico, August 1987.)

4. The combination of new technologies in agriculture (biotechnologies and biogenetics) and a widespread subsidies program have also brought prices down.

5. Marginal as producers also: the GDP of New England, in the United States, with its 12.5 million people, is the same as that of India with its 750 million.

6. The liberalization of financial markets among the OECD countries was the driving force behind the application in this field of the technological advances. While in 1971 the Euromarket consisted of $80 billion, financial flows are now twelve times as big as the trade ones. (See P. Drucker, "El cambio en la economía mundial," *El Mercado de Valores*, August 25, 1986.)

7. As named by Clairmont and Cavanagh, in "Services, the last frontier," *Trade and Development Review*, no. 4 (April 1986), UNCTAD, Geneva, pp. 149–182, to refer to the merging of manufacturing and services TNCs.

8. Gibbs, "El debate internacional sobre servicios."

9. This point has been emphasized by international organizations such as UNCTAD, ECLA (Economic Commission for Latin America), and SELA (Sistema Economico Latino-Americano), as well as by independent writers such as V. Ventura, "Produçao e Comércio de Servicios, Notas Conceituaes," paper, 1986, and Dorothy Riddle, *Service-Led Growth* (New York: Praeger, 1986).

10. SELA, "Servicios y el disarrollo de América Latina," *Papeles* 2 (1985): 1-11.
11. For a full discussion in this respect, see F. de Mateo "La Política Comercial de México," in A. Violante and R. Davilla, *México: Una Economía en Transición* (Mexico City: LIMUSA, CNE, 1985).
12. For a further disaggregation and the items included therein, see INEGI, *Cuentas Nacionales*, reproduced in F. de Mateo, "México: El Sector Servicios. Informe Prelininar," CEPAL, January 1987.
13. Traditional manufacturing is loosely defined as activities producing consumer goods; intermediate manufacturing includes activities used mainly as inputs by other activities; while modern manufacturing includes some durable consumer goods (such as automobiles), capital goods, and newly developed activities.
14. E. Rouzar reached similar conclusions for "other services." See Rouzar, "El Sector Servicios: Comportamiento y Articulacion Económica, 1970–1982," *La Economía Mexicana* 5 (1983).
15. However, it may also be seen that, as expected from Figure 8-2, there is autocorrelation between other producer services and intermediate manufacturing. The latter is also autocorrelated with modern manufacturing.
16. The authors want to thank Carlos Piñera, Luis Rangel, and Eduardo Sánchez for the econometric help provided to obtain the figures cited here.
17. This section is based on calculations by Jorge Hernández.
18. For an analysis of these services, see F. de Mateo, "La Telemática: posibilidades de cooperación entre Argentina, Brasil y México," ECLA, June 1987.
19. There are even national development programs for activities such as tourism, transportation, and communications, and *maquiladora* industries, among others.
20. The position of the Mexican delegation so far in the Uruguay Round has been that the Punta del Este Declaration refers only to trade in services, not FDI. Moreover, the position of this delegation has been that if there is to be discussion about international flows of factors of production, they should refer exclusively to labor flows.

THE URUGUAY ROUND SERVICES NEGOTIATIONS IN SEARCH OF A FRAMEWORK

INTRODUCTION, BY JONATHAN D. ARONSON

The GATT was designed with goods, not services in mind. Indeed, movie services are the only service sector explicitly mentioned in the GATT Articles. Interest in the possibility of treating services in the context of trade negotiations emerged in the late 1960s and increased after the insertion of services into U.S. trade law in 1974. Traded services were addressed in a few places in the Tokyo round codes in so far as traded services were tied to trade in goods.

The United States stepped up the pressure to put trade in services high on the trade negotiating agenda after William Brock was appointed the U.S. Trade Representative in 1981. At the GATT ministerial meeting in late 1982 trade in services was one of the three most important and controversial issues. The meeting began a process that culminated four years later in Uruguay. Despite continued objections by a number of developing countries led by Brazil and India, the GATT trade ministers mandated negotiations on services separate from negotiations on other issues but under the GATT umbrella.

Part III of this book explores the emergence of trade in services as a negotiating issue in the GATT and suggests how negotiations might most profitably evolve. In addition, it contains one more specific case study that illustrates the problems and opportunities that will face GATT negotiators concerned with trade in services. Although many of the authors in this part are involved in the actual negotiations, it should be stressed that all of the chapters represent the personal views of the authors and not the official views of their institutions.

The first chapter examines the development of services as a trade issue. Kalypso Nicolaïdis shows how the United States' initial pressure for service negotiations resulted in substantive and strategic learning about services among other industrial and developing countries.

The next two chapters, by two of the key figures in the effort to launch services negotiations, focus on what could be accomplished in multilateral negotiations on services. Raymond Krommenacker, counselor to the GATT Group of Negotiations on Services Division, reviews the issues that will need to be covered in the context of preparing a multilateral framework for trade in services. In particular he reviews the five-point 1987 program underway in the GATT to consider 1) definitional and statistical issues, 2) broad concepts on which principles and rules might be based, 3) coverage of the multilateral framework, 4) existing international disciplines and arrangements, and 5) measures and practices contributing to or limiting the expansion of trade in services. Geza Feketekuty, counselor to the U.S. Trade Representative, elaborates further on the issues to be resolved during multilateral trade negotiations. Feketekuty suggests ways that negotiators could approach some of the most difficult aspects of these extremely complex negotiations.

Finally, the case study in Chapter 12 examines the limits of both public and private negotiations involving telecommunications services. This sectoral approach may also begin to show what can be accomplished for sectors within the context of the GATT negotiations.

Taken together these four chapters demonstrate the tremendous advances in thinking about and negotiating on trade in services issues that has taken place over the past several years.

We provide the full text of the Uruguay Round Declaration which is extensively referred to in Chapters 9, 10 and 11.

MINISTERIAL DECLARATION
ON THE URUGUAY ROUND
PART II
NEGOTIATIONS ON TRADE IN SERVICES

Ministers also decided, as part of the multilateral trade negotiations, to launch negotiations on trade in services.

Negotiations in this area shall aim to establish a multilateral framework of principles and rules for trade in services, including elaboration of possible disciplines for individual sectors, with a view to expansion of such trade under conditions of transparency and progressive liberalization and as a means of promoting economic growth of all trading partners and the development of developing countries. Such framework shall respect the policy objectives of national laws and regulations applying to services and shall take into account the work of relevant international organizations.

GATT procedures and practices shall apply to these negotiations. A group on negotiations on services is established to deal with these matters. Participation in the negotiations under this part of the declaration will be open to the same countries as under Part I. GATT Secretariat support will be provided, with technical support from other organizations as decided by the Group of Negotiations on services.

The Group of Negotiations on services shall report to the Trade Negotiations Committee.

.

9 LEARNING WHILE NEGOTIATING
How Services Got on the Uruguay Round Agenda

Kalypso Nicolaïdis

The Uruguay Round of Multilateral Trade Negotiations is now well underway in Geneva. Services are indeed negotiated separately from all other items but the *are* part of the ongoing multilateral negotiations. The story of how "trade in services" got on the agenda is one of intensive intergovernmental bargaining, lasting over half a decade, with players having to engage in thorough learning about the issues at hand and their own interest while at the same time trying to extract concessions from their counterparts.

During all these years, governments needed to reach concensus on one key question: Should they engage in a negotiation exercise covering international services transactions or not? Although this question ultimately required a simple yes or no answer, a complex foreshadow negotiation took place in Geneva to determine the criteria, rules of reference, and international setting that would characterize the services negotiations to be. There are few cases in history where parties to a negotiations had been so uncertain about the terms of the debate while having to conduct it. Yet, in September 1986, ministers from 92 countries signed a declaration with far-reaching consequences, yet with little increased certainty about what those consequences would be. This chapter explores the intertwined patterns of learning that led to such a result. (The next two chapters in this book analyze the substantive issues pertaining to the current negotiations in greater detail.)

161

THE INITIAL NEGOTIATION PHASE: BACKGROUND AND NATIONAL POSITIONS

Up to the mid-1970s, international services transactions had been widely ignored by policymakers as well as economists. At the domestic level, services were generally considered either as the low productivity sector in traditional macroeconomic models[1] or as more prone to be consumed collectively, partly outside the market logic.[2] In any event, their tradeable character was overlooked. Historically, it can be argued that services as infrastructures, such as financial or transportation services, have always been a key factor in the expansion of world trade but they were seen as inputs to trade rather than trade as such. Because services consist mainly of human activities where supply must "meet" demand on a geographic basis, they were regarded as products that could not easily travel across borders. Typically, international economic textbooks did not mention—and often still don't—trade in services in their analysis of international economic activities, except insofar as they described services imports and exports as items of the balance of payment.[3] While "invisibles" had actually accounted for 25 percent of world trade statistics for decades, this share did not earn them attention until radical technological developments in the 1970s turned them into the "engine" of world trade. Services were becoming "transportable," hence tradeable and therefore fashionable. Before assessing the source and impact of such a change, we will first take a closer look at the regulatory and institutional context in which those changes were taking place.

The 1970s and Services: An Institutional Void

Governments around the world had mostly been concerned about keeping their regulatory control in the services sector. Many services had traditionally been highly regulated and sometimes directly controlled by governments. Unavoidably, protectionism was a byproduct of this high degree of state involvement, which itself was, and still is, legitimated on the basis of national concerns relating to security and sovereignty, monetary policy, protection of privacy and national identity, regulatory needs, or the existence of natural monopolies as in the case of telecommunications. Given this context, service-exporting industries were faced with discriminatory barriers to trade ranging from unequal treatment on the part of public services monopolies to opaque regulations. More generally as international services transactions encompass a communication component and an investment component, they were hindered by discriminatory regulations pertaining to both of these components.

In spite of the trade-related impact of national regulations, service trade was a topic largely left out of the scope of institutionalized cooperation among states. At the international level there was no issue identified as "trade in services" as a whole, and as a matter of fact the term developed largely as a result of negotiations preceding the Uruguay Round. The services issue is one of those examples of world bargaining unavoidably shaping inquiries within the world of academia. Actually, services had indeed been dealt with at the international level but only in terms of harmonization goals as opposed to liberalization goals. A number of international institutions had a mandate pertaining to particular services but none of them dealt with services as a trade issue. Their role had been to establish common roles and monitor services according to definitions of the issues at stake, which were very much in phase with domestic regulations themselves. For instance, the Chicago Convention regulating international aviation had to do with ensuring safety in the air and optimal flight conditions around the world for various national carriers, not with ensuring the maintenance of an international competitive environment. The International Telecommunication Union had presided for more than a century over market sharing arrangements between governments, which implied devising norms for interfacing (common standards, joint pricing, and so on), not for competing in the same geographic areas. Most important, the General Agreement on Tariffs and Trade (GATT), set up in 1947 to supervise trade liberalization, did not apply to services trade. Yet from 1973 to 1979, the Tokyo Round's emphasis on nontariff barriers with regard to trade in good was one of the elements that led to a growing awareness that such nontariff barriers had a much greater scope, extending into the services sector. Indeed, given their very nature, services were almost exclusively subject to nontariff barriers (it is interesting to note that the first book written on the topic of protectionism and services was titled *Invisible Barriers to Invisible Trade*, and published at the time of the Tokyo Round).[4] As a matter of fact, in the 1974 Trade Act the U.S. Congress had actually included services in the negotiation mandate given to the executive branch. Yet, both in the eyes of the United States and in those of other GATT contracting parties, there were at the time more urgent matters to deal with under the general label of nontariff barriers. Hence, services were either totally ignored in the drafting of the various Tokyo Round codes, or incorporated marginally and as an afterthought, as in the case of the Code on Customs Valuation.

Spreading throughout the 1970s, the technological revolution in the communications sector led to the increasing attention given to international services. The electronic merging of computer and communication technologies was helping to overcome the problems of information storage and distance transmission of data that greatly increased the productivity of all information-intensive services, and led to such services being increasingly tradeable. Furthermore, as many firms went through an externalization of their services activities, these services came to be traded in their own right by independent firms who sought to follow their clients abroad—a phenomenon best described as the "cohorte of multinationals"—and to seek out local clients. Services, by the early 1980s, started acquiring in many OECD countries a high-tech image. The new capabilities offered by communication services not only were leading to major changes in the speed, efficiency, and global integration of provision of most services but also had a major impact on world-scale processes of production in general.

Multinational corporations were the first actors to recognize and use the potential offered by these new technologies in order to integrate their worldwide and cross-sectoral activities. hence, the significance of traded services started to be attributed not only to their actual share in world trade but to their impact as multipliers for global economic growth. During the second half of the 1970s, these transnational corporations started voicing their concern regarding the discriminatory character of national regulations in services. They argued that the lack of international rules and discipline in this issue area was a major impediment to their activities.

Initial Pressures on the Part of the United States

The technological and economic changes described above where most obvious in the case of the United States, and American transnational corporations were instrumental in highlighting both the great potential for evolution in the area of international services trade and the gap between such potential and current patterns of trade. As they saw it, this gap was due to the complete lack of any institutional setting to ensure some trade discipline. An alliance was formed between major U.S. service firms in tourism and finance (American Express, Citibank, Merrill Lynch), insurance (American International Group), data processing, shipping, high technology (IBM), who soon became the strongest allies to free trade advocates in the U.S. government.

Simultaneously, by the early 1980s, U.S. policymakers were beginning to see larger trade deficits, while the invisible trade balance kept exhibiting surpluses. They started adopting the notion that comparative advantage lay for the U.S. in moving toward highly knowledge-intensive services production and that in the upcoming restructuring of the international division of labor, the United States should be a major exporter of services. National regulations around the world were viewed as major impediments to this American repositioning in international division of labor. Hence, at the level of U.S. policymakers, trade liberalization came to be viewed as an important international policy goal. But lobbying activities on the part of actors in the manufacturing sector had increasingly been flirting with protectionism, and prospects of deemphasizing the trade policies related to goods in favor of services were perceived a threat to most of the politically active industries in the United States. A victory on the international front was needed to convince Congress that large returns could be had in resisting protectionist temptations.

After its aborted and half-hearted attempt to start talking about services in the Tokyo Round, the first move of the U.S. government was to establish a trade in services committee in the OECD Secretariat in 1979.[5] In 1982 the Reagan administration raised the U.S. policy thrust in matters of international trade liberalization. This administration's attitude toward multilateralism was characterized by a great deal of skepticism at that point but, in spite of its current inefficiencies, the GATT was seen as one of the few international regimes that did not find its raison d'être in international "competition management." The last trade round under the GATT, the Tokyo Round, had been completed in 1979, after six years of discussions. In the following years the world trading system had been under great strain. In the context of the worldwide recession, the early 1980s were characterized by alarming prophecies regarding the deterioration of the world-trading environment. An aggressive policy in the field of services was seen as a means to give momentum to the trade system as a whole and one of the ways to deal with internal structural adjustment problems.

In the fall of 1982, U.S. negotiators introduced the issue of services liberalization in the GATT, which was holding its first ministerial meeting since the launching of the Tokyo Round in 1973. Launching a new trade round was not explicitly proposed until a few months later, but it was clear that the United States was looking to expand to trade in services the scope of liberalization under the GATT supervision. An offensive policy on "new" issues such as services and intellectual property was a necessary counterpart to the more defensive stands of the United States on more traditional issues, in order to curtail current protectionist pressures at home and increase the support of free trade constituencies domestically. From that point on, the U.S. government's arguments in support of a new round had a different emphasis depending on whether they were presented at home or in international forums. At home, the government stressed the fact that the GATT needed to be strengthened in *all* sectors of activities. Abroad, however, the U.S. initiative was perceived as seeking a grand tradeoff with developing countries, consisting of an acceptance to roll back existing U.S. protectionist measures inconsistent with the GATT and to liberalize the importation of low-technology goods, commodities, and agricultural products, in exchange for Third World countries' opening up their market in the field of services. As for the form of the services regime the United States was trying to push forward at this point, it had the following characteristics:

1. Liberalization would be conducted according to the original GATT principles and norms. Stretching it a little, this amounted to adding "and services" to "goods" in the GATT charter.

2. Hence the future negotiations of a services agreement were to be conducted directly under the GATT umbrella and according to

the general setting and procedures of the trade round along with other items, so as to allow concessions across services and goods.

Initial Reactions of GATT Trading Partners

U.S. negotiators quickly realized that their push was premature and that the ground had not been sufficiently prepared. EC countries had little interest in launching a new round, primarily because they felt vulnerable on agriculture but also because, a priori, they were wary of the possible implications of engaging into service negotiations. This included, for instance, the future status of their postal, telegraph, and telephone monopolies (PTTs). Internationally, and given the psychological response to the 1982 recession, EC countries were very unsure of their potential to compete in high-tech and information-intensive services with the United States or Japan, seen as further ahead on the learning curve.

Maybe more to the point, the European Community didn't know quite what to make of the services issue. It had indeed been participating for a while in the initial efforts conducted under the OECD secretariat, along with other OECD countries. But there were no experts or administration officials to be found in the capitals who had devoted any serious attention to the issue. Not until fall 1982, was an interdivision working party set up in the EC commission in Brussels to study the EC stakes in this area. The Community's lack of position on the issue was determinant given the fact that the EC negotiates as a whole in the GATT. At the level of member countries the investment in understanding policy implications of services was also very low. There was a general feeling, however, that contrary to what the United States was arguing, traditional GATT principles and rules (such as national treatment) were not well adapted to address the new problems posed by services trade. Not only had service trade never been supervised by GATT, but analysts questioned GATT's ability to provide supervision. The difficulties in defining services themselves and gathering relevant data, in identifying the boundaries between trade and investment, in addressing new modes of protection, in accounting for the rapid pace of technological change in these sectors, and the like, were seen as major hindrances. Despite the best efforts of U.S. negotiators, the EC was only willing to go along with a minimalist decision at the 1982 ministerial in the form of a declaration inviting contracting parties to undertake national examinations and exchange of information on services. This move was a way of buying time and put off until the 1984 yearly session of the contracting parties the decision regarding "whether any multi-lateral action in these matters is appropriate and desirable."

As far as they were concerned, developing countries—which at this point appeared basically united—went along with this minimalist decision since it did not involve any commitment on their part. Yet they clearly stated that in their view, multilateral action in this field was neither appropriate nor desirable. They felt that there was no reason for them to go along with the U.S. demand until their most pressing concerns were addressed, that is until they saw all previous commitments related to their goods exports enforced under the GATT. On services per se, at best they felt that such negotiations did not really concern them, and at worst, they were afraid that a service regime aiming at liberalization would amount to unilateral concessions on their part, a one-way compromise due to their lack of competitiveness in this field. More deeply, sovereignty concerns could appear as even more prominent than in the case of Europeans for countries that often had lacked time to develop well-grounded national regulations pertaining to services; quite apart from their potentially protectionist dimension, the very existence of such regulations could be seen as a means to control the effect of a forthcoming liberalization. In this context, the revered "gains from trade" unfortunately appeared as a zero-sum prospect.

These arguments were stressed most vocally by some of the most advanced developing countries such as India and Brazil, traditional spokespeople for the Third World. In their most pessimistic assessment, developing countries thought that "negotiations in services might contribute to a new international division of labor . . . which would permanently exclude us from passing on to a post-industrial or a service-oriented economy, which is what is happening in the developed world," as expressed by a Brazilian negotiator. Finally, many developing countries opposed a goods-for-services quid pro quo in terms of actual concessions during the negotiations, fearing that such a framework would allow and legitimize retaliation against their exports of goods, when and if they would eventually decide to protect and develop their own service industries.

Hence, the basic position of the developing world in 1982 was the following: Services have no place in GATT because 1) GATT liberalization principles did not apply in this area, and 2) developing countries do not accept the prospect of a goods-for-services quid pro quo.

THE CONVERGENCE PHASE: SUBSTANTIVE AND STRATEGIC LEARNING IN THE GATT

During the phase that followed, the gap between the positions of most parties to the negotiations was progressively reduced.[6] What is most striking, however, is that this convergence was less due to a general lowering of the aspiration levels of parties in order to meet each other halfway but, rather, to a learning process that led actors to redefine their interests. On one hand, actors changed their beliefs about the actual role and characteristics of international service flows and how these related to their national interests; we might call this substantive learning. On the other hand, actors were able to better assess what type of final agreement a multilateral negotiation would actually lead to—that is what including service, in a new trade round actually entailed; we might call this strategic learning.

This complex learning process in turn led negotiators to uncover potentials for agreement in the fact that their actual interests could be broken into subdimensions, which could serve as the basis for concessions acceptable to all sides (as will be shown in the last section of this chapter).

The United States versus Other OECD Countries

The single most important factor in explaining the evolution of OECD countries position between 1982 and 1986 is the role played by substantive learning processes in changing perceptions of national interests. In a nutshell, given the coming need to take a position at the international level, OECD countries "started doing their homework," which led them to an increased awareness of their own potential gains in liberalizing services.

Learning occurred through a great number of channels. In 1983, the Colombian ambassador to the GATT, Felippe Jaramillo, convened the first of a series of meetings on services attended by all key GATT players. Officially, the Jaramillo group existed simply to facilitate the exchange of national information on services. Unofficially, it became the GATT's forum for trying to decide if services should be a formal GATT priority. Ambassador Jaramillo ran the session on his own authority, since, as he put it, "an active participation of the GATT secretariat would have meant implicitly admitting the competence of GATT in this field," but it was understood that the group had the blessing of the GATT organization. By early 1986, 16 developed countries had submitted their national studies on services, a phenomenon that went together with a great increase of the number of senior officials and staff working on services within national administrations. The EC commission had also engaged into extensive consultation and work at the conceptual and statistical level to come up with a global position. Conceptual and statistical work was also undertaken in other international institutions in which OECD countries were active (IMF, World Bank, UNCTAD, OECD, BIS). This work led in part to the realization that services were greatly undervalued in balance-of-payment statistics and that the small degree of disaggregation of service trade had hidden the importance and peculiarities of very important and growing transactions lumped together in trade statistics as "other private services" (finance, consulting, engineering). Many countries came to realize the importance of trade surpluses in these sectors. These efforts in the public sector were accompanied by numerous publications and a suddenly exponential involvement of academia, including attempts to identify the major determinants of international trade in services through the reconceptualization of trade theory in order to make it applicable to services. Whether bold or cautious, the new explorers shared the feeling of being involved in a totally new field of enquiry.

National interest is not defined by the state as a unitary actor. Changes in the perception of interest are due in part to the fact that different groups are given more voice and hence influence, at the domestic level as a consequence of the international climate. In most European countries, for example, existing groups such as chambers of commerce were encouraged by their U.S. counterparts to speak out and present reports. Service industries, and in particular export industries, started forming lobbying groups that took an increasingly active part in policy debates. Numerous commissions of social representatives or ad hoc groups of experts started competing in expressing recommendations. As services was increasingly identified as an important issue by policymakers, the traditional regulatory approach started to give way to other arguments based on international competitiveness. In addition, following the U.S. model, debates on the implementation of deregulation policies at the national level unleashed pressures for liberalization at the international level. For instance, bringing telecommunications under the scrutiny of international trade discussions had the major effect that the tariff and technology decisions came to be seen as not only under the responsibility of engineers, technicians, and PTT ministries but also, and increasingly, of ministries of economy, industry, or commerce. In this context the concern of private multinational firms were given greater attention.

Seen from the international systemic level, the very rapid cognitive evolution on the part of policymakers was a top-down phenomenon. That is, the placement of an issue on the international agenda meant that there was a need to respond to it. In turn, these developments constituted major pressures for change in terms of the policy choices facing governments around the world and highlighted the intrinsic interdependent character of such choices at the international level.

Japan was the first OECD country to support the U.S. position, to the point of sending delegations in Third World countries explaining this position. Obviously, Japan with its limited natural resources was quickly attracted by the idea of freeing up foreign markets for its invisible exports, for instance in the financial sector. Many "small" developed countries like Switzerland and Canada also followed suit in 1984–85. In March 1985, the EC trade ministers issued a declaration in favor of a new GATT round, which stated "on possible new topics for negotiations . . . trade in services seems suitable for inclusion." Given that the EC negotiated as a whole within the GATT, such a common understanding was crucial.

In fall 1985 the GATT contracting parties gave a preparatory committee until summer 1986 to come up with an agenda for the new trade round to be adopted at a ministerial meeting in September 1986. Whether services would be part of this draft ministerial "declaration of intent" became the focus of the negotiations, even though discussions on services were not officially included under the mandate of the PrepCom. At that point, the EC was at least as vehement in the United States in refusing to consider launching any trade round of which services would be excluded. In a speech that summer, Willy De Clerq, EC commissioner for external affairs, stated that the

EC was "the biggest world exporter of services." As the ministerial meeting to be held in Punta del Este (Uruguay) approached, the most prominent difference of position remaining between the United States and European countries concerned the attitude to be taken toward moderate and nonmoderate developing countries.

Hence, within a three-year period, all OECD countries had come to support service negotiations; yet as they better understood the stakes they also found more ground for stressing GATT's limitations in this field. Countries that had originally been very cautious started feeling more comfortable as a common understanding about future negotiations was developed: ideally, following a very unspecific declaration of intent, a great deal of creativity and concept formation would have to be allowed in one way or another. In this light, agreeing to negotiate had become less commital than originally perceived. Hence, the convergence in accepting services as a priority issue did reflect an awareness that interests of OECD countries were compatible but not that governments had similar views as to what a service regime would look like.

In other words, while OECD countries engaged into a great deal of substantive learning by redefining their interests to fit new visions of the world, their perception of the existing game was also colored by strategic learning: the initial U.S. proposal didn't need to be accepted at face value and GATT principles did not need to be naively transposed to services. American negotiators themselves had evolved in this regard. Concerns regarding state sovereignty, consumer protection, needs for standards, and the like, led Europeans in particular to stressing the need for some regulatory harmonization concurrently with liberalization. Adapting traditional GATT norms (such as national treatment) and devising new concepts (such as market access) would allow for continued relevance of any agreement in the face of the pace of technological and institutional change. Little by little, it became clear that such a view could prevail.

In addition, by identifying U.S. barriers to trade in services (such as different states' legislation in banking), other countries were acquiring more leverage and bargaining chips. The role played by the United States during the negotiations was twofold: on one hand, the services issue was raised while the U.S. international role shifted from hegemony to leadership. The United States was no longer ready to make side payments to compensate potential losers and accept greater costs than others in order to shape a liberal international economic order; but it was still able to put an issue on the international agenda and use the power of persuasion to influence other actors' perception of their own interests.[7] On the other hand, the U.S. government also had the means to change its partners' perceptions of the bargaining set by worsening their nonagreement alternatives: U.S. initiatives at the bilateral level were a model of what to expect if GATT partners did not accept to play; either through the design of across-the-board services liberalization agreements (such as the bilateral agreements signed with Israel in 1985 and discussed with Canada before the 1986 ministerial) or through sectoral deals with developing countries (such as the 1985 pressures to open the Korean insurance market).[8] The induced European fear of being left out in the event of a major stalemate on the multilateral route, contributed to the EC's changed perception of interest.

At a more general level, during such negotiations over future negotiations, countries try to influence each other's learning processes in various ways. Strategic learning leading to greater confidence over one's ability to shape further negotiations is, paradoxically, often advantageous to weakened negotiating counterparts. For instance, it was in the U.S. interest that European governments realize that a service agreement would not automatically imply domestic telecom deregulation à la U.S.A. Indeed, Europeans let the door open to negotiating telecommunication services as their case became stronger against considering them as a direct, rather than indirect trade issue. Actually, Europeans did learn, but mostly by refining their own paradigm regarding the issue; that is, by working on an intra-European consensus and having to defend it.

Developed versus Developing Countries

Discussions on service were marked from the beginning by a high level of mistrust toward the United States. In the fall of 1985, developing countries still opposed the inclusion of services under the mandate of the preparatory committee. Hence, until the Punta del Este ministerial meeting in September 1986 to launch the trade round, discussions on services officially followed a separate track. In the mind of developing countries the issue was not ripe for negotiations and "exchange of information" would have to be continued much longer before anyone would really understand what services were all about. No developing countries ever presented a national study in the informal Jaramillo group, in part because many of them did not have the technical ability to do so. Available means for learning were definitely asymmetrical.

On the other hand, consensus had been reached among developed countries during 1985. Why then was the support of developing countries so important? The United States preferred the GATT as a negotiating forum for services because of its being legally binding and universal (unlike the OECD) as well as directly geared at trade liberalization. Yet with the GATT came a tradition of consensus. In addition, there had been a pledge at the end of Tokyo Round that developing countries would, from then on, be more involved in GATT decisionmaking. Not fulfilling this pledge would be a sign of major failure. This did not imply that developing countries would have to be part, at least in a first phase, in the services regime itself. The situation was paradoxical: usually regimes can be set up with a small number of states initially and expand membership later. In our case, while only a critical number of states would be needed to maintain a service regime itself, its initial setup under the aegis of GATT necessitated wide participation, hence a change of attitude on the part of developing countries regarding their interests (substantive learning) and their own impact on the outcome (strategic learning).

The first expression of strategic learning on the part of developing countries was with regards to the implicit linkage between goods and services negotiations. In the short term, many developing countries were interested above all in negotiations on textile, steel, voluntary export restraints, and other protectionist measures on goods or agricultural product. They felt that this type of liberalization was of urgent necessity, especially in view of the debt crisis. As they also realized that the United States, the EC, and Japan were not going to start a new round without seeing services included, this short-term positive linkage came to prevail for a number of developing countries, including the Asian newly industrializing countries, Latin American countries such as Colombia, Venezuela, and Uruguay, and Caribbean basin countries. Driven in part by the fear that the United States might deliver on its protectionist threats, those countries considered that they had a lot to gain in a new round, even if that meant broadly trading off goods for services in the short term. In addition, they could see their diplomatic stand greatly enhanced in the international trade community by playing an independent and constructive role in breaking the deadlock arrived at in the negotiations. This led in June 1986 to the split between the so-called moderate developing countries and the so-called hardliners, that is, India, Brazil and a few other countries. During summer 1986, an alliance was formed between moderate developing countries and small developed countries, which soon came to include the big three (the United States, the EC, Japan). These countries called themselves the friends of the new negotiations, and during a whole month, worked together outside the GATT building in the EFTA (European Free Trade Agreement) headquarters on a draft agenda for the upcoming round. Moderate developing countries agreed to the need to set up a regime in services, while leaving open the question of applicability of GATT rules to services. The paragraph on services negotiations was bracketed in the draft declaration, reflecting the fact that it would be up to the higher decision-making level to decide. The other dimension of strategic learning in this phase was that many developing countries realized that they could influence future services negotiations in a way much more congruent with development goals; this was reflected in the wording of the paragraphs on services in the draft declaration presented by the self-styled friends of the new negotiations.

There was also a great deal of substantive learning on the part of moderate developing countries. While most developing countries, apart from countries like Singapore, were far from persuaded in the fall of 1986 that opening up their service markets was in their best interest, many had come to realize the importance of service inputs for their national economy and accepted that some degree of international cooperation could be helpful in that sense. For many small developing countries lacking research capabilities, the continued learning process during the presumably lengthy negotiations of the regime itself, along with the technical support on the part of GATT and UNCTAD, could be of great help in shaping domestic service strategies. Some also realized that their interests might be different than those of their traditional spokesman, Brazil and India, which were large countries with their own regional service markets, and hence with vested interests in no further expansion of liberalization of trade in services.

Yet most developing countries even after agreeing to the compromise still had long-term concerns related to possible goods-for-services quid pro quos on specific concessions and fears of legitimate retaliation once these cross-issues concessions would have been made. Hence, while linking goods and services as far as the launching of the round was concerned, they also thought it was in their interests to "delink" the future negotiations in services from other items under discussion, as concerns exchanging specific concessions.

The hardliners' refusal to go along with the summer compromise of moderate countries could be described as a willingness to move further along the strategic learning curve. Their strategic learning had occurred through their probing the negotiations ground in order to find out how far they could go in keeping services outside the GATT framework and rules. They continued to be convinced that as long as developed countries—and their multinational firms—had a major say in the shape of a future services regime, it would be difficult to dream up clauses that would channel the market forces unleashed by liberalization toward serving development in less favored regions of the globe. On the other hand, there was the question of how isolated they could afford to be on the international scene. The United States had clearly stated that consensus was not worth compromising on its goal and that it intended to be true to the results of the constructive collaboration with Third World moderates during the summer of 1986.

Disaggregating Issues at Punta del Este

Ultimately, no one had an interest in the GATT becoming, or appearing to become, a U.S. hostage. While having taken part in the compromise with moderate developing countries, Europeans felt the process could not, after so many years of effort, stop short of a consensus. During the month preceding the Punta del Este deadline, the EC put all its efforts into working out a compromise position with the hard-liners. Their respective delegates concocted a "common working platform" that basically sketched out the notion that services and goods negotiations could be conducted under the Uruguay Round under two separate tracks, with services falling outside the GATT umbrella, avoiding compulsory reference to GATT principles.

Finally, the United States abandoned its all-or-nothing position: while insisting that the service negotiations be conducted under the traditional GATT procedures, under the overall Trade Round time frame and with the GATT organization technical support, its delegates in Uruguay agreed that under such conditions services could formally fall outside the GATT as a Treaty.

On this basis, consensus was finally reached among all 92 trade ministers: the Punta del Este ministerial declaration was composed in two parts, but served to launch a "single undertaking." Most important for the hard-liners, services negotiations were explicitly bound to aim at the "development of developing countries," with liberalization presented as a means for such an end.

The declaration of intent left a much wider margin of maneuver to negotiators than envisaged by the United States. Brazil and India agreed to this open-ended solution before the United States did, as they became aware that this result was the most they would obtain and that their exclusion from the ministerial compromise itself would have been a worse outcome. For them, forcing the United States to back up from its initial position was indeed a political victory (until the last minute at Punta del Este, there were more opinions against than for yielding in the U.S. delegation). U.S. negotiators ultimately agreed to this compromise as they realized that they could present it at home as a "procedural accommodation," a small cost for making Punta del Este an international success. To sum up, we must stress that the learning process allowed parties to explore ways of disaggregating issues that could transform apparently totally opposite initial positions into compatible ones. This is illustrated in Figure 9–1.

First, parties learned to disaggregate the issue as to whether services were ultimately to be included under the GATT. Basically, the ministerial declaration would allow to leave options open, until the end of the negotiations. Countries did put services under the auspices of the GATT as an organization hosting the multilateral trade round, but not as a treaty, as shown in Figure 9–1, part a.

Second, the initial U.S. stress on the importance of treating goods and services under a single negotiation, implying a "grand tradeoff," and the fear of developing countries that this link would imply retaliation, were both addressed in the final instance. The final agreement kept the priority dimension of each party's position, as shown in Figure 9–1, part b.

The irony is that the final form of the linkage might actually serve its opponents. The clear ruling out of tradeoffs served U.S. officials well since they could dismiss the question that was always put to

Figure 9-1. Disaggregating Issues at Punta del Este.

a. Under the GATT umbrella?

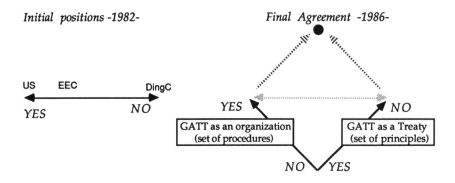

b. A goods versus services tradeoff ?

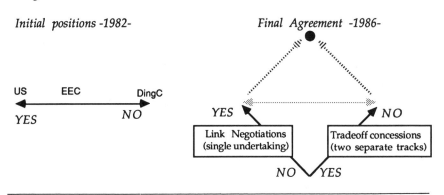

them domestically as to "what sector would pay the price for services." On the other hand, the developing countries could start wondering if the endgame "single political undertaking" was not to their advantage as it allowed to keep the success of the service agreement hostage to satisfactory results for their traditional goods exports.

In keeping with the French saying, "There could be no treaty without conflicting mental reservations," those two sets of compromise may have been efficient because they allowed for some ambiguity. Ultimately, parties may well be faced with the need to collapse again the dimensions that had, at least implicitly, been solved separately at Punta del Este. The fact that ambiguity helped reach agreement on a declaration of intent might turn out to be less a reflection on the lack of real convergence than a witness to the fact that parties realized then that they needed to allow for the learning process to go on.

NOTES

1. Not before the 1930s did economists introduce the notion of a *tertiary sector*, relating it to a stage analysis of economic growth. Refer to Alan Fisher, *The Clash of Progress and Security* (London: Kelley, 1935), and Colin Clark, *The Conditions of Economic Progress* (London: Macmillan, 1940). At the end of the 1960s, with economists such as J. Fuchs introducing the term *services* in *The Services Economy* (1968) did the set of activities described under this label begin losing its residual and homogenous character. Not until the end of the 1970s, however, with the advent of a neoindustrial approach to services and the apprehension of the importance of advanced services in the production process, did capital-intensive and information-intensive services come to be seen as key to industrial productivity.
2. The view that the increased consumption of services was at the heart of a major socio-political, rather than an economic change was first put forward in Daniel Bell's seminal *The Coming of Post-Industrial Society: A Venture in Social Forecasting* (New York: Basic Books, 1973).
3. See for instance C.P. Kindleberger and P.H. Lindert, *International Economics* (Homewood, Ill.: Richard D. Irwin, 1978); or R.E. Caves and R.W. Jones, *World Trade and Payments* (Boston: Little, Brown, 1981). The authors usually refer to what is traded under the labels "commodities," "goods," "merchandise," "bundle," or "manufactured products." Whether failing to single out services amounts to excluding them from the analysis is debatable. What is clear is that the authors did not have in mind the specific characteristics of services when discussing trade theoretical issues.
4. Brian Griffith, *Invisible Barriers to Invisible Trade* (London: Trade Policy Research Center, 1975).
5. While at the same time pushing toward a greater trade emphasis in the work conducted by OECD's Division on Information, Communication, and Computer Policies.
6. For a more extensive description of the final phase of these negotiations refer to K. Nicolaïdis, "Launching the Uruguay Round," Case Study, John F. Kennedy School of Government, Harvard University, Cambridge, Mass., 1987.
7. A U.S. Trade Representative deputy once described U.S. negotiators as "missionaries," literally bringing the message to their OECD partners.
8. There were also significant unilateral actions such as the 1984 Trade and Tariff Act that authorized the president to give high priority to the negotiation of bilateral and multilateral agreements governing trade in services.

10 SERVICES NEGOTIATIONS From Interest Lateralism to Reasoned Multilateralism

Raymond J. Krommenacker

The General Agreement on Tariffs and Trade (GATT) is a multilateral contract subscribed to by 96 governments that together account for more than four-fifths of world trade. Its basic aim is to liberalize world trade and place it on a secure basis, thereby contributing to economic growth, development, and welfare. The General Agreement is the only multilateral instrument that lays down agreed rules for international trade. Since 1948 GATT has also functioned as the principal international body concerned with international trade relations, negotiating the reduction of trade barriers and other measures that distort competition.

The contractual rights and obligations that GATT embodies have been accepted, voluntarily, in their mutual interest, by the member countries. Overseeing the application of these rules is an important part of GATT's activities. In successive multilateral negotiations in GATT, the rules have been refined and obstacles to trade progressively reduced.

This chapter reviews some of the issues to be covered in the context of preparing a multilateral framework for trade in services.

The ministerial meeting on the occasion of the Special Session of the Contracting Parties to the General Agreement at Punta del Este

The author is grateful for the comments received from persons who made time available for discussions. The views are his own and do not commit the GATT in any way.

181

(Uruguay) from September 15 to September 20, 1986, adopted a declaration, part II of which launches negotiations on trade in services. The ministers decided that the negotiations on trade in services would not take place within the legal framework of GATT but that nevertheless GATT procedures and practices would apply to those negotiations.

The negotiations have a threefold purpose: first, the expansion of trade in services under conditions of transparency and progressive liberalization; second, the promotion of the economic growth of all trading partners; and, last, the promotion of the development of developing countries. As regards the ways and means of implementing the results of the negotiations, the declaration states that it is the ministers who shall decide at the end of the negotiations. In other words, all options concerning the legal status and institutional framework of an international agreement on services remain open until the ministerial decision is taken.

Participation in such an agreement will depend on the type of agreement that can be reached at the end of the negotiations, in particular on the nature of its normative provisions and the degree of progressivity of liberalization. By contrast, the General Agreement was signed on October 30, 1947, by 23 countries that had just negotiated a first reduction in customs duties. Among the signatories were 11 developing countries. It took 39 years for the number of member countries to reach the figure of 96.

In considering the substance to be included in the multilateral framework on trade in services, there are many precedents that can be referred to by the negotiators of the Group of Negotiations on Services. There are the wide variety of existing regulations and of the planned regulations in the European Economic Community (in telematics—the combination of telecommunications and informatics—as well as in the other services), in particular in the context of the process of establishing a single internal market by 1992.

In addition to these regional EC activities, there are a great number of reforms at the national level, such as the French draft legislation on telematics to be adopted by the Legislature in 1988 (which would represent a major change to the law signed by King Louis-Philippe on May 2, 1837, institutionalizing telecommunications monopoly, whose provisions have inspired numerous foreign legislations). Most important, there exist two bilateral agreements.

The agreement between the United States and Israel is of a non-binding nature. Under it, detailed discussions are being held on some service sectors in order to test the practices in these services against the principles enunciated in the agreement and to identify the areas in which there may be inconsistency. In addition, the Canada-U.S. Free Trade Agreement of October 1987 provides for the first time a set of disciplines covering a large number of service sectors.

Yet another sectoral specific bilateral agreement is reflected in a law of the Japanese Diet implemented on April 1, 1987. The law titled "Special Law on the Handling of Legal Matters by Foreign Lawyers" incorporates the results of the negotiations held between the United States and Japan.

Existing national, bilateral, and regional activities reinforce the growing importance of liberalization issues in the trade in services between trading partners. This current state of affairs might be categorized as one of interest-lateralism: where processes in which shared interests motivate economic policy actions of a national, or a bilateral, or a plurilateral nature. Interest-lateralism is key to the Uruguay round negotiations on trade in services because it provides a full-scale laboratory for testing principles and rules to verify their applicability to the multilateral framework for services under negotiation.

For 1987, a program for the initial phase of the negotiations serves as a frame of reference for the discussions. The program consists of five elements:

1. Definitional and statistical issues
2. Broad concepts on which principles and rules for trade in services, including possible disciplines for individual sectors, might be based
3. Coverage of the multilateral framework for trade in services
4. Existing international disciplines and arrangements
5. Measures and practices contributing to or limiting the expansion of trade in services, including specifically any barriers perceived by individual participants, to which the conditions of transparency and progressive liberalization might be applicable

In 1988 the negotiating program will carry forward further on the basis of the examination of the five elements, as well as other issues arising therefrom. In this process, submissions and statements by delegations will be addressed with a view to achieving concrete progress in the negotiations in accordance with the negotiating objectives in the ministerial declaration.

The first and third of these elements should make it possible to sketch the outlines of a possible agreement in its vertical and horizontal dimensions. The vertical dimensions concerns the definition of trade in services. Do we need to go beyond the traditional notion of transborder trade? If so, how far? Should the definition include the notions of commercial presence, temporary residence, and intellectual property transactions? The horizontal dimension relates to the coverage of the multilateral framework. What types of services should be covered by the multilateral agreement and by possible sectoral disciplines?

Creating a typology of services is difficult because of the uncertainties inherent in such an exercise arising from the continual emergence of new types of services resulting both from the merging of traditional services and from the impact on services of the application of technological developments, particularly in the spheres of telematics and space.

Another element of the program for the initial phase of the negotiations concerns "broad concepts on which principles and rules for trade in services, including possible disciplines for individual sectors, might be based." Under this heading, the object is to examine and develop appropriate concepts that take fully into account the unique nature of services. It will involve establishing an appropriate balance between the objectives of expansion of trade in services and the objectives of development of developing countries, and of economic growth of all trading partners. Some concepts and issues have already been studied in part, such as transparency, nondiscrimination, national treatment, market access, treatment of monopolies, suitable character of a regulation, exceptions and safeguards, application of the agreement in the case of federated states, infant industry, and restrictive business practices. These concepts, however, relate to only one aspect, and it is obvious that the negotiations will have to produce principles and rules relating to a larger range of concerns. In the present initial stage of negotiations reference is also made to other possible concepts such as "progressive liberalization," "mutual advantage for countries," and "economic development." Substantial discussions are still needed to deepen the meaning and to test the applicability of these concepts.

Without prejudging the deliberations of participating countries, it is useful to highlight seven important issues.

The first important issue is *national treatment*. Services are complicated because they touch on the operations of foreign service firms (or their dependencies) *in* the markets of purchasing countries, in addition to the local treatment of services sold across borders. Therefore, before agreement can be reached on a national treatment principle applicable to services, it must be clear whether and to what extent services traded on an investment/establishment basis will be covered in the negotiations. Moreover, it may be necessary to distinguish between national treatment and equivalent treatment, given the fact that in certain circumstances the sheer granting of equal operating rights to dependencies of foreign firms is not sufficient to equalize conditions of competition. In such cases, national treatment may be a necessary, but not sufficient condition for effective market access.

In the course of the negotiations, the point has already been made that, since the introduction of national treatment principle in the multilateral framework of trade in services would mean full elimination of protection, such an introduction could only be a long-term goal. Consequently, this principle may not be included as an obligation in the multilateral framework. Instead, this principle could be used as a criterion to judge whether particular perceived obstacles to trade in services should be eliminated or not.

The second issue relates to state intervention in services production and trade. This has so far arisen mainly in connection with telecommunications monopolies. In this context, the question is how to draw the boundary between basic services (subject to regulations limiting or excluding competition) from value-added networks (open to domestic and foreign competition) since it may appear that services that are basic from one point of view are added from the other and vice versa in the context of the networks generated by the emerging global information economy. But state intervention also has wider implications for the development policies of certain countries where other services activities such as banking, insurance, and some types of transport are nationalized. This issue is related to the issue of motivations for regulations, and as in that case, the problem to be solved through negotiation is: Where does one draw the line between measures that restrict market access and measures taken for "other" purposes? In other words, is there any scope for deregulation and how does one define the parameters of the process?

Third, negotiations also need to address the issue of *labor migration*, in two ways. First, what is the possibility that firms operating abroad will temporarily employ staff from their home country to perform specific service functions or carry out specific service projects, such as construction contracts? Second, broader issue of labor movement may also need to be tackled, at the request of labor-exporting countries. The problem may be to distinguish between primary factor movements unrelated to specific service outputs and those that are related. Different solutions may be called for in these cases. Another problem would be to distinguish between highly sophisticated and nonspecialized labor services.

Fourth, the *treaty-making power* of central governments deserves particular attention insofar as in certain federal states the regulation of major services sectors such as banking and insurance falls within the competence of political subdivisions. This is not a new problem in the GATT; up to now, however, the Contracting Parties have not formally given an interpretation of the scope of these provisions. In any event, it does not seem conceivable that services sectors falling under local jurisdiction in certain countries could be excluded from negotiations on that account alone.

Fifth, *development-related issues in services* is another issue to come up in the negotiations. The need for special treatment or an appropriate escape clause or some development-related concepts would appear to depend on the type of arrangement concluded. An alternative approach may be to build on the premise that while all trade expansion may not further development, much of it can do. Negotiators will be challenged to identify the conditions under which the services trade expansion promotes development. Attention will have to be paid to the positive and negative interlinkages between trade and development, the different situations in different services sectors and the stages of development reached in different countries.

A sixth issue is whether a *tradeoff* between trade concessions on goods and trade concessions on services will be undertaken. This problem relates not only to the eventual outcome but also to the conduct of negotiations, and it therefore has as much to do with modalities as with objectives. Some governments believe that some degree of tradeoff must be involved, at least implicitly. For some governments the question is important from the point of view of the kind of support they can muster from their private sectors.

Seventh, issues of *transparency and dispute settlement* are important in the GATT and other international and regional forums that have a long tradition in the treatment of notifications, consultations, surveillance, and dispute settlement procedures of trade in goods and economic policies. For example, in addition to the obligations contained in the OECD Codes concerning various services, the 1985 OECD Declaration on Transborder Data Flows seeks transparency in regulations and policies relating to information, computer, and communications services affecting transborder data flows. The governments of OECD member countries have agreed to cooperate and to consult with each other in carrying out this work.

Existing practices of transparency and dispute settlement in GATT show that this notion is inseparable from those of notification, consultation, and surveillance. The question is whether the existing practices could be transposed mutatis mutandis from trade in goods to trade in services with respect to a priori notifications, the possibility of commenting proposed laws and regulations, reverse notifications, periodic multilateral reviews of reservations and derogations, domestic reviews, and juridical proceedings, and the setting up of national Services Enquiry Points (SEP) with the mandate of answering all reasonable enquiries regarding any adopted or proposed laws and regulations governing specific services and services transactions.

The fourth element of the program for the initial phase of the negotiations concerns *existing international disciplines and arrangements*, in such service sectors as *civil aviation, maritime transport,* and *telecommunications.* These international agreements govern certain aspects of trade in services. Consequently, the task is to examine the relationship of these international agreements with the objective of the negotiations on services. For instance, in telematics, at least two major international disciplines have direct relevance to this fourth element, namely the International Telecommunications Satellite Organization and the International Telecommunication Convention.

Finally, the fifth element of the program deals with *government measures and the practices of private firms*, including specific barriers contributing to or limiting the expansion of trade in services. One object is to examine the relationship between the regulatory frameworks existing in the various countries and the objective of expansion of trade as construed in the ministerial declaration. It seems necessary to reach agreement on how to deal with national regulations concerning services and their effects on trade in services, because this element will play a central and decisive role in any multilateral agreement. The way in which such measures and practices promote trade also needs consideration.

The negotiators are engaged in a complex task, especially as several major service sectors, and consequently a multitude of types of services transactions, have been identified so far. Nevertheless, in the context of the global market that is emerging, the present negotiations will determine the exact nature of the multilateral trading system governing trade in services for decades to come and of the issues resulting therefrom for the trading partners in various categories of services.

The bulk of international services transactions is now taking place in a legal vacuum, without any link between one set of national regulations and another. Trade flows can be suddenly interrupted at the whim of a ministerial or legislative act of any country, and the absence of common disciplines means that only bilateral negotiations, sometimes influenced by arbitrary considerations, can restore them.

Because of the globalization of markets, there is a growing interest in bringing about consistency between the regulations of different countries in order to ensure a continuation of a process that promises a great deal of growth and well-being. To move progressively from a context of interest-lateralism to an interwoven network of rights and obligations, symbolic of reasoned multilateralism, is the challenge being thrown down to businessmen, scholars, and government representatives interested in promoting the expansion of trade in services.

11 DEALING WITH TRADE IN SERVICES IN THE URUGUAY ROUND

Geza Feketekuty

Modern technology has changed both the tradeability of services and the role of services in the international economy. Public recognition of the new role of services, has created a growing consensus that trade in services, like trade in goods, can create economic gains, and that a reduction of barriers to trade in services, like past reductions in barriers to trade in goods, can boost economic growth. This led to a decision by countries that belong to the GATT to address trade in services in the Uruguay Round of Multilateral Trade Negotiations in September 1986. The ministers adopted a fairly detailed mandate for the negotiations, in which they agreed that the negotiations should lead to the development of a general framework of principles and rules for trade in services.

In developing a framework for trade in services, trade negotiators will be able to utilize many of the key concepts that have proved useful in liberalizing trade in goods. A framework agreement for trade in services will also need to take account of the unique characteristics of international trade in services. While services have become more

The author is Counselor to the U.S. Trade Representative, but the views expressed here are his private personal views and not those of the U.S. government. The author wishes to thank Albert Bressand, who contributed to the development of many of the ideas included in this chapter, including the role of networks and the need for customization in trade in services.

tradeable, trade in services is in some fundamental aspects different from trade in goods, and barriers to trade in services are in many ways different from barriers to trade in goods.

This chapter is devoted to the development of an analytical or conceptual framework for analyzing the policy issues that arise in connection with the negotiations on trade in services.

THE ANALYTICAL BUILDING BLOCKS

The Traditional Treatment of Trade in Services

As a starting point, we need to review traditional forms of trade and models of trade by theorists and policymakers. Until fairly recently, international trade theorists and trade policy officials did not concern themselves with trade in services. In part this reflected an implicit judgment that international transactions in services could not be very important and, in any case, served largely a supportive function with respect to international flows of goods, people, money, and information.

Traditional models of the world economy focused on trade in goods and on international movements of factors of production such as labor or capital. Since factors of production are essentially means for producing services, these models, in effect, accommodated exports and imports of many services by allowing for an international flow of the means for producing services. International payments generated through the production of services abroad by "foreign" factors were treated as factor payments. Traditional models could also accommodate international trade in services associated with trade in goods, such as shipping or insurance, by treating such services solely as domestic inputs into the production of internationally traded goods.

The treatment of trade in services as either trade in goods or as international factor movements had major policy implications. It meant that policy issues related to trade in services surfaced only in connection with trade in goods or with international factor movements. Trade negotiators, for example, concerned themselves with barriers to trade in marine insurance only in so far as such barriers affected trade in goods.

Impact of Modern Technology
on Trade in Services

Major changes in technology associated with the flow of information and money, as well as the transportation of people and goods, have significantly expanded the volume of international trade in services in recent years and enhanced its importance for economic growth and prosperity. Advances in computer and communication technology, for example, have made it possible to transport information and money in the form of electronic signals over great distances virtually instantaneously. This new capacity to send money and information efficiently over large distances has significantly reduced the need for physical proximity between producers and consumers of many services, though it has not entirely eliminated the need for close contacts. This is because most services have to be customized for each individual consumer on the basis of information provided by the consumer, and such information is often best obtained through an on-the-spot assessment of the consumer's needs and circumstances.

The need for face-to-face contacts between producers and consumers of services living in different countries can often be satisfied by international travel by either the seller or the buyer of services. It has become a reasonable proposition for either the buyer or the seller of many services to travel to another country explicitly for the purpose of acquiring or delivering services that continue to require close proximity between producer and consumer. In this regard, advances in transportation technology have had as much of an impact on trade in services as modern communications and data processing technology.

In light of the growing economic importance of trade in service, the economic cost of barriers to such trade have become much higher. Looking at barriers to international transactions in services only insofar as they affect trade in goods or international factor movements has become less acceptable because it fails to highlight the costs of such barriers in terms of lost opportunities from international specialization in services. It has also become politically unacceptable to an increasingly important economic group in society, namely businesses engaged in international trade in services.

New models thus need to be developed that will focus on international trade in services as a distinct set of international transactions, raising a distinct set of policy issues. The initial contributions to the economic literature on trade in services have tended to treat trade in services as something similar to trade in goods: it has thus been shown, for example, that the theory of comparative advantage could be applied to services in order to demonstrate that trade in services will lead to mutual economic gains by the countries participating in such trade. While the proponents of such views have recognized that trade in services is different in some respects from trade in goods, they argued that these differences do not lead to logical inconsistencies with the theory of comparative advantage. The theory of comparative advantage and other traditional models are not adequate, however, for analyzing all of the issues that relate to trade in services, given some of the unique characteristics of such trade.

Trade in Services as a Flow of Goods, People, Money, and Information

The key to understanding trade in services is to focus on the means for storing and transporting services from one place to another. A first characteristic of tradeable services is that they become storable and transportable by being incorporated in goods, people, money, or information: they are thus "transported" from one country to another by goods, people, money, or information that have "absorbed" services.

All international trade in services is thus linked to an international movement of people, information, money, or goods.[1] In order to become tradeable, services either have to be applied to people, information, money, or goods (which then provide the means for transferring the services involved to another country), or the services have to be used to move people, information, money, or goods from one country to another. We might call the first category of international trade in services "trade in value-enhancing services" and the second category "trade in support services."

The easiest way to conceptualize trade in services is to think of it in terms of an application of value-enhancing services to goods (as in repair services), people (as in educational services), money (as in financial management services), or information (as in data processing services) in the exporting country, and a transfer of the "enhanced" goods, people, money, or information to the importing country with the help of internationally traded "support services." Another way to look at trade in services is in terms of trade in the economic benefits created by the application of services in the exporting country.

International Trade in Services and Foreign Investment

Another important characteristic of trade in services is that it usually requires the establishment of local facilities in the importing country. While modern technology has made it physically possible to supply many services, from a remote location, most services require a degree of customization for the individual buyer, and this makes it sometimes necessary, and frequently advantageous, to establish local facilities as a point of contact between the foreign export business and the local consumer. Government restrictions on foreign investment in services can therefore create barriers to trade in services.

Generally, retail sales of services to households and to small and medium-sized companies are most dependent on the establishment of local facilities in the importing country and are therefore most affected by restrictions on foreign investments in service facilities. On the other hand, large purchases of services by large international corporations are least dependent on access to local facilities by a foreign supplier. Large corporations can dilute the added transaction cost of buying services abroad, since the added cost of buying abroad does not bear a direct relationship to the value of the transaction: a business executive who travels to New York to negotiate a loan or who travels to London to negotiate an insurance contract can as easily negotiate a contract for $10 million as for $100,000. Large corporations thus can most easily bypass barriers that take the form of restrictions on foreign investment, or restrictions on the sale of services by foreign enterprises in the importing country.

Trade in Services and International Network Competition

Another characteristic of some services, such as basic telecommunication services and transportation services, is that they have to be produced locally, through the utilization of local facilities. Many have argued that these services are not tradeable and therefore should not be subject to trade negotiations. Those who take this view argue that the regulation of such service providers is a purely domestic issue. Others have argued, however, that many of these services are supplied today by international enterprises that maintain facilities in a large number of countries, and that the terms under which such international enterprises can compete with each other are by necessity an international commercial issue. While the services supplied by such enterprises do not fit the traditional notion of trade, they are not purely domestic utilities in the traditional sense.

International competition among firms that maintain an international network of facilities has many of the same economic characteristics as trade and raises many of the same policy issues as trade. Their economic advantage and competitive strength is that they facilitate the delivery of services that an individual or a business wishes to buy in many different countries. A tourist is clearly better off if he or she can use the same credit card or traveler's check in many different countries. A firm doing business in a dozen countries is likely to find it cheaper and more convenient to deal with the same accounting firm, insurance company, bank, or telecommunications company. There is therefore a need to develop an analytical and policy framework for addressing issues related to international network competition.

INVISIBLE BARRIERS TO INVISIBLE TRADE

Trade in services is largely invisible because it is usually impossible to see the services that have been absorbed by the people, information, money, and goods crossing the border. An observer who is at the right spot at the right time might see the goods, money, people, or an information medium crossing the border, but such an observer would not be able to identify the services that are being exported or imported. This has a number of important real-world implications. Not only is it difficult to measure the flow of services, but it is also difficult to control the flow of services across the border. In order to assert control over the flow of services across its border, a government can adopt one of two strategies: it can extract more information about the people, money, and information crossing the border and use that information to control the flow of services, or it can control all goods, people, money, and information crossing the border. This creates a major dilemma for democratic governments: How deeply should they pry into the affairs of their citizens and to what extent should they control the free flow of information, people, and money just in order to control the flow of services?

Most democratic governments of advanced countries respect the rights of the individual and recognize the need to limit the amount of information that individuals should be required to report to the government. This means that governments find it far more difficult to limit imports of services purchased abroad than to limit domestic sales of imported services. Most barriers to trade in services are therefore embedded in domestic regulations that control the sale of services.

A government can also try to establish restrictions on purchases of services by its citizens in foreign countries, but it can enforce them only through a comprehensive foreign exchange control system or through a comprehensive system for regulating the consumption of particular services. For example, the government can refuse to allocate foreign exchange to the purchase of foreign architectural services, or it can insist that only architectural plans signed by a domestically registered architect can be used to construct a building. A government can also refuse to allocate foreign exchange for the purchase of insurance abroad, or it can insist that only insurance sold by an approved insurance company can satisfy the requirement for compulsory auto insurance, or that only a will signed by a local lawyer will be recognized by the courts.

Barriers to trade in services are thus intermingled with domestic regulatory measures that control the production, sale, and consumption of services, and such barriers therefore tend to be as invisible to the average person as trade in services itself. This only compounds the skepticism that there is anything to talk about with respect to trade in services.

Trade in services that are conveniently purchased abroad are subject to far fewer restrictions than services that are most conveniently purchased in the importing country, since the government of the importing country will not have any effective means for controlling the sale of services produced abroad to its citizens. In contrast, if the sale takes place in the home country of the customer, the laws and regulations of the importing country will fully apply to the sale.

TOWARD A MULTILATERAL AGREEMENT

International Trade in Services in the Uruguay Round

The Uruguay Declaration, which contains the negotiating mandate for the Uruguay Round of Multilateral Trade Negotiations, establishes three levels of objectives for the negotiations on trade in services. At the operational level, the Declaration says, "Negotiations in this area shall aim to establish a multilateral framework of principles and rules for trade in services, including elaboration of possible disciplines for individual sectors. This conclusion resolved a major debate over the feasibility and desirability of negotiating trade issues in services as diverse as banking, insurance, professional services, data processing, and transportation within a common framework. Some argued that each service sector raises unique issues that have nothing in common with other sectors and that it makes no sense to negotiate such issues under the common heading of trade in services. Others argued that many of the principles and rules of the GATT could be applied to trade in services and that a general framework of principles and rules would be more likely to succeed in achieving a broad liberalization than a sector by sector approach. The language in the Uruguay Declaration supports the traditional trade policy view while recognizing that effective negotiations will ultimately have to get down to a sector-by-sector focus.

The Declaration goes on to say that the purpose of negotiations on trade in services is to achieve an "expansion of such trade under conditions of transparency and progressive liberalization." This makes it clear that one of the key objectives of the negotiations is to expand trade in services through a process of liberalization.

The last part of the long sentence on objectives establishes the negotiations "as a means of promoting economic growth of all trading partners and the development of developing countries." This is a statement of conviction that liberalization of trade in services and the development of an agreed framework of rules for trade in services can advance the economic growth of all countries as well as the develment of developing countries.

The fear was often expressed that a GATT framework agreement on trade in services would undermine the achievement of national regulatory objectives. The Declaration addresses these concerns by stating that "Such a framework shall respect the policy objectives of national laws and regulations applying to services." By focusing on the objectives of national laws and regulations rather than the laws and regulations themselves, the language of the Declaration leaves open the possibility that the liberalization of trade might require changes in the way national laws and regulations implement policy objectives. This is a distinction the GATT has made with respect to the application of technical and regulatory standards to internationally traded goods.

Conceptual Framework for Trade in Services

Some have argued that despite basic differences between goods and services, an agreement in services should follow the basic structure of the GATT framework for goods: that trade barriers should be imposed only at the border, that the protection provided by border measures should be quantifiable like a tariff, and that national treatment should prevail with respect to domestic regulations.

A straight application of the GATT rules to services would not be workable, however, for several reasons. First, the conversion of discriminatory regulations into tariffs would absorb too much energy and political capital without generating significant economic gain. Second, tariffs would be difficult to collect since governments cannot easily identify cross-border flows of services. Third, governments will not agree to an a priori application of national treatment to all domestic regulations since that would eliminate the most effective means of protection in one step. Moreover, it will not be easy to agree what national treatment means in the case of highly complex regulations that inevitably have a different effect on different enterprises.

Each element of the GATT framework, however, contains an underlying principle that could be applied to trade in services in another form and accomplish the same purpose. The goal of the GATT framework—making import barriers more visible, more focused, and more price-sensitive—should also be a goal of the framework of principles and rules that is developed for trade in services, while adapted to the unique aspects of trade in services.

Identifying Barriers to Trade Barriers in Services

The clear identification of barriers and their separation from domestic regulations would substantially facilitate the process of negotiating their reduction. There has to be a process for determining which regulations are negotiable and which regulations are not negotiable. The clear identification of barriers would also reduce the protective effect created by uncertainty associated with the treatment of foreign service providers. If any regulatory decision can be turned into a protective device arbitrarily, how can a firm calculate the costs of doing business abroad?

Separating import restrictions from domestic regulations will also encourage good government by clarifying decision-making responsibilities within a government. It will force governments to identify the officials responsible for trade decisions on one hand, and the officials responsible for domestic regulatory decisions on the other. It will also force governments to develop distinct ground rules for making each set of decisions.

In sorting out protectionist measures from legitimate domestic regulations it will be necessary to consider both the protective effect of a measure and the domestic regulatory objective. Neither criterion by itself is likely to provide a sufficient basis for identifying the measures that should be covered by negotiations. Whether or not a measure creates an impediment to trade is best established on the basis of its actual effect on trade. The negotiability of such a measure, however, depends on the extent to which the protective element can be removed while preserving legitimate domestic regulatory objectives. A process of identifying barriers therefore should include both a procedure for identifying measures with restrictive trade effects and a procedure for identifying the domestic regulatory objectives served by these measures.

Exporting countries are probably in the best position to determine restrictive trade effects, and the importing country is in the best position to identify the contributions to the achievement of domestic policy objectives. A natural division of labor thus suggests itself. Exporting countries should be asked to draw up lists of regulatory measures in importing countries that create impediments to trade, and importing countries should be asked to identify the extent to which such measures are essential for the achievement of domestic policy objectives. Naturally, both groups of countries would be asked to explain and defend their claims.

Going through a process of reconciling perceptions of exporting countries and importing countries will be an extremely useful exercise for both. Exporting countries will obtain a better understanding of the regulatory systems of importing countries, and importing countries may find that many practices they have always accepted as the normal way of doing things in fact are restrictive measures.

In summary, the identification of barriers to trade in services will identify the regulations subject to negotiation, reduce the likelihood that purely domestic regulations will be used as hidden trade barriers, and lead to better government by clarifying the process and criteria whereby to distinguish between domestic regulatory objectives and trade objectives.

National Treatment—the Core Concept in A Trade Regime for Services

The GATT principle that all barriers should be at the border, for the sake of logical consistency, requires a complementary principle that domestic policy measures should not become trade barriers; that is, domestic policy measures should not be used to protect domestic industry. This companion principle is the so-called national treatment principle, which requires governments to treat imported goods that have satisfied border measures as if they would have been produced within the country.

Since it is not practical to require that barriers to trade in services be erected at the border for all the reasons discussed above, the national treatment principle also needs to be adjusted for services. Applying it across the board would be tantamount to ruling out the possibility of protecting domestic service industries, and this would not be acceptable to many governments. The underlying concept is crucial to development of an effective regime for trade in services, however, and the only question is how the GATT national treatment principle should be modified to fit the requirements of a service regime.

We argued above that the basic rule for trade in services should be that barriers to trade in services should be clearly identified, i.e., that they should be fully transparent. One could build the national treatment principle on this basic rule, by requiring countries to provide national treatment for all measures not identified as barriers.

There is an important reason, however, why governments may not be willing to go quite that far. A commitment to provide national treatment may not result in equivalent market access when countries have very different regulatory regimes. A domestic regulatory regime that allows open competition, for example, provides more trade opportunities than a domestic regulatory regime that limits competition.

A commitment to provide national treatment for any given area of services could thus become the subject of negotiation. A country could, for example, commit itself to provide national treatment with respect to certain policy instruments and not others. In addition, a government could commit itself to a ceiling on the protection provided through the application of protective policy tools. The negotiations would thus consist of two components, a negotiation over the list of policy tools for which governments would bind national treatment and a negotiation over the extent of protection offered through the application of policy tools not bound by a national treatment commitment.

In summary, the most important challenge for the negotiators of a trade agreement in services is to develop a framework that will achieve clarity and establish limits with respect to the trade effects of domestic regulations, without getting into a detailed negotiation of domestic regulations.

Reciprocity and Most Favored Nation Treatment

The GATT framework provides a basis for a bilateral exchange of tariff reductions on the basis of reciprocity, and at the same time it makes the results of such bilateral negotiations available to all other GATT member countries on a most favored nation (MFN) basis. This hybrid system combining reciprocity and MFN treatment should be incorporated in the framework for trade in services.

First, all the provisions of the General Agreement on Trade in Services would apply equally, on a MFN basis to all countries that agree to adhere to the obligations of the agreement. Second, each country would be expected to table a list of services for which it is willing to grant national treatment to all member countries on a MFN basis, subject to enumerated barriers and reservations.

As is currently the case with respect to negotiations on goods under the GATT, each country will have to evaluate the commercial value of the commitments it is offering, versus the commercial commitments it is being offered by other countries applying a general reciprocity test. If the value of commitments made by others is inadequate, a country can adjust its offer by not making as many reductions in barriers affecting some services, or by withholding commitments on other services.

Inevitably the scope for a general exchange of commitments on a general MFN basis is constrained by the value of the commitments made by the most restrictive countries and by the large differences among regulatory systems. Countries with relatively few regulatory restraints will be reluctant to provide full national treatment commitments in sectors where other important member countries maintain tight regulatory controls.

A framework that gives all participants the same level of benefits regardless of the restrictiveness of the domestic regulatory system will not fully exploit opportunities for trade liberalization. The service framework therefore needs to leave open the possibility for countries with a relatively similar regulatory regimes to negotiate supplementary agreements that require adherence to a tighter discipline. Any country that adheres to the general agreement should have a right, however, to join such an agreement provided it is prepared to accept its obligations. This is usually referred to as conditional most favored nation treatment.

International Flows of Information, People, and Money

In addition to the pervasive role of regulation, trade in services differs from trade in goods in terms of its dependence on an international movement of information, people, money, and goods. It is hard to conceive of a more emotionally charged agenda.

The framework agreement itself cannot establish substantive, legally binding commitments in any of these areas. It should, however, establish the principle that governments should provide as much freedom of movement for information, money, and people, and as much freedom for foreign investment as is consistent with the achievement of national policy objectives.

Foreign Investment and Foreign Trade

As discussed earlier, international trade in consumer services typically requires an extensive presence in the local market, and foreign exporters therefore usually find it necessary or advantageous to establish themselves in the foreign market and to invest in local facilities, or at the very least to establish a local presence through local representatives and agents.

This raises the emotional issue of foreign investment. Like all other issues of an equal degree of sensitivity, the foreign investment issue will need to be broken down into its component parts if it is to prove manageable. First, a framework agreement should define a minimum presence in the importing country that would be granted to all foreign suppliers that have been granted national treatment. Such a minimum presence should include legal establishment (insofar as is required by local regulations as a precondition for selling specific service products), establishment of local representative offices, the ability to use local business enterprises as agents for distributing and supporting the services product, and any investments that have to be made to satisfy regulatory requirements. This minimum presence could be incorporated in the definition of national treatment included in the framework agreement.

Beyond minimum presence, the framework agreement could make provisions for the exchange of higher levels of commitment, notably in sectors for which foreign investment is absolutely essential, such as banking and most consumer services.

The Network Dimension of International Trade in Services

The issue that arise from network competition fall between the responsibilities of trade officials and the responsibilities of regulatory officials. To the extent an international firm managing a network provides services that fall within the traditional concept of a public utility, the management of that network raises international regulatory issues. But when such policies affect the development of network facilities essential for international commerce and the terms of network competition, they raise issues that look like traditional trade issues.

International trade agreements and international regulatory agreements in various sectors serve different governmental purposes. Each set of rules constitutes, in effect, an extension of national laws to the international level in a particular policy sphere and is based on a distinct set of assumptions. While national laws and regulations naturally reflect each country's own political and economic philosophy, every government has to face more or less the same set of issues in a given area of policy, and this commonality of purpose is reflected in the rules of the GATT and rules of sectoral organizations such as the ITU and ICAO. Trade officials and regulatory officials are also expected to play distinct roles in the policymaking process of their countries, and by extension in their international activities.

Trade officials have a dual role in the government—to act as guardians of the country's general commercial interest and simultaneously to act as guardians of a system of trade rules that permit market-based competition among enterprises from different countries. The strength of a trade policy approach is in its emphasis on competition and the removal of obstacles to such competition. Negotiations in the GATT can best supplement and complement negotiations in sectoral organizations with a regulatory focus by focusing on the ground rules for competition.

The principal purpose of international negotiations among regulatory officials is to establish a basis for the interconnection of national telecommunication networks and to reconcile conflicts among national regulations that could pose an obstacle to the operation of an international network. The underlying assumption of international regulatory agreements in various sectors is that services offered to the public are a public utility and that the international rules of the game should support the achievement of domestic regulatory objectives. Regulatory officials responsible for international issues in national administrations generally have the dual role of acting as guardians of national regulatory objectives and as guardians of the network as a public utility.

Hence trade officials are best equipped to deal with issues that relate to international competition among commercial enterprises, while regulatory officials are best equipped to deal with issues that relate to the reliability of the services produced by individual firms.

CONCLUSION: STRATEGIC ISSUES

As we saw earlier in this chapter, the structure of barriers affecting trade in services is quite different from the structure of barriers affecting trade in goods. Restrictions on trade in goods have generally been imposed at the border and not at the point of sale or consumption inside the country. The situation in services is the reverse.

This raises an important issue for negotiating strategy. Should the first priority in the negotiations be to keep cross-border flows relatively free of restraint, or should it be on reducing the detailed regulatory restraints on the sale of services by foreign enterprises inside the importing country? On one hand, it could be argued that there are few cross-border flows that are not tied to the establishment and operation of facilities in the importing country, and that governments will not find it any easier in the future to impose effective restraints on cross-border movements. On the other hand, it could be argued that technological changes will make it more and more practical to buy services abroad and to transfer such services through channels of communication. Since there are few barriers to such transfer today, a relatively modest negotiating effort could forestall the imposition of disruptive new restrictions on cross-border sales of services through communication channels.

The choice between one strategy or another is clearly not an either/or situation, but a question of emphasis. Opinion in the business community on this issue is clearly divided. There are those who argue that you should not try to fix what is not broken, while others are concerned that governments will come under increasing pressure from affected domestic industries to restrain imports of services based on cross-border information flows.

A related issue concerns the degree of emphasis that should be placed on services that are traded internationally through a flow of information, as against services traded through a flow of people or money. Many services based on the flow of information require or benefit from the establishment of local facilities in the importing country. Services being largely customized products, they may call for face-to-face meetings between producer and consumer even when transmitted through communication channels over great distances. But issues related to the movements of people and money raise many sensitive policy issues outside trade in services, and it can be expected that officials responsible for these policy areas will be very reluctant to accept changes in these policies.

All in all, it is clear that traditional trade concepts are not sufficient for analyzing trade in services and will have to be supplemented by new concepts that can address the unique features of trade in services, including 1) the international movement of people, information, money, and goods that is essential for trade in services to take place, 2) the close relationship between trade in services and foreign investment in services, and 3) the network dimension of trade in services.

NOTES

1. The term *money* is used here as a surrogate for financial assets. All future references to a movement of money as a vehicle for trade in services should similarly be interpreted as a shorthand reference to international movements of financial assets.

12 BILATERAL TELECOMMUNICATIONS NEGOTIATIONS

Jonathan D. Aronson
Peter F. Cowhey

The real issues about managing international telecommunications stem from changes in domestic politics, regulatory philosophy, and technology. This chapter discusses these changes and then reviews some of the current bilateral telecommunications negotiations involving the United States.

BACKGROUND

For decades the system for managing telecommunications services domestically and internationally functioned smoothly because the technology on which services were based was changing relatively slowly and the services were homogeneous and easily distinguished from one another. The same basic range of services was offered in all countries under similar regulatory conditions. All this has changed.[1]

In the past two decades technological breakthroughs stimulated the emergence of a world information economy and led to fundamental changes. One consequence was the erosion of boundaries within and among sectors. Most notably, communications, computer, and broadcast technologies are merging.

This is an abridged version of a paper prepared for a Conference of the IIC Telecommunications Forum, New York, November 5–6, 1987. Reprinted with permission of the IIC.

Just as dramatic is the revolution occurring in regulatory philosophy. Many countries have split apart their post and telecommunications authorities and opened up competition in customer premises equipment. Other countries are considering privatization of some services, the introduction of more competition in selected segments of the market, and liberalizing some mix of broadcast and data communications services.[2] Most sweepingly, the United States, the United Kingdom, and Japan now permit facilities competition in the provision of basic services.[3] Governments also are beginning to create competitive international transmission facilities. New fiber optic cables and satellites will permit non-PTTs to bargain aggressively to secure their rights to own or lease capacity.

Before 1984 the traditional U.S. regulatory bargain resembled the bargains struck in other countries. The old regulatory bargain benefited the public switched telephone networks (PSTNs) and their favored equipment suppliers (AT&T's Western Electric in the U.S. case). It also favored smaller users at the expense of larger users. But as communications became more vital to the global operations of large users, they started to rebel against subsidizing small users.[4] Simultaneously, the computer industry, and especially IBM, grew restless with the old bargain.

Once interests in the U.S. market were changed, interests of comparable groups in other countries also substantially changed in a similar manner. To some extent, transformation in the United States spilled over into other countries.

The interests of players changed in important ways. The public switched telephone networks (PSTNs) realized that they need to develop customized, value-added communications services, because changing technology permits enhanced services to encroach increasingly on their basic service domains. They began to see that to prosper they had to follow their biggest customers abroad. This reality is pushing U.S. public networks into offering new specialized services to large customers that bypass their own public networks. The new regulatory bargain also discourages continued cross-subsidization of smaller users and equipment companies.

Large users understand that for them to reap the full benefits of U.S. deregulation, the advantages won in the United States must be duplicated abroad. Backed by computer and terminal equipment manufacturers, large users are lobbying for freer competition in telecommunications services, freedom to choose terminal equipment, and the end of cross-subsidies by PSTNs. Similarly, makers of transmission and switching equipment now understand that to be world leaders they must increase their global market share by penetrating foreign markets and by preventing competitors from using their protected home markets to finance onslaughts abroad.

Other countries' companies gained access to the U.S. market, but U.S. firms did not win comparable access abroad. (The U.S. trade balance in telecommunications equipment moved from a surplus of nearly $225 million in 1982 to a deficit of more than $2.0 billion in 1986.[5]) A new U.S. agenda for international telecommunications emerged.

Obviously, U.S. preferences cannot be achieved in international negotiations if telecommunications policies elsewhere are static. Without outside allies, U.S. will and diplomatic might are insufficient to rewrite the global telecommunications regime. But, the interests of domestic groups in other countries were also altered when the United States moved toward telecommunications deregulation. Differences in national politics and market structures cause variations from country to country, but the broad changes in interests in other countries are fairly clear.

1. To protect their competitive advantage, large users everywhere are starting to demand terms for service and terminal equipment equivalent to those available in the United States.

2. PSTNs are realizing that they will lose their commanding domestic position unless they coopt their large users. They are starting to reduce cross-subsidies to smaller users and equipment makers and are experimenting more aggressively in organizing data services and acquiring equipment and technology for their networks. The barriers keeping out foreign switching and transmission equipment are weakening in many markets. The barriers keeping out terminal equipment are falling in virtually all markets.

3. The markets for computers and for terminal equipment are becoming intertwined, forcing all players to redefine their own systems for data communications and to allow customers greater freedom to choose their own equipment.

4. Makers of switching and transmission equipment realize that in the future their national networks must be compatible with foreign networks.

National suppliers now also recognize that their PSTN may someday abandon them if they do not match world equipment standards. Although every non-U.S. company would prefer the U.S. market to be open to competition and its own market to be closed, few firms can risk being shut out of other major industrial markets in order to keep their home markets closed. Therefore all of these players are susceptible to pressure to gain their support for limited liberalization of their home markets.

U.S. GOVERNMENT BILATERAL NEGOTIATIONS

In recent years the United States has participated in four major sets of bilateral talks covering telecommunications. These talks are important in their own right and also may provide important precedents for multilateral negotiations in the GATT and ITU.

Market-Oriented Sector-Selective (MOSS) Talks with Japan

Under international pressure, NTT was the only telecommunications monopoly to accede to the Government Procurement Code negotiated during the Tokyo Round of GATT trade negotiations. In 1981 the United States and Japan signed an Agreement on NTT procurement. The agreement was renewed in December 1983 and again at the end of 1986. Nonetheless, total Japanese imports of U.S. communication equipment has been roughly constant in real terms since 1983. In 1986 NTT purchased about $250 million of foreign equipment. Overseas purchases accounted for only 2 percent of its total purchases.

The Market-Oriented Sector-Selective (MOSS) talks on telecommunications grew out of a meeting between Prime Minister Nakasone and President Reagan on January 2, 1985.[6] The first phase of the telecommunications talks, which mainly addressed terminal equipment and network services, were placed on the fast track because they would be covered by legislation designed to liberalize the Japanese telecommunications market. Before the law went into effect on April 1, 1985, the United States and Japan negotiated intensively to remove potentially discriminatory aspects of the new Japanese tele-communications regulatory structure. The United States sought greater transparency in Japanese rule-making and standard-setting processes, a reduction in the actual number of standards, and the lib-eralization in the market for terminal equipment by adopting the U.S. standard of "no harm to network." The United States also asked the Japanese to accept foreign test data on telecommunica-tions equipment and tried to persuade the Ministry of Posts and Tele-communications not to enact significant equity restrictions on for-eign ownership or to impose cumbersome registration procedures.

The second phase of the MOSS talks began in mid-1985 and con-centrated on wireless communications, including radio frequency allocation, pagers, and cellular telephones. U.S. negotiators sought to simplify Japanese licensing and approval procedures, broaden oppor-tunities for foreign companies to provide third-party services, and to promote the acceptance of foreign test data. The second phase of talks concluded in January 1986. However, the two governments continued to hold follow-up talks. In 1987 these talks focused on the introduction of international value-added services between Japan and the United States.

Phase 1 negotiations resulted in the simplification of application and approval procedures for terminal equipment and the creation of an independent agency to determine the conformity of technical standards. Foreign firms were allowed to own 100 percent of the equity of value-added networks (VANs) and registration procedures for VANs were streamlined. During the second phase of talks Japan inched toward self-certification, offered greater transparency in administration of rules regarding radio transmission and established an organization to issue individual approvals of radio equipment. Pri-vate firms were allowed to buy U.S. satellites.[7] The main outcome of the MOSS follow-up talks was the modification of the Telecom-munications Business Law to allow international value-added services between the United States and Japan. On September 1, 1987, an amendment of the Telecommunications Business Law entered into force to allow international VAN businesses to be operated.[8]

Negotiations were difficult and prolonged. Success was most likely when American firms worked with the government to fight for entry. For example, Motorola has won 25 percent of the Japanese domestic market for pagers. Major barriers in Japan hampering U.S. VANs have fallen and some U.S. firms report progress in the PBX market.

However, more often Japanese agreement to allow competition under the MOSS or other guises has not led to major sales. For instance, during the MOSS talks the Japanese promised to allow foreign participation and ownership of shared mobile radio systems. Unfortunately, getting a license was an operation in frustration for Motorola. The firm suspects that it will eventually get a license but that the lag will be "just enough for the Japanese to catch up technologically in their product offering."[9] Similarly, the MOSS talks helped persuade the Japanese to adopt a "no harm to network" approach for the attachment of terminal equipment, but this concession has so far not resulted in major new sales contracts.

Market Access Fact-Finding (MAFF) and Technical Bilateral Talks

Historically, the U.S. government raised issues concerning telecommunications almost exclusively with ministries of posts and telecommunications. To better understand the structure and regulation of telecommunications with the countries that present the most important markets for U.S. telecommunications products and services, the Reagan administration initiated wide-ranging fact-finding talks that exchange of technical, policy, and legal information. The United States intended "to stimulate involvement of senior policy-level officials in other countries beyond the traditionally parochial interests of the PTTs."[10]

Since 1983 the U.S. government has held formal Market Access Fact-Finding (MAFF) bilateral talks on telecommunications matters with West Germany, Italy, Spain, and Sweden. Technical bilateral consultations have also been held with France and the Netherlands. Generally, during MAFF talks the U.S. government has concentrated on six main concerns related to access to the telecommunications markets of foreign countries: 1) the lack of fair and open competition for government procurement, 2) a restricted market for value-added services, 3) the lack of equitable ISDN (Integrated Services Digital Network) tariff rates for value-added service providers, 4) standards that go beyond ensuring against harm to the public network, 5) the lack of transparency for draft telecommunications regulations, and 6) restrictive procedures for the testing, certification, and attachment of terminal equipment for the public network.[11]

Because these are discussions, not negotiations, it is difficult to assess their impact. At minimum they have focused attention in other countries on the possible benefits of liberalization. Conceivably they have pressured other countries to move faster than they would have otherwise. The MAFF talks with West Germany certainly were the most intense, focusing pressure on West Germany to implement an eight-step market liberalization program. For example, the Germans began to allow competition in the low-speed modem market, eliminated the 50 percent domestic data processing requirement and drafted more liberal PBX specifications.

In most other cases the United States seems to have acted as a cheerleader for domestic interests favoring liberalization. The talks threw light on new Italian legislation liberalized maintenance of terminal equipment, on Dutch plans to liberalize its PTT structure starting in 1989, and on the draft Spanish Law on Telecommunications. The French used the talks to brief the United States about its Audiovisual Reform Law passed in August 1986 and to clarify its goals in establishing the Commission Nationale des Communications et Liberté, an independent regulatory agency modeled after the U.S. Federal Communications Commission (FCC), in January 1987.

Similar discussions (not formally labeled as MAFF talks) have been initiated with other countries such as the People's Republic of China leading to a mutual cooperation agreement with the NTIA on May 16, 1986.[12] In addition, the United States has engaged the United Kingdom and the European Community in several meetings since 1983.

The U.S.-Israel Free Trade Agreement

On April 22, 1985, the United States and Israel signed a Declaration on Trade in Services in conjunction with a Free Trade Agreement covering trade in goods that established a set of principles for trade in services between the two countries. The effort devoted to this exercise was remarkable considering that except in tourism there is limited trade in services and few pressing commercial differences separating the two countries. It was pursued in part to help define issues that would need to be addressed in broader negotiations on trade in services in the Uruguay round of GATT negotiations.

The Declaration covered broad principles: open market access, national treatment (and its application to domestic regulations), the behavior of public monopolies, due process, problem solving, and the negotiation of binding commitments. Subsequently the United States and Israel entered into negotiations on three sectoral annotations covering tourism, telecommunications, and insurance.

The draft telecommunications annotation sets out both suppliers' interests and users' interests and distinguished "between the interests of small and large users and suppliers. The most important definitional issue, however, has . . . been the dividing line between basic telecommunications services and value-added telecommunications services."[13]

The U.S.-Canada Free Trade Agreement

On October 3, 1987, U.S. and Canadian negotiators agreed to a comprehensive trade agreement. Enhanced telecommunication services are an important element of the pact, which took effect after being approved by Congress and then Parliament. Significantly, there is almost nothing on telecommunication equipment in the agreement, nor are basic services covered. (The United States, hoping to erode Canada's Northern Telecom's dominance of the Canadian equipment market, wanted the agreement to cover telecommunications equipment. But the United States insisted that basic services be excluded. Canada took the mirror position. Ultimately both sectors were excluded.[14])

Negotiations with Canada about domestic and international long-distance services are complicated because, like state regulators in the United States, the provincial regulatory authorities are articulate defenders of small residential users. However, provincial politicians have comparatively greater political power in Canada than do state politicians in the United States. Moreover, the provinces have local phone companies (often owned by the provincial governments) with comparatively higher cost structures for long distance than the ones in federally regulated areas. Therefore, in many cases they also are representing the interests of their phone companies.

The negotiations took place against a changing regulatory picture in Canada. At the outset, Canada had almost no competition in basic services. It had tried to liberalize competition in value-added services. The Canadian policy, however, did not lead to a boom in providers of value-added services because of restrictions on competition in facilities and on shared use and resale of circuits. The new competitive policy announced in July 1987 promised to remedy many of the problems. They authorized complete freedom of competition in value-added and information services by Type II carriers. Although Type II carriers may not own transmission facilities, they will be allowed to lease and use facilities services as they wish. Furthermore, Type II carriers may be owned totally by foreigners.

The biggest potential for disrupting the sectoral trade agreement and the regulatory arrangements for telecommunications services would be an effort by Bell Canada to emulate the U.S. model and pursue its largest customers abroad. It became clear by the summer of 1987 that a Canadian move into the U.S. service market was in the cards. Bell Canada had reached a tentative agreement with Ameritech, a regional Bell operating company, for a joint venture in information services. More important, the Canadian negotiators demanded a unilateral right for Canadian firms to build facilities or resell long-distance services in the United States. The Canadians would not offer U.S. firms a reciprocal privilege and justified their position by noting concessions on other issues.

U.S. negotiators resisted Canadian demands to include international basic services in the bargain, limiting the agreement to enhanced and computer services. U.S. negotiators won access to the telecommunications infrastructure for American providers of enhanced and computer services on a national treatment basis. Canadian firms received identical guarantees in the U.S. market. In addition, the U.S. industry sought guaranteed minimum rights for providers of enhanced services. U.S. firms fear that Bell Canada will try to dominate Teleglobe (the newly privatized carrier for Canada's international telecommunications services) and then push for control of Telecom Canada (the consortium for domestic long-distance services owned by Canadian phone companies) as well. If this occurred, U.S. value-added network providers would have to rely on a facilities system controlled by their strongest competitor, Bell Canada (now that Bell Canada is free to offer VANs). For its part, Canada excluded the provincial market for enhanced and computer services (about 30 percent of the total) from the deal.

A second barrier to free entry is the limits on bypassing Canadian networks by using U.S. based value-added networks. Canada insists on local data-processing in some sectors such as banking. Thus, even free access to U.S. value-added networks would not end all required local data-processing. The U.S. financial industry registered complaints during preparation for the trade talks. More fundamentally, the Canadian government and phone companies have long-standing policies that limit the crossing points for telecommunications from the United States to Canada to official network carriers. Current federal rules and phone companies' practices make it impossible to rely on U.S. value-added networks to handle data shipped from a Canadian origin to a Canadian destination. (One-way transit in either direction is permissible.)

Canadian regulators, in essence, tried for a long time to protect the basic network while slowly opening up data services to greater competition. The smaller Canadian providers of enhanced services feared potential competitors from the United States as much as they opposed any domestic barriers to competition. But a significant base of support for competition emerged. Loopholes in the old regulations permitted larger users to bargain aggressively about the terms and prices of services. Yet these users still faced significant cost disadvantages compared to their U.S. counterparts. This made them a constituency for further reform that produced increased competition in basic services while reinforcing their commitment to international free trade in value-added services. Nonetheless, the talks have shown that reciprocal free trade in basic services is hard to achieve, although some one other than the United States is now suggesting putting basic services on the table. Moreover, an agreement on equipment or value-added services is likely to force continuing reforms of domestic regulatory systems of both countries.

CORPORATE-GOVERNMENT NEGOTIATIONS

In addition to bilateral government talks and negotiations, it is useful to highlight cases of interactions between private firms and foreign governments. In several cases corporations seeking access to foreign markets sought and received assistance from the U.S. government. The case of AT&T's unsuccessful effort to purchase the CGCT company from the French government in 1985–86 was a case in point. Here we review the case of MCI and U.S. Sprint.

MCI and U.S. Sprint have a serious problem competing in the lucrative international long-distance telephone market. During 1986 AT&T held 82 percent of the $50 billion U.S. domestic inter-LATA long-distance market, MCI had an 8 percent share, and U.S. Sprint totaled about 6 percent. Allnet captured 1 percent with the remainder spread among smaller companies.[15] However, AT&T still managed to hold on to over 97 percent of the international market. Although both MCI and U.S. Sprint had signed numerous operating agreements by mid-1986, they still had not cracked three key markets: Canada, West Germany, and Mexico. Consequently, MCI, U.S. Sprint and others entered into discussions with the telecommunications authorities in these three countries.

Canada allowed MCI and U.S. Sprint to offer northbound traffic starting in 1983 and 1984, respectively. But although MCI and U.S. Sprint could transmit calls from the United States to most major Canadian markets, they received no return traffic from Canada. This made the Canadian traffic unprofitable for the Other Common Carriers although they had to provide the service in order to win attractive U.S. customers. U.S. Sprint claimed potential losses of $50 million in 1985–88.[16] Although Canadian carriers worried that the entry of the OCCs would open the way to ingenious ways to bypass the domestic Canadian long-distance network, Canada modified its policy in late 1986 to end the complaint when U.S. Sprint demonstrated that it was willing to force the issue onto the bilateral trade agenda. MCI and U.S. Sprint began receiving return traffic almost simultaneously in April 1987.

West Germany was tougher to crack. The Bundespost was content with its dealings with AT&T and did not want to deviate from its preferred monopoly-to-monopoly dealings. Moreover, until the Witte Commission report was officially submitted to Chancellor Kohl in late summer 1987, the Bundespost had little incentive to announce concessions. Why should they give ground and get no credit for their action? However, in the spring of 1987 the Bundespost agreed to meet with four U.S. carriers: U.S. Sprint, MCI, TRT, and FTCC, to consider operating with alternative long-distance carriers but insisted that they would all have to share a single gateway. Ultimately, with the help of the education process that took place in the MAFF talks and continuing discussion in Washington of sanctions against Siemens' U.S. operations, the Bundespost agreed that under some circumstances more than one alternative gateway would be permitted. Preliminary agreement with the carriers was reached in July 1987 and the decision to permit additional carriers was announced in September 1987.

The Bundespost agreed to the establishment of a common gateway for telephone traffic between West Germany and the United States that would not be routed via AT&T. U.S. Sprint was chosen to operate the common gateway and MCI was promised that it could open its own independent gateway. In return the Bundespost wanted guarantees that quality standards would conform to international levels, that U.S. Sprint would provide all interested U.S. carriers with reasonable and fair access, that the U.S. carriers would cover the additional costs incurred by the Bundespost in establishing the gateway, that all U.S. subscribers can be reached via the common gateway and that at the beginning only automatically switched terminal traffic would be permitted. Trial operations began in 1988.

As of January 1, 1989, MCI and U.S. Sprint have failed to reach agreement with Mexico to provide service. U.S. Sprint, which has a higher percentage of business in the Southwest than MCI, is particularly interested in establishing long-distance service. However, Telefonos de Mexico S.A. de C.V. (Telmex) has until recently shown little interest in allowing more competition.

Telmex enjoys a particularly favorable revenue split with AT&T. Its profits have increased in recent years (to about $51 million in 1985) as the peso was devalued because charges on international long-distance calls are denominated in dollars.

Some changes may be in the wind. The financial centers in the Mexican government ordered a study of the communications services for the *maquiladoras* (export zone factories) that are so important to foreign exchange earning. In June 1987 Joaquin Munoz Izquierdo, previously the head of Pemex, became president of Telmex. And the new President of Mexico, Carlos Salinas, has singled out telecommunications as an example of the need to reform and rationalize public services in his campaign speeches.

Throughout 1988 the Mexican government was being lobbied on three fronts by foreign governments. First, outside vendors of network equipment (especially France) were encouraging a comprehensive plan for the transition to integrated digital services network. Second, several U.S. providers of data communications equipment and services were urging Mexico to consider some measure of privatization of value-added services (or co-financing of the services with the private sector even if they remained a public monopoly). Third, Sprint, MCI, and other common carriers were having continuing discussions about access to the Mexican market.

Implications and Conclusion

There are five important implications of the process that we have described.

1. There is an emerging "green belt" that girdles the globe for financial and communications services. It ties together the major U.S., British, and Japanese finance and service centers. Other countries are deciding to what extent they will plug into the network. Canada has just opted to join it. West Germany is now considering such a plan.

    The services industries have formed a coalition for reform of communications rules in these services centers. Often they have been allied with the computer industry and with large manufacturing firms that are major users of information systems.

2. Usually the United States assumes that all good things come together. In its bilateral negotiations it has bet that freer trade in equipment helps the sale of value-added services, and vice versa. It also has assumed that it has a competitive advantage in VANs that will help define the information system in a way that will make the virtues of U. S. equipment more salient. No one knows that these assumptions are valid. Perhaps, as in other technology markets, the cost and reliability of equipment is more vital than customized, state-of-the-art communications technology. Or, perhaps the Japanese will be formidable competitors in value-added services in the United States. Thus, in the future the United States may have to make tradeoffs among the items that it so freely packages together today. This could shift the terms of the telecommunications debate.

3. The forces favoring reform are formidable. The technological marriage of broadcast, computers, and communications will endure. Its precise terms may vary, but the merger makes it unlikely that even an enlightened monopoly could make optimal choices about society's use of the communications system. Moreover, the political infrastructure (including interest groups that cut across national boundaries) already exists to mobilize these interests for reform.

4. U.S.-style deregulation of telecommunications is viable but the absence of policies to complement deregulation may be a prob-

lem. Japan, for example, is using a variety of funding and regulatory decisions to force creative experimentation that goes beyond what the marketplace might yield. This may induce better coordination among interests that often are locked into a strictly adversarial relationship in the United States. Both the pattern of industrial organization in Japan and government oversight have been at work. In short, increased competition does not rule out continued innovation in communications, and government has a role to play.

5. The U.S. initiatives have posed some important questions about the relationships between bilateral and multilateral diplomacy. European states are right in asking if a cohesive international order can emerge from so much bilateralism. But many of the questions posed by telecommunications negotiations require fundamental innovations in what we mean by trade, investment, and regulation. Indeed, we argue in *When Countries Talk*[17] that these negotiations are indirectly introducing guaranteed rights to foreign investment, new degrees of oversight of domestic regulation by foreign trade rules, and guarantees of the rights of users (as opposed to producers). These constitute a new intellectual and political agenda for world trade negotiations. They require a great deal of experimentation, and bilateral initiatives are in some sense "controlled experiments" to figure out what can and should be done in the multilateral negotiations.

The real trick is to find a way to guarantee that the United States does not play off bilateral and multilateral negotiations against each other in an effort to reap an unending string of new concessions. This can only happen if the United States begins to articulate an overall vision of the future world communication system that can help orient negotiators. In the heyday of the IMF fixed exchange rates there were many serious disputes on how to run the system. But everyone understood the broad U.S. vision of what role the IMF should play. No one has such confidence today about communications, and therein lies much of the political problem.

NOTES

1. Ann Hutcheson Reid, "Trade in Telecommunications Services: The Current Institutional Framework and the Potential for Change," paper pre-

pared for the Committee for Information, Computer, and Communication Policy, Organization for Economic Cooperation and Development, ICCP (85)12 (Paris: OECD, September 9, 1985), pp. 16–25.

2. For example, France has decided to partially privatize the French broadcast system, to allow additional private firms to enter the market, and to introduce more competition in data services. In 1987 Canada privatized Teleglobe Canada, its international service provider, and is likely eventually to license a second domestic long-distance company. And countries as diverse as the Netherlands, Spain, Italy, Chile, Turkey, Australia, and Sri Lanka are exploring increased competition in at least some aspects of the telecommunications business. Even the German Bundespost, in the wake of the Witte Commission Report, is experiencing some liberalization.

3. The United Kingdom has granted Mercury, a subsidiary of Cable and Wireless, permission to compete with British Telecom at home and abroad. After 1989 other firms may also be allowed to compete. Similarly, the Japanese government has authorized several groups to compete in the domestic long-distance market with Nippon Telegraph and Telephone (NTT) and two to compete with Kokusai Denshin Denwa (KDD) in the provision of international telecommunications services.

4. The politics of telecommunications is significantly influenced by the fact that roughly 5–10 percent of all users generate half of the long-distance traffic in industrial countries and use of international long-distance services is even more concentrated.

5. In 1986 U.S. exports were about $1.1 billion while imports were nearly $3.1 billion. Testimony of Deputy U.S. Trade Representative Alan Woods before the subcommittee on Communications of the Senate Committee on Commerce, Science, and Transportation, February 28, 1987 (Washington, D.C.: Government Printing Office, 1987), p. 5.

6. Four sectors were initially chosen—telecommunications, electronics, pharmaceutical/medical equipment, and forestry products.

7. In addition a MOSS Telecommunications Oversight Committee with both U.S. and Japanese representatives has met eight times since September 1986. The Committee identifies problems, monitors implementation, and develops further information that can help in updating MPT's administrative, regulatory and policy changes. Testimony of Deputy U.S. Trade Representative Alan Woods before the subcommittee on Communications of the Senate Committee on Commerce, Science, and Transportation, February 28, 1987 (Washington, D.C.: Government Printing Office, 1987), p. 5.

8. Entities wishing to operate an international VAN business in Japan are required to 1) register themselves as international Special Type II telecommunications carriers; 2) conclude agreements with foreign partners concerning the provision of international VAN services, which must be approved by the government; 3) submit notifications of their service tariffs to the government; 4) acquire nontariff-based circuits from international

Type I telecommunications carriers, who have obtained approval of the contract on the provision of circuits from the government. "New Regulatory Framework in Japan Concerning the Provision of International Value-added Services," delayed contribution by Japan to the ITU's CCITT Working Party III/5, Question 21/III, D-146, Ottawa, October 21–23, 1987. This issue was only resolved in late 1988 after a year of further negotiations.

9. Testimony of George Fisher, Senior Executive Vice President, Motorola, before the subcommittee on Communications of the Senate Committee on Commerce, Science, and Transportation, "International Telecommunications," hearings, February 28, 1987, pp. 94–101.

10. The State Department also designated 14 key posts abroad for telecommunications: London; Paris; Bonn; Rome; Ottawa; U.S. Mission to the EC, Brussels; U.S. Mission to the OECD, Paris; U.S. Mission to the U.N., Geneva; Tokyo; Beijing; New Delhi; Nairobi; Mexico City; and Brasilia. Each post now has a "telecommunications attaché." Testimony of Diana Lady Dougan, Coordinator and Director, Bureau of International Communications and Information Policy, U.S. Department of State, "International Telecommunications," Hearings, February 28, 1987, pp. 31–32.

11. "Market Access Fact-Finding Technical Bilateral Talks," background U.S. government paper, Department of Commerce, October 19, 1987.

12. "U.S. Telecommunications Team Report on November, 1986. Visit to China: First Implementation Phase of U.S.-China Protocol on Cooperation in the Field of Telecommunications," National Telecommunications and Information Administration, U.S. Department of Commerce, March 1987.

13. Geza Feketekuty, *International Trade in Services: An Overview and Blueprint for Trade Negotiations* (Cambridge, Mass.: Ballinger, 1988).

14. Ironically, it is usually the United States that wants to include basic services on the agenda and the PTTs that resist.

15. Communication Workers of America, *Information Industry Report* 1, no. 1 (July 1987): 8.

16. USTR announced that it would press for acceptance of basic principles about the right of entry rather than fight on behalf of a specific carrier. USTR had to be sensitive to the concerns of AT&T, which has invested in the expectation that the U.S. government was not going to take sides among U.S. carriers.

17. Jonathon D. Aronson and Peter F. Cowhey, *When Countries Talk: International Trade in Telecommunications Services* (Cambridge, Mass.: Ballinger, 1988).

IV FUNDAMENTAL CONCEPTS OF A SERVICE ECONOMY

INTRODUCTION, BY JOHN B. RICHARDSON

The growth in academic literature on the service economy since 1983 has been little short of phenomenal, indeed its production may well be one of the most rapidly expanding sectors of services. Increased knowledge of how the service economy operates, increased insights into its specific characteristics, and partial theories to explain its operation have all emerged. But the result is somewhat anarchic, and inconsistencies are manyfold because those working in the area are often starting from differing assumptions. Their work may be based on an intellectual mindset derived from the analysis of a manufacturing economy or on a variety of implicit, even unconscious hypotheses about the nature of services, which may be incompatible with each other. There is a clear need for a new paradigm, for a coherent intellectual foundation for further analysis.

In this situation, the first essential is to understand the fundamental differences between a predominantly manufacturing economy and one in which service activities are dominant. The two chapters in this part are designed to throw light on one essential feature of the services economy, the element of pure risk and uncertainty. Orio Giarini probes the underlying structural differences that characterize the service economy, and he identifies its stochastic nature, in which uncertainty is an inevitable and accepted component, and the management of pure risk an essential element.

Gerard Dickinson provides the pragmatic pendant to Giarini's more theoretical approach. He demonstrates how the phenomena

223

described in general terms by Giarini can indeed be observed in practice in the rapid changes currently making the financial services sector so exciting.

In looking for links between the analysis of these chapters and other work on services, the concepts of complexity and interdependence need to be kept carefully in mind. Over and over again in the literature, the thesis is repeated that many growing service functions are associated with the management of complexity. All stages in the process that allows a product to satisfy consumer needs—research, design, production, distribution, marketing—have increased in complexity and generated a need for more sophisticated service functions to manage them. This increasing sophistication has led to increased specialization and increased specialization in an economy leads, as it has always done, to increased interdependence between its components.

One aspect of this interdependence is an increased vulnerability of the overall system to a malfunction of one of its parts. The associated pure risk is thus an inevitable by-product of interdependence and it generates a systemic need for risk-reduction services and for insurance inside an economy.

Another aspect of interdependence is, of course, that created by interlinkages between countries. As this international interdependence grows, so too does the vulnerability of the system to disturbances caused by malfunctions in the international monetary system. The same needs for risk-reduction services (in this case intergovernmental or intercentral bank cooperation) and for insurance of the associated risks (as described in detail by Dickinson) are apparent.

Paradoxically, as the risks involved in this process grow, so does the need to lay them off through reinsurance, which itself increases the degree of interdependence of the world economy.

It is Giarini's thesis that we will succeed in understanding these phenomena and in building theoretical models to explain them only if we are prepared to abandon the idea that theories of static equilibrium are the solution and start constructing models that accept that nonequilibrium is the norm. With some justification he regards this as the equivalent of the scientific revolution that separates Heisenberg from Newton.

A new paradigm for understanding the services economy is unlikely to emerge to create order out of anarchy until theses like this have been thoroughly tested and either accepted or rejected by a broad consensus of workers in the field of services.

13 THE SERVICE ECONOMY AND THE MANAGEMENT OF RISK

Orio Giarini

The evolution of the insurance industry in the last two decades is a typical example of the relevance of the service economy concept. Until the 1970s, everybody, including people in the insurance industry, accepted that insurance policies covering life risks or material damages were a typical secondary product in the traditional economic sense and that they could only expand once the basic needs were satisfied by material production. However, during the fifteen years following 1973, when the growth of GNP in the world dropped from an average of 6 percent to less than 3 percent per year, the overall sales of policies continued to grow at a rate of 5 percent per year. If insurance consumption were of secondary importance, the slowdown in other activities and in particular in manufacturing would have produced more than a proportional reduction in the sales of insurance, according to Engels' law.

In fact, Engels' law reproduces the traditional industrial economics paradigm according to which services are a secondary type of economic good and can only be consumed after the basic needs are satisfied through the so-called essential economic activities (agricultural products and industrial manufactured goods). Even if we allow this law to be still valid in some specific cases, when some types of consumption (including industrial products) only arise after a certain level of wealth, it completely misrepresents the function of services, which are essential today to make even the most basic goods avail-

225

able. We would stress the fact that today many situations of poverty and even hunger in the world are due more to the bad functioning of services than to the mere existence of agriculture produce and manufactured goods per se.

The explanation for the continuous growth of insurance activities, even in periods of declining overall growth, lies precisely the nature of the modern production system, which depends on services as key tools to guarantee its proper functioning. At a very advanced technological level of production, where risks and vulnerabilities are highly concentrated and represent an essential managerial challenge, insurance has become a fundamental precondition for investment. Similarly, at a more general level, social security, health, and life insurance have by now achieved the status of a primary need in most industrialized countries.

THE SERVICE ECONOMY AS A SYSTEM AND THE MANAGEMENT OF VULNERABILITY

The very process of development of technology in the modern economy has led to a more and more complex system, where logistics, organization, and information have become fundamental issues. Considering the economy as a service economy also allows better appreciation of the contributions made by contemporary technology: the latest technological advances have their greatest impact on systems concerned with the communication and organization of information, which is exactly what is needed in order to better manage the development of present-day economies. All this is quite different from the direction that technology had taken during the classic Industrial Revolution, when all that appeared to matter was how to investigate and improve the stages of production that transformed raw materials into finished goods.

The notion of system has become essential in the service economy. Systems produce positive results or economic value when they function properly. The notion of systems operation (or functioning) requires the consideration of real time and the dynamics of real life. And whenever real time is taken into consideration, the degree of uncertainty and of probability that conditions any human action becomes a central issue.

Any system working in order to obtain some future results is by definition in a situation of uncertainty, even if different situations are characterized by different degrees of risk, uncertainty, or even indetermination.[1] But risk and uncertainty are not a matter of choice: they are simply part of the human condition and activity. Rationality is therefore not so much a problem of avoiding risk than bringing uncertainty to manageable levels in given situations.

Furthermore, the very systemic nature of the modern economy and the increasing degree of complexity of technological developments require a deeper and deeper economic understanding and control of the increasing vulnerability of these systems. Unfortunately, the notion of vulnerability is generally misunderstood. To say that vulnerability increases parallel to the increase of the quality and performance of modern technology might seem paradoxical. In fact, the higher level of performance of most technological advances relies upon a reduction of the margins of error that a system can tolerate without breakdown. Accidents and management mistakes still happen, even if less frequently, but their effects have now more costly systemic consequences. Opening the door of a car in motion does not necessarily lead to a catastrophe. In the case of a modern airplane, it will. This shows that systems functioning and vulnerability control become a key economic function where the contributions of economists and engineers must be integrated. In a similar way, problems of social security and savings for the individuals have to take into account vulnerability management at a personal level.

The notion of vulnerability is also relevant with regard to the notion of productivity. In fact, the notion and measurement of productivity is an important issue for the service economy. It is clear that if the economic value depends on the proper functioning of a system, the notion of productivity cannot simply be linked to the quantity of inputs compared to the quantity of measurable outputs, but rather to the *quality of performance.* Hence, vulnerability is a factor conditioning real productivity in the industrial economy, a quality where specific indicators of results have to be integrated with price indicators.

In any case, it is clear that the question of measuring quality in economic terms is becoming a major issue in itself, which is an obvious additional indication of the emergence of the service economy.[2]

THE NOTION OF RISK IN THE
INDUSTRIAL REVOLUTION AND
IN THE SERVICE ECONOMY

The risk-taking attitude was not studied as a basic theoretical issue by the first great economists. Rather, it was discussed as a general cultural reference, concerning much more sociology than economics. The general theory of economics did rather privilege the notion of general equilibrium, excluding uncertainty and risk by definition. Schumpeter made some more explicit references to the risk-taking entrepreneur and through his theory of cycles hinted at some sort of economic disequilibria. Only in 1921 did Frank Knight write a first comprehensive book on the subject.[3] But also in this case, the risks that he discussed were limited to the "entrepreneurial" (subjective) type. The field of the "pure" (objective) risks, due to the vulnerability of systems was still considered too secondary to be treated as a priority, among the managerial objectives of the firm. The difference between entrepreneurial and pure risks is discussed in more detail below.

More recently, economists such as Kenneth Arrow[4] have begun to take a closer look at the reality of the uncertainties that may undermine any economic policy or managerial decision. Just as Ricardo and Smith drew practical examples of their theories from agriculture and small-scale manufacturing, today's economists refer to the management of risk and uncertainty by insurance institutions and in the social welfare or health sectors as a natural reference point.

The increasing economic impact of vulnerability is leading to a widespread reconsideration of some basic concepts in economic activity, where the fundamental point is the need for a better understanding of the conditions for modern economic risks and uncertainties to be managed. The worldwide development of risk management is a sign of this process.[5] Basically, it represents a reaction to the new nature and dimension of the risks that condition our economic and social environment.

Obviously the more traditional risks considered in economics (that is, the entrepreneurial risks) have also been subject to considerable change, particularly with reference to the occurrence of sudden fluctuations of greater and greater amplitude. This phenomenon is visible in the financial field, where it is defined as volatility. It is the consequence of concentration and of ever larger markets, where smaller and smaller variations tend to have proportionally greater destabilizing effects. Hence a general increase in uncertainty.

But the overall increase of uncertainty in the economy and of the need to manage risk in a more professional way, as a basic element of the economic strategy, is linked to the present relevance of pure risks. This, again, is the consequence of the need to manage the functioning of systems, typical of the service economy. In fact, the development of vulnerability and of pure risks is a key characteristics of the service economy.

Modern technology is at the source of the growing management problems in dealing with pure risks in many ways:[6]

1. Increases in the economies of scale have mainly been due to progress in technology. The gains in productivity throughout the period of the Industrial Revolution were enormous, but the increased concentration of production also increased the vulnerability of production systems to small disturbances.

This is an area where risks and vulnerability are increasingly of the pure type: they need a statistical universe of occurrences in order to assess probabilities in a given time and space dimension. Lower frequency and higher size of risks make them more and more difficult to manage; uncertainty increases.

2. Specialization has been a key factor for industrial progress, but an excess of specialization has today resulted in systems that are increasingly interdependent and vulnerable, leading to a high growth of consequential losses (losses deriving from the nonfunctioning or malfunctioning of a system). Furthermore, specialization can reduce the adaptability to changing market conditions of a machine or installation and can impose more severe maintenance and repair requirements that may be difficult to implement under some operating conditions. Gains from specialization may be partially offset or even outweighed by the lack of flexibility that results.

3. Operating reliability has made great progress due to advances in technology. However, minor variations and small accidents in one component can lead to disasters in a complex system, even if these accidents occur less frequently due to the higher operating reliability.

4. The quality of many products has been greatly improved by modern technology. However, this same improved quality for a spe-

cific task may increase the problem of its recycling when a product is thrown away. The human and economic environment, as Alfred Marshall puts it, is more like a biological process than a mechanical one. An improvement in one sense may introduce a disequilibrium in another: this is the lesson brought home by the problems of pollution and hazardous waste management control.

These examples have in common a shift of emphasis from the traditional entrepreneurial risks to pure risks, a large part of which become insurance markets. We can thus expect to find a reflection of these developments in the practice of insurance business, which in fact is passing through a period of quantitative and qualitative change and development unequaled in its long history.

Risk has become more and more concentrated at levels where the vulnerability is such that the overall uncertainty of the economic process increases. How many boards of trustees today dream of the decision possibilities experienced 20 years ago? Consumers are also reluctant to become consumers of risk. The unique situation in the field of product liability and malpractice in the United States, although amplified by a specific legal environment, starts to have its effects on other parts of the world. This is a typical trend of demand in the service economy: the consumer is more conscious that tools and products designed for given purposes and even experts are only of value when the result of their "utilization" is positive. The fact that their utilization might give negative results is refuted and gives rise to requests for compensation.[7] Product liability is a great issue in the United States, where litigation has led in some cases to extremely high and even excessive compensations. Chemical and pharmaceutical companies have a special problem in this area.[8]

Doctors, lawyers, and other experts are sued in court for malpractice and have to compensate their clients if found guilty.[9] In Europe a recent EC directive[10] is the result of 10 years of discussions and preparations to manage the expanding phenomenon of the increasing perception by the public that producers of economic wealth have to be liable for delivering a product yielding negative results. Once again, in the contemporary economy, it is "product performance" that has economic value, that counts, rather than simply the existence of a product or service.

The problem of environmental hazards, which very often is linked with the question of transportation and storage of dangerous materials, is part of the same type of risks and vulnerabilities that our modern society has to face.[11]

COMBINED STRATEGIES TO MANAGE BOTH PURE AND ENTREPRENEURIAL RISKS

The connotations of the notion of risk in the service economy cover a much larger ground than the notion of risk current in the Industrial Revolution. In the latter case, the key risk normally referred to is entrepreneurial or commercial risk; in the service economy, it is extended to pure risk.

Entrepreneurial risk is one where the people involved in an action can influence its goals and the way the action develops by deciding to produce, to sell, to finance, and so on.

Pure risk is out of reach of those involved in an action. It depends on the vulnerabilities of their environment or of the system in which they are working, and it will materialize by accident and by hazard. This notion of pure risk is strictly linked to the notion of the vulnerability of systems which we have developed in the preceding paragraphs and is typical of the service economy.

One of the great differences between neoclassical economics and the new service economy is not only that entrepreneurial risk is taken into account (as in the case of Frank Knight), but that the notion of the economically relevant risk is extended to include the notion of pure risk. The notion of risk, globally, has therefore two fundamentally different but complementary connotations.

For any important economic endeavor, the consideration of both notions of risk is today on an *equal* strategic level (again linked to the notion of systems and of vulnerability). An appropriate risk management action needs to identify each category of risks in its own right, evaluate how they interreact, and design an appropriate global risk management strategy.

The demarcation line between pure and entrepreneurial risks is the notion of moral hazard.[12] This notion has long been understood by insurers when they have to face damages produced by those suffering them with the purpose of making money out of them. An example is the case of somebody burning his own home to collect the insurance; such cases account for more than 20 percent of fires.[13] Economists look at this notion from another point of view as a spin-off of their studies on economic incentives: moral hazard is equivalent to studying the negative result of incentives. One important case concerns the level of social insurance for unemployed people who might stop looking for another job if the level of compensation is too high.[14] Many economists who have dealt with public policy are entering into the field of moral hazard (the negative effects of incentives) and can profit from the experience of insurers in this field.[15]

RISK AS A POSITIVE FACTOR AND THE CHALLENGES OF UNCERTAINTY: AN ATTITUDE AND A PHILOSOPHY FOR STIMULATING PROGRESS[16]

A main, probably the most relevant, feature of these changes in the socioeconomic environment toward a service economy is their relation *to advanced scientific thinking* and of discoveries in this century. More generally, this has to do with the relationship between social and natural (soft and hard) sciences that embodies the cultural background of our knowledge, views, attitudes, and behavior with regard to our individual and community life.

When economics became a specific and recognized social science (in a process started by the definition of value by Adam Smith in 1776), its key inspiration and reference were the cultural and scientific assumptions of the day. Economics proved a useful tool for analyzing, understanding, and systematizing the ongoing process of the Industrial Revolution.

Let us recall just a few of these basic assumptions. Newton had provided the notion of equilibrium as a basic reference for understanding the universe. This static equilibrium survived until Einstein started the modern Scientific Revolution by adding time as the fourth dimension of space.

Heisenberg and the quantum theory introduced the notion of indeterminate systems, thus overcoming the objections of Einstein, who was still striving for a universal model of scientific knowledge that would eliminate uncertainty. And in 1983 Ilya Prigogine wrote:

We are more and more numerous who think that the fundamental laws of nature are irreversible *and* stochastic: that deterministic and reversible laws are applicable only in limiting situations.

He further wrote that:

> Over the last decade we have learned that in nonequilibrium conditions, conditions, simple material can acquire complex behavior . . . today, our interest is shifting to nonequilibrium systems, interacting with the surroundings through the entropy flow.[17]

There can no longer be any scientific justification for considering a state of equilibrium in economics (as referred to the Newtonian model) as the premise of economic analysis. In some cases equilibrium might be desirable, but economic progress could well depend much more on specific and *desirable states of nonequilibrium* in cases where the isolated industrial system opens up to a multiplicity of new functions and interactions typical of the service economy. The key economic question of the future might well become not "How shall we achieve a perfect (certain) equilibrium?", but rather "How shall we create or stimulate productive nonequilibrium situations?", situations which, contrary to Newtonian philosophy, have a real-time dimension. However, the model still subsumed by the mainstream of current economic thinking has as its fundamental paradigm the hypotheses of perfect equilibrium and of certainty that belong to the static Newtonian scientific model.

Unfortunately, this means that the current economic model often refers to scientific premises that science itself has long ago abandoned.

Intuition suggests the idea that modern societal and economic development depend not so much on achieving perfect, determinstic, and sure objectives, but rather on developing creative activities, in a world where uncertainty, probability, and risk are *given* conditions, providing a circumstance of real opportunities and choice.

This would not be a step backward toward irrationality. Quite the contrary, more intelligence, more rationality, more initiative are required to cope with situations of uncertainty, which after all are the daily experience of every living being. The simplistic vision of mechanized preprogrammed robots belongs much more to a deterministic world. The attempt to achieve abstract "certainty" and "perfect" information can only lead to a dogmatic, pseudoreligious system on the one hand or, on the other, to the annihilation of all intelligence, to the destruction of all hope for development and creativity. The marriage of contemporary scientific thinking with social sciences, and in particular with economics, in an increasingly complex world that is interactive even beyond the limits of planet earth, is providing a rich source of moral and intellectual stimulus for reconstructing an image of the future. Learning to face uncertainties and to manage risks under these new horizons might in turn lead to a quantum leap in the human condition.

Even in terms of equity or of social justice, the problem is not to produce or sell or distribute *security*, which is in any case a self-deceiving system in political terms (look at the dictatorships of our century) as well as economic terms (excessive state or community protection has limited the capacity of social institutions to provide security and has rendered them increasingly vulnerable, inefficient, and ultimately the agents of greater global insecurity). Equity has more and more to do with increasing the physical and cultural capacity of individuals and communities to face uncertainty: the very risks that confront all living species render them creative. *Absolute poverty* is a situation in which no risk can be faced, no choice taken.

And finally in cultural terms: no enterprise is built by dreams alone and none without. Action, successful action, is by necessity guided by practical circumstances. But the goal of any action is defined, implicitly or explicitly, by the deep nature of the human being, his dreams, his vision of life, his culture. The dynamics of life, the challenge of risk and uncertainty, require from us today a new creative effort leading to the reconstruction and the reconquest of the notion of progress, which the philosophies and the ideologies of certainty have shuttered so much and almost destroyed. There is no real human culture other than that to be found in the real-life process of creation, in, that is, the producing and continuous testing in each of our many endeavors of an image of the future we would fashion for ourselves.

NOTES

1. The definitions adopted in this chapter are the following: Risk represents a probable occurrence or event of subjective nature (following a decision to act or not to act) or of objective nature (independent of one's decision) influencing a given system at different levels of magnitude. Uncertainty measures the degree of confidence one can have in a given probability. Indetermination refers to systems or situations that lack any possibility of being defined.

2. See, for instance, the chapter "Quality, Productivity, and Strategy" in Richard Normann, *Service Management* (New York: John Wiley and Sons, 1984); see also the chapter "Services and Productivity" in Dorothy Riddle, *Service-Led Growth* (New York: Praeger Special Studies, 1986); the chapter "Measurement of Output and Productivity in the Service Sector," by John Kendrick, in Robert Inman, ed., *Managing the Service Economy* (Cambridge, England: Cambridge University Press, 1985).

3. Frank Knight, *Risk, Uncertainty and Profit* (Chicago: University of Chicago Press, 1971 [originally 1921]).

4. See Kenneth Arrow, "Risk Allocation and Information," The Geneva Papers on Risk and Insurance no. 8, June 1978, pp. 5-19, and its bibliography.

5. See Norman Baglini, "Risk Management in International Corporation," Risk Studies Foundation, New York, 1976; see also the special issues on Risk Management of The Geneva Papers on Risk and Insurance no. 2, August 1976; no. 22, January 1982; no. 23, April 1982; no. 35, April 1985; no. 37, October 1985; no. 45, October 1987.

6. Orio Giarini, "Développement économique et croissance des risques," The Geneva Papers on Risk and Insurance no. 22, January 1982.

7. See S. Shavell, "Accidents, Liability, and Insurance," Harvard Institute of Economic Research, 1979, Discussion Paper no. 685; "Liability, Insurance, and Safety Regulation," The Geneva Papers on Risk and Insurance no. 43, April 1987 (special issue).

8. See the book by Arthur Hailey, *Strong Medicine* (London: Pan Books, 1985).

9. See R. Jackson and J. Powell, *Professional Negligence* (London: Sweet and Maxwell, 1982).

10. The European Community, Directive on Product Liability, 1985.

11. See H. Kunreuther, ed., *Transportation, Storage, and Disposal of Hazardous Materials*, papers from a conference at IIASA, Laxenberg (Vienna) (Philadelphia: Wharton School, University of Pennsylvania, 1986).

12. Among many other references, the subject has been presented in an annual lecture of the Geneva Association, in a paper by Joseph Stiglitz titled "The Pure Theory of Moral Hazard" (The Geneva Papers no. 26, January 1983).

13. See Andrew Tobias, *The Invisible Bankers* (New York: Pocket Books, 1982).

14. There is a delicate economic and social tradeoff. A high level of compensation for unemployment might be socially desirable, but it is also desirable not to use working taxpayers' money beyond a certain level that might *favor* unemployment by eliminating the need to find a job.

15. See Stiglitz, "The Pure Theory of Moral Hazard."

16. This section is taken from a new report on "The Limits to Certainty—Facing Risks in the New Service Economy," working paper for the Risk Institute Project, Geneva, 1988.

17. Quotations from papers circulated at the Seminar on Complexity organized in Montpellier by the United Nations University and the IDATE, May 1984.

14 CORPORATE RISK MANAGEMENT IN THE AGE OF GLOBAL NETWORKS

Gerard M. Dickinson

Rapidly changing environments over the last decade have increased the financial and insurable risks faced by industrial and commercial enterprises. Not only have volatile financial and commodity markets been in evidence, but the incidence of insurable losses has grown due to more complex production and distribution systems, greater employee and public dishonesty, and a higher likelihood of being sued for negligence.

But the riskiness has not been confined to a higher probability of loss, the scale of potential loss has also risen sharply. As corporations grow, organically or through acquisition, risk exposures increase. When this is accompanied by a greater internationalization of operations, additional risks are produced. The restructuring of operations to improve competitiveness has often entailed more investment in new technologies, and many of the new technologies have their own economies of scale, particularly in research and development.

It has been the interplay of increases in the causes and likelihood of loss and the greater scale of potential loss that has caused the total risk facing industrial and commercial enterprises to grow. Indeed, risk management services are developing in scope, diversity, and sophistication within corporations, as well as in the form of specialized external services and through general purpose financial instrument markets. Providing the information, skills and software required by the risk management function is one of the engines for growth in a service-intensive economy.

CHANGING ORGANIZATIONAL
EMPHASIS ON RISK

Since the late 1970s, both nonfinancial corporations and financial institutions have placed a greater emphasis on risk management than in earlier times. Decisions in risk management have often been reactive; top management has recognized the need to put greater corporate resources into the risk management function, not infrequently because a large loss had already occurred within the organization. This greater corporate emphasis has been reflected at two levels in many organizations. First, risk analysis has been incorporated more specifically into the strategic planning process, which itself had been gaining in importance due to more complex and competitive environments. Second, as the number of risks that can be transferred through insurance or hedged through new types of financial instrument has increased, corporate treasury departments have begun to look at a much wider range of risks and to do so in a more structured way than hitherto. Risk management is now no longer restricted to insurable causes of loss, but to the whole range of financial and insurable risks.

It has become increasingly recognized that there should be coordination between all risks that can be transferred or hedged outside the group, as well as those that cannot. This has resulted in a change in the policy emphasis within many firms. Risk management decisions are now taken at a higher management level than previously. Moreover it became increasingly evident that in order to be effective, risk management systems have to be more centralized in a number of areas. Assessment of risk exposure can only be done accurately for the group as a whole, and the same applies to decisions about levels of internal risk retention. Moreover, the purchasing of external insurance and financial instruments for hedging purposes is better coordinated and more economic if carried out centrally. Tax considerations have also played a key role in the funding of risk management programs that has reinforced this centralization tendency.

Furthermore, it became clear that there were benefits to be gained if the insurance purchasing of the group was carried out through a wholly owned subsidiary—that is, a "captive" insurance company servicing the insurance risk management needs of the corporation. Similarly, some of the larger groups felt that some of the corporate treasury functions, including the purchase of financial instruments for hedging purposes, could be best carried out by a captive finance company or investment bank. Offshore tax havens often served as locations for such captive or in-house financial institutions, providing not only fiscal benefits but also being less subject to regulatory control.[1]

The greater emphasis on risk management in nonfinancial corporations has had a major impact on the financial institutions that supply them with risk-transfer facilities. The centralized purchasing of insurance and hedging programs has strained the capacity of the supplying institutions. Moreover, organizational changes within the financial institutions themselves have been necessary in order to accommodate the new modes of purchase through captive insurance companies and captive banks.

As enterprises in their own right, financial institutions have also placed a much greater emphasis on the risk management function than previously. Because financial asset or liability management is central to their overall management, they have been much affected by volatile financial markets. Moreover, because they are subject to government regulation in view of their fiduciary role in the financial system, they have had to define their risk management function more broadly than nonfinancial corporations. They not only have to manage risks inherent in their asset/liability positions, but also to concern themselves with risks that could breach regulatory thresholds.[2] Financial instutitions have to contend with the fact that they could be deemed to be technically insolvent by regulatory authorities while they do not believe this is commercially the case.

INCREASED RISKS FACED BY FINANCIAL INSTITUTIONS

Let us now turn to the main risk-absorbing financial institutions and to the different risks with which they are faced. We will examine three groups of financial institutions: commercial banks, property and liability insurance companies, and life insurance and pension funds.

Commercial Banks

Traditionally, the major risk facing a commercial bank has been the potential rapid withdrawal of its deposits, a run on the bank. Because of the growth of interbank markets and of domestic and international money markets, this maturity-transformation risk has now been reduced significantly. Networks among banks have been set up that have allowed funds to be raised fast enough to cope with such risks.

On the other hand, default risks on loans have considerably increased in the last decade, not only due to the sovereign debt problem. Corporate customers have found it cheaper to raise their short to medium-term debt directly on the growing eurocurrency markets and domestic money markets.[3] This gradual drift of the larger and more creditworthy corporate borrowers away from the banks' lending portfolios has indirectly increased the credit risk in the remaining loan portfolios. In turn, attempts to replace this loss of business have meant that the banks have been forced to search for alternative borrowers, which has tended to mean higher potential default rates.

Interest rate risks have also been growing, not only because of inherent interest rates volatility but because of the structural changes in the borrowing and lending patterns of banks. As commercial banks themselves have been tapping the wholesale deposit markets on the one hand and having to tailor loans to suit client needs on the other, they have had to take interest rate risks in order to accommodate the preferences of borrowers and lenders. Expectations of borrowers and lenders regarding interest rates differ, and so do time horizons and risk preferences; hence banks have been required to assume a mismatch in the mix of floating- and fixed-rate borrowing and lending. In the past few years, interest rate risks that arise from this mismatch have been exacerbated by competitive pressures on the banks to lengthen the maturity structure of their assets.

Currency risk exposures have also increased, especially for international banks. Competitive pressures have not always permitted them to match currencies in their international borrowing and lending, a problem exacerbated by maturity mismatching. Increased international expansion of operations have added to these currency risks. Commercial banks being providers of currency risk hedges for nonfinancial corporations, and indeed for nonbanking financial institutions, have been required to set up more extensive risk transfer mechanisms to accommodate the growing risk exposures being placed upon them.

Property and Liability Insurance Companies

The growth of multinational firms through mergers and acquisitions and the centralization of the insurance-buying function have increased the size of risk exposure for insurance suppliers. Techno-economic changes in infrastructure projects, means of transportation, methods of energy production, telecommunications systems have compounded this issue of vulnerability inherent in size. One area of insurance that has grown dramatically since the early 1980s has been liability insurance—that is, insurances for negligence claims brought by customers and others against corporations and professional partnerships. The frequency of these claims has increased on account of changing social and cultural attitudes, while the scale of claim payments has escalated due to generous court settlements and changes in legislation.

More generally, as developed in Chapter 13, the growth of the service sector, including the financial institutions themselves, has given rise to further risks. New technologies have generated new insurable risks, as in the case of risks of breakdown in computer and communications systems and computer fraud, which have greatly increased demands on insurers.

Property and liability insurers do not directly face risks on their asset holdings as part of their intermediation role. For the most part they invest their funds in a range of relatively liquid securities, which can be sold at short notice in order to be able to pay a large claim. However, insurers do expose themselves to capital market fluctuations when investing in equities or in longer term bonds; but insurers take these potentially profitable risks voluntarily, often to strengthen their capital base and hence increase their ability to underwrite higher levels of insurable risk in the longer term with less need to raise external equity capital.

Life Insurance Companies and Pension Funds

Life insurance companies and pension funds are major financial institutions through which retirement and other long-term saving takes place. They provide individuals directly (and with respect to their pension funds, corporations indirectly) with investment risk diversification benefits over a long time horizon. Most of the assets of life insurance companies and pension funds are held in the form of long-term bonds, equities, and property investments. Hence, the major risks that these financial institutions face are capital market risks.

Short-term fluctuation in investment values on capital markets do not pose serious operational risks for these institutions; in fact they have no intrinsic need to sell assets until their liabilities mature, which is well into the future. Some pension funds under short-term management contracts may be concerned with short-term fluctuations in capital market values—since their performance may fall below a specified standard—but this is a commercial risk facing the fund manager and not a risk intrinsic to the pension fund itself.

The main investment risks of these institutional investors are long term. Life insurance companies have built into their insurance and annuity contracts interest rate guarantees that necessitate that they earn a minimum rate of return on their assets in the long term, or otherwise become insolvent. Pension funds also face similar constraints but to a lesser degree, since their liabilities remain the ultimate financial responsibility of the organization whose employees are beneficiaries under the pension fund's scheme.

A major point must be stressed here. Both life insurers and pension funds are ultimately concerned that the savings they invest should maintain their purchasing power in the long term. This has meant an increasing proportion of funds being invested not only in domestic equities but also in international equities. In part the internationalization of pension fund investment reflects the uncertainty concerning which national economies will be buoyant in the very long term. The massive flows of long-term capital by U.S., Japanese, and European pension funds outside their national capital markets reflect this search for wider diversification. Indeed the process of globalization of bond and equity markets reflects to a significant degree a response to the needs of these major investing institutions.

THE INNOVATORS AMONG FINANCIAL INSTITUTIONS

Investment banks, especially those based in New York, have been major innovators during the last decade. They have provided an interface between their nonfinancial corporate clients and other financial institutions, as well as between financial institutions themselves. They have been an important conduit for nonfinancial corporations wishing to directly access capital and financial markets. Indeed they have largely contributed to the creation of certain financial markets, such as swap and options markets. Many of the financial instruments developed to cope with increasing volatility in financial markets have been the product of research and development carried out within these organizations. Investment banks, including the subsidiaries of international banks, have seen their own risks increase from their own trading activities,[4] in addition to their traditional underwriting of new capital issues and the placing of securities.

Major insurance broking firms, which are mainly located in the United States and the United Kingdom have played a similar innovative and intermediary role in insurance markets. They also maintain close links with corporate buyers of insurance and have been instrumental in establishing, and indeed managing some of the captive insurance companies set up by large multinational firms. These brokers have, moreover, played a major role in developing the global reinsurance networks through which large risks can be spread.

MECHANISMS FOR TRANSFERRING THE RISKS OF FINANCIAL INSTITUTIONS

In the last few years, financial institutions have sought to handle risks in a number of new ways:

Cooperative Arrangements with Other Financial Institutions in the Same Sector

There is indeed scope for cooperation among competing financial institutions, particularly with regard to risk, given that risk-spreading is far from being a zero-sum game. The evolution of the interbank market, at first within national markets and then internationally, is an example of how banks have set up a system to reduce deposit withdrawal risks. Loan syndication and the networks set up to spread the risks associated with the underwriting of new capital issues, both in domestic and subsequently in international capital markets, are visible witness to this trend. Collection and sharing of information for credit risk assessment, clearing systems for settlements, and shared communication systems are all examples of activities related to risk-sharing.

The need for risk-sharing arrangements was recognized early on by insurance companies. Awareness of catastrophic losses, often caused by natural hazards, preceded that of risks engendered by economic interdependence. Reinsurance networks that serve to lay off large risks grew up initially regionally and then became international. A number of insurance companies have always specialized in reinsurance, while many of the major international insurance companies have now set up their own specialist subsidiaries, which take in risks of their current and prospective competitors.

Cooperation in Risk-Sharing between Noncompeting Financial Institutions

Financial institutions that operate in different parts of the financial system have increasingly sought to assist each other in risk-sharing in selected areas. The most noticeable example of this is the risk-sharing arrangements between commercial bank and insurance companies, particularly property and liability insurance companies.

Insurance companies have assisted commercial banks with the management of credit risks associated with growing volume of letters of credit, guarantees, and other off-balance-sheet liabilities and assets.[5] As bank regulatory authorities require more of these contingent payables and receivables to be brought onto their balance sheets in measuring their capital adequacy ratios, this will stimulate the demand for more support from insurance companies.

Insurance companies have played a role in guaranteeing assets of potential borrowers in order to increase their value as a collateral to the bank. One might argue that these value guarantees, and indeed the willingness to purchase assets should the need arise, is mainly a risk benefit for the corporate borrower. But it does assist the bank too, since in the event of default on a loan, the bank can more readily sell the collateral at a guaranteed value and hence minimize its lending risk.

Insurance companies in a more general way have played an active role in providing insurance protection to banks faced with the need to introduce new information technologies. As mentioned previously, the risks associated with breakdown of computer or communications systems for settlement or for transactions activity as well as computer fraud risks have been absorbed by the insurance industry. Indeed without the existence of an insurance sector willing to absorb these risks, the speed of technological innovation may well have been slower.

While to a less significant degree—which is not surprising—banks have also supplied some risk-related services to insurance companies. Speed of settlement and the need to have mobile central funds are essential to the risk-absorption role of these insurance companies. Large international banks grant letters of credit and guarantees for reinsurance transactions that are acceptable to insurance regulatory authorities, hence facilitating the international movement of funds within reinsurance networks. In their normal lending role, they supply short-term finance to permit the speedy settlement of large losses incurred by insurance companies and assist in freeing funds blocked by exchange control regulations. Banks' currency risk management services have also been increasingly used by insurance companies as their operations have become more international in nature.

Finally, life insurance companies and pension funds, because they naturally hold bonds and equities as parts of their investment portfolios, have grown to play an important part in networks absorbing the risks associated with the underwriting of new capital issues that are used by investment banks and merchant banks, both in domestic capital markets and increasingly in international capital markets.

The Growing Role of Financial Instruments as Methods of Risk-Spreading

As commonly recognized, during the last decade, volatility of interest rates, exchange rates, and capital market values has created a need for new ways of spreading risks, and hence spurred creativity in devising new financial instruments; the size of these risks has been such that they could not be handled by financial institutions alone.

With regard to interest rate risk management instruments, *interest rate financial futures*, introduced in the mid-1970s, were an important initial development. They drew on principles and mechanisms of futures on commodities, which had existed for decades. The limited flexibility in financial futures, in particular the loss of the upside potential and their inefficiency with regard to partial or contingent hedging led to the introduction of *interest rate options.* Options on futures contracts were gradually introduced, which increased the flexibility of the futures contracts themselves. Banks have hence created tailor-made instruments, but have used traded instruments to lay off their own subsequent risks onto speculators.

Interest rate swap markets have grown explosively since their introduction in 1982, allowing exchanges between fixed-rate and floating-rate risk obligations. Further developments in interest rate risk management took place in the early 1980s with the development of (*Forward Rate Agreements*) (FRAs) which were essentially customized financial futures.

Commercial banks having their main asset/liability management intimately tied up with short- to medium-term interest rate risks were active participants in these markets. They did so on their own account but were also involved to a growing extent in supplying directly to, or acting as an intermediary for, nonfinancial corporate clients who wished to hedge their interest rate exposures. Given the many instruments competing to satisfy interest rate risk management needs of clients, banks have also been increasingly drawn into *advisory services.*

Similarly, a plethora of financial instruments to manage exchange rate risks have emerged. Banks have supplied currency hedges for centuries through forward markets, and at a minimal risk by covering themselves in the underlying cash markets. The provision of forward contracts still remains an important part of the currency risk management of both banks and their corporate clients. Futures on selective currencies have also emerged although their role is somewhat limited; their fundamental weakness is linked to the fact that they are mainly denominated in U.S. dollars. Hence, currency risks not involving the dollar make these instruments extremely expensive, since hedging entails purchasing two sets of instruments. *Currency options* have provided greater flexibility than futures, or indeed forwards. Currency options grew rapidly on a traded form on selected exchanges since their introduction in the Netherlands in 1978 and spread to the exchanges in the United States, London, and Singapore. However, because traded options are also denominated in U.S. dollars and because corporate customers want more tailor-made currency options, investment banks and specialist departments of the major commercial banks have been required to supply them directly. Again, some of the attendant risks faced by the supplying banks have had to be laid off in the traded options and futures markets. *Currency swap markets* have also evolved to provide long-term currency hedges for corporates and for financial institutions.

Financial instruments aimed at the capital market risks faced by life insurance companies and pension funds have also been developed. Initially, the futures contracts on long-term bonds were introduced in part for this purpose. To provide a hedge against broad market movements in share prices, *index futures* (futures based usually on a weighted average of shares) were introduced in the United States and later in the United Kingdom. Again, to increase flexibility on these future instruments, options contracts on these futures instruments were introduced. To some degree, the capital risk market hedges supplied to life insurance and pension funds have not fully met the underlying needs of these institutions, since these hedges are only short term, whereas the investment risks of these institutions are long term in nature. Nevertheless they have played a role in allowing fund managers to lock in some of the gains from the appreciation in market values in the short term, without the need to sell the underlying securities.

Financial instruments have also been created to spread credit risks faced by banks. *Swap markets* have provided a mechanism for indirectly reducing credit risks for banks in their own borrowing capacity. Provided they are fundamentally sound, commercial banks, well known in their own domestic markets, can raise funds in those markets on better terms than foreign banks.

The benefits accrue essentially from the fact that credit risk assessment is subjective and lenders to banks can only assess the risks on the basis of available information. In effect, *the swap mechanism affords a net information gain*, which in turn causes a reduction in perceived credit risk. *Asset swaps* have played a role in cases where the risk balance between borrowing and lending portfolios is thought to be suboptimal, in the light of changing circumstances. The fact that loans often have legal characteristics that limit their direct exchangeability has led to financial innovations such as the securitization of bank debt.

Insurance contracts are, of course, financial instruments and have evolved with changing demand. In addition to the information-technology risks, particular areas of innovation have been in the fields of liability insurances (both product liability and professional indemnity insurances), legal expenses insurance, credit insurances, and political risk insurances. Insurance companies have been extending their activities into bonding, in both the field of fidelity (honesty) and the field of surety (performance).

Reinsurance, as it has grown, has also changed its contractual terms. There has been a tendency for reinsurance portfolios to move toward an excess of loss and other nonproportional forms that afford a purer form of risk transfer than surplus line, quota share, or other forms of proportional reinsurance. Large individual risks have been increasingly separated out for individual reinsurance arrangements or for a more direct type of risk-sharing through co-insurance. More generally, keen competition in insurance and reinsurance markets has tended to widen the scope of coverage, with insurance policies embracing more and more causes of loss.

COMPUTER SOFTWARE IN RISK MANAGEMENT

Associated with the growth of financial instruments has been the development of software systems by specialist service companies, and indeed departments within major investment banks. These systems are not of themselves a means of risk transfer but provide a framework to assist in better decisionmaking.

Models exist tailored to the management of bond portfolios, such as bond immunization models, targeted mainly at life insurance companies. These models can access external financial data to show how the returns on bond portfolios can be optimized subject to earning a chosen minimum rate of return. With the power of modern computer systems, bond portfolios can be constructed allowing for tax, regulatory, and other constraints on asset choice.

In the last few years, there has been a growth in *portfolio insurance* or dynamic hedging models that provide a system for hedging against short- to medium-term downward movements in common stock values. Essentially, these models are a simulated put option on a diversified equity portfolio.[6] The role of these portfolio insurance models will be limited, however, not only because of the thinness of futures markets for trading but for a technical reason: the risk-free rate for these investors is not the short-term money rate but is a long-term bond rate matched to the maturity structure of their liabilities.

Insurance brokers and specialized service companies such as risk management consultants have also been developing software to assist large corporations in managing insurable risks and will gradually be adapting them for small to medium clients.[7] The focus of these models is to assist in risk pricing and flexible funding of insurance programs and in helping to formulate more economic decisions on the balance between risk retention and risk transfer.

LOOKING TO THE FUTURE: THE ROLE OF SECURITIZATION AND GLOBALIZATION AS A MEANS OF SPREADING RISKS

Whatever the nature of the risk, whether it be from exchange rate and interest rate movements, capital market fluctuations, credit risk exposures, or the broad range of insurable risks, there has been an increasing tendency of financial institutions to search for ways of spreading these risks internationally. In order to be spread, risks have to be made legally transferable and hence capable of being securitized.

The securitization process not only breaks down risks into smaller sizes in order to effect greater spreading but is a prerequisite to tradeability. Risks that can be securitized and traded can then be spread internationally. The existence of modern computer/communications technology allows for globalization of risks to take place. But in order to increase intrinsic tradeability there is a need to develop secondary markets, recognizing that all investors, including investors in risk-bearing instruments, prefer to have a market in which they can sell their commitments, should they wish to do so. This demand for flexibility is in part due to uncertainty about their own future needs and to the recognition that their perceptions may change in light of new information, but it is also a basic psychological need of individuals in that they do not like to be locked into situations. This process of risk spreading through securitization and their subsequent globalization has been an underlying feature of many of the financial instruments that have been spawned during the 1980s. This pattern is likely to continue in the future.

Paradoxically, one interesting area where this trend has not extended to date is with respect to insurance contracts themselves.

There are legal restrictions on the transferability of many direct insurance contracts, mainly due to the fact that the holder of the contract often has to have an insurable interest; concerns about moral hazard against insurance companies, and antigambling laws in some countries, inhibit the securitization of most insurance contracts. Reinsurance contracts are technically less restricted, but the securitization of reinsurance contracts poses a different problem. A risk instrument must be clearly assignable to a risk class: a buyer or seller must know that he is trading in a commodity that is homogeneous in risk. Reinsurance portfolios are very heterogeneous and it is difficult to decompose such portfolios into tradeable securities. Despite these restrictions on the potential securitization of insurance contracts, there are bound to be certain types of insurance risk that will be securitized. Only time will tell what they are, but risk management services can be expected to continue to develop, in scope, depth, and sophistication, thereby providing a pillar of a volatile service and risk-intensive economy.

NOTES

1. Since the mid-1980s changes in the tax and regulatory system in the United States have been introduced that discourage the use of offshore captives and encourage onshore captives. This trend is likely to continue in other parts of the world.

2. A specific example here is the increased emphasis by regulatory authorities on capital adequacy. Commercial banks, in particular, have wished to take on additional risks, and have felt able to do so with their existing capital base. Yet they have been forced to take certain activities off balance sheet because of the impact that these activities would have on the statutory capital adequacy requirements.

3. As an example, new and more flexible forms of borrowing, such as Note Issuance Facilities (NIFs) in euromarkets have allowed large corporations, and indeed governments, to borrow in most of the major currencies.

4. These trading activities are not part of their risk intermediation role but are speculative activities with a view to increasing profitability.

5. An area of cooperation is in factoring. Many of the larger commercial banks around the world have set up factoring subsidiaries that take on the client credit risks of major corporation. In turn, there has been a growing tendency for banks to lay off credit risks above a certain level with specialist insurance companies, analogous to the way that insurance companies lay off their risks to reinsurance companies.

6. Rather than purchase a put option on the index to hedge against a fall in equity values, which is not feasible in practice for large investment funds, these portfolio insurance models allow managers to simulate the characteristics of a put option by creating, in effect, their own hedge. In order to effect the hedge under the model, managers—because of lower transaction costs—often purchase financial instruments, in particular futures on stock index instruments, rather than trade in the stocks themselves.

7. An essential feature of all successful models in this area is that they focus on the portfolio as a whole and not on individual risk exposures or sub-portfolios.

V THE EMPIRICAL AND METHODOLOGICAL CHALLENGE

INTRODUCTION, BY JOËL BONAMY AND ANDRÉ SAPIR

The need to improve the data on services and on services trade has been widely emphasized.[1] The inclusion of this issue as a priority item of the Group of Negotiations on Services (GNS) in the Uruguay Round of Multilateral Trade Negotiations gives it a new political dimension. The context for improving data is complex and could be the subject of an entire book. We focus here on three dimensions: How can international statistics be used? How can their production be harmonized? What is the measurement methodology?

The first point of view we need to take into account is that of the user, although we are all aware that, in the field of services, the user is himself a producer. In other words, statistics can only be improved if they are utilized. Claude Fontaine explores the possible uses of international statistics to their very limits, on the basis of his broad-ranging experience with regard to manipulating and comparing statistics across time and space (through studies covering 25 years and 18 countries).[2] He reflects upon the degree of comparability of international organizations' statistics: based on the assumption that international statistics cannot be more extensive than national ones, he first analyzes the causes of heterogeneity among national service measurement methods. Whether nomenclatures are concerned or the frontiers between activities, or the use and updating of input-output tables, practices and interpretations are so diverse that harmonization has become a formidable job, whose degree of detail and reliability Fontaine tries to assess for us.

The OECD, SOEC (Statistical Office of the European Community), UN, and IMF tables are sifted to the requirement for more in-depth understanding of recent evolutions in terms of value-added, intermediate and final demand for services, trade in services. The conclusion is one of distress, or at least of such an impoverishment of comparable information that only important progress in national statistics, international dialogue, and the combined efforts of national agencies could succeed in significantly improving the situation.

Under the auspices of UNSO[3] (United Nations Statistical Office), several countries[4] and international organizations[5] have buckled down to this task. It would be premature to propose a summary of the work in progress at this point, especially given that several questions remain unanswered. Adrien Lhomme, however, offers in Chapter 16 a complete analytical description of work undertaken on international nomenclatures. He brings to light the complex challenges involved in attempting to harmonize nomenclatures developed independently, by different organizations, at different points in time, and according to different objectives. While there are problems to be solved, what must be emphasized here is the advantage of an approach grounded on what already exists or, more precisely, on the empirical nomenclatures employed rather than on some theoretical nomenclature. Because the work is meant to respond to users' needs, it is hoped that its results will be used without being subject to diverse interpretation; if the latter were to be the case, we would only be led back to our starting point.

There are numerous gray areas but one of the most important questions we need to ask is whether the emerging system of nomenclature will be both detailed and flexible enough to integrate over time changes in products and activities observable today but not yet described with enough precision. This is particularly the case with new information and communication services, with the emergence of "compacks" (complex packages of services or of goods and services), or with the current transformation of actual production units (this refers in particular to the concept of networks). Concretely, it is becoming obvious that harmonization, while not requiring a tabula rasa of the existing system, involves at least a reformulation of many of the most basic operations. The current agenda of those working on harmonization leaves great hope for completion of this first phase by 1990–92, consisting of reviews of nomenclatures, national accounts, and balance-of-payment manuals.[6] Thus we could expect a take-off beyond the "degree zero" of statistics in the last decade of this century.

This leaves one bothersome issue that will not be discussed in this chapter, that of the actual implementation of these new devices for measuring services. For, as we said previously, this involves highly increased efforts in each country concerned. This concern is all the more justified as the protagonists of the work on harmonization in the developed countries themselves point to the lack of adequate funding.[7] Hence, the breadth of the efforts necessary must not be underestimated.[8]

What will happen in most of the developing countries? The needs stemming from current international negotiations work as incentives, but they must be preceded by a greater awareness of key role of services in the development process. The approach taken by UNCTAD,[9] particularly through the assistance provided to developing countries undertaking in-depth studies on the role of services in their development, takes this problem of measurement very much into account. Shouldn't this effort benefit from technical support on the part of countries that are most advanced in improving their statistical systems on services?

Even if one remains reasonably optimistic about the combined efforts of the international community and the prospect of getting, in the medium term, comparable data with a high degree of detail and reliability, there still remain a number of conceptual and theoretical problems. Does one know what should be considered as service "outputs"? Can the productivity of services be assessed? Aren't the effect and quality of services actually the source of comparative advantage, and, as such, the real stake of the Uruguay Round negotiations?

Figures always represent a risk of oversimplifying problems. In this vein, a better understanding of the specific characteristics of services leads to solutions that are considered "homogeneous" with those for goods: nomenclatures of activities and products drawing a continuous spectrum from goods to services, identical solutions for treating services and goods in national accounts and balance of payments. One can thus ask what is the economic significance of the distinction between goods and services.[10]

In raising this problem one reopens the Pandora's box of measurement questions. In this part, Jacques de Bandt draws our attention to the following paradox: on one hand, we can observe a lower productivity growth for services than for goods, while on the other hand, productivity levels are relatively higher for services than for other activities. This brings to bear the statistical illusion of volume-based measurement, the idea that it is possible to measure separately prices and volumes of the various components of services activities. Once again, we come back to the economic specificity of services: the non-separation between output and production processes, the importance of coproduction so-called "servuction,"[11] which implies that there is no volume of production per se, services being integrated into the activity of other units. Henceforth, product and productivity can only be indirect.

The issue of the "service effect" must be of major concern, highlighting the need for research which would be freed from the archetype of nonproductive services. This being the case, the question of services productivity, prices, and, even more important, quality must be brought back as a focus of a broader endeavor that includes measurement issues but, even more fundamentally, the issue of how to integrate services as part of growth and development policies.

NOTES

1. Notably B. Ascher and O.O. Wiehard, "Improving Services Trade Data" in Orio Giarini, ed., *The Emerging Services Economy* (New York: Pergamon Press, 1987).

2. Claude Fontaine, *The Expansion of Services: A Quarter of a Century in France and the Developed World*, 3 vols. (Paris: Rexervices, 1987).

3. Ad hoc work group on services statistics.

4. West Germany, Australia, Canada, the United States, France, the Netherlands, the United Kingdom, Sweden.

5. IMF, OECD, OSCE, UNCTAD, UN.

6. It should be pointed out that in 1990, the term fixed for the Uruguay Round, there will be no improved data, considering the breadth of the task described by C. Fontaine (Chapter 14) and A. Lhomme (Chapter 16). This should be taken into account by the GNS and will have a great influence on final negotiation outcomes.

7. Important budgetary restrictions endanger the quantitative and qualitative progress of measurements: deregulation has sometimes had the perverse effect of suppressing the legal base of statistical collection. Cf., for the United States, J.M. Aanestad, "Statistical Data on Services," in W.O. Candilis, ed., *United States Services Industries Handbook* (New York: Praeger, 1988).

    More fundamentally it should be pointed out here that the gap that exists between the statistical effort on services and the importance of the services sector in the economy is enough to explain the poor quality of data and argues for a reallocation of funds within the budgets of statistical offices.

8. Efforts are evaluated for an average country like France, by sector, to amount to a 50-member team including five high-level statisticians. See the communication presented by J. Albert, "Current Statistics on Services and the Means of Developing Them on an International Scale," paper presented for the UNSO workshop, Stockholm, November 1987.

9. UNCTAD (United Nations Conference on Trade and Development), "The Service Sector: Production and Trade, Policies Which Influence International Transactions and Underlying Factors," CNUCED, TD/B/941.

10. T.P. Hill, "The Economic Significance of the Distinction between Goods and Services," IARIW (International Association of Researchers on Income and Wealth), Rome, August 1987.

11. Theorized by A. Barcet, *The Rise of Services: Towards an Economy of "Servuction,"* CEDES (Centre d'Echange et de Documentation sur les Activities de Services), Economie et Humanisme, Lyon, 1987.

15 SERVICES MEASUREMENT
The Main Lessons from
International Comparisons

Claude Fontaine

The issue of service measurement is obviously too vast to be dealt with in an exhaustive manner in the present chapter. The main concern here will be to elaborate on the difficulties met in a recent study on the growth of services.[1] The following thoughts and remarks are meant in the spirit of constructive criticism. Rather than assess developments over the past 10, 20, or 30 years, which would in all probability reveal marked progress in data acquisition on services by international organizations, I have undertaken to demonstrate the weaknesses and deficiencies of data acquisition today. In this way, I prefer exposing the other face of the issue. Much remains to be done if progress is to be made in this field.

In order to conduct international comparative analysis of service activities and their evolution over time, it is clear that one must first turn to the official statistics published by international organizations. They are more accessible than national statistics and, more important, they have the advantage of being, a priori, *harmonized*, that is to say, classified under a unique nomenclature. This advantage, however, has its reverse side and limits, which are due in large part, but not solely as we will see, to the heterogeneity of the measures taken by the different countries inasmuch as international statistics can't be more detailed than national ones. Before elucidating the limits of international statistics, let's take a look at the problem of heterogeneity in the national statistics.

259

SERVICE MEASUREMENT AND
INTERNATIONAL HETEROGENEITY

I would venture to say that there are few measurement problems specific to nonfinancial market services save those related to the high proportion of small businesses in certain service sectors—problems such as insufficient coverage by professional organizations and the high turnover rate of businesses. Such phenomena explain, in part, one of the most important deficiencies in conjectural analysis today, where the weight of services has become predominant: the absence or mediocrity of statistics on short-term evolution in service production. Another alleged snag regarding services is that of establishing a relevant measure for the evolution in service prices, that is to say a measure "at constant quality" thereby including evolution in terms of volume. It is true that the price of services provided to businesses is poorly measured in France and other countries, and that the criterion for "quality" is, for many services, indeed a difficult measure to define (see the next chapter). But the task is the same when one undertakes to measure the evolution in public works or durable goods whose characteristics are constantly changing. It is equally important to note that prices of services consumed by households tend to be regularly recorded and are no more a problem than food or manufactured commodities prices. Moreover, the measure of prices is, from one point of view, simplified in the service sector: there are no intermediaries between producers and consumers of services; the production price and the consumer price (by households or businesses) are not differentiated, except for taxes.

The Nomenclature Issue

The problems raised by international comparisons are not due to the aforementioned particularities, but rather to the heterogeneity in the national nomenclature system for service headings, to their unequal degrees of detail, and to the fact that measures or estimations are taken regularly in some countries while episodically in others. What is at issue here is not the nature of services but the relatively short history as well as the recent explosion of service sectors. As new sectors are born, each country establishes, at its own pace, a criterion for appraisal and a procedure. Every nomenclature takes into account the diversity of services with a variable time lag depending on the country. The "youth" of services and the "new" terrain are expressions that may seem excessive in referring to an industry already predominant in industrialized nations. Doubtless, it won't be long before standardized classification tables appear, and so oblige all of the developed countries to measure these services accordingly. However, international cooperation is not enough; there must also be improvement in national statistics. A number of services other than such traditional sectors as telecommunications or wholesale retail trade are still poorly accounted for, even in major industrialized nations. It is surprising to find that in the United Kingdom, for example, the national accountants seem incapable of distinguishing "business services" from "credit" or "insurance" services.

The choice of nomenclature headings and their correct application, though tedious tasks, are of the utmost importance to statistical studies, since the possibility of establishing a breakdown by "kind of activity" in order to obtain detailed measurement based on income tax returns or surveys depends on an identification number attributed to each business unit, which is the key to finding the right entry in the nomenclature tables. The problems stem from two contradictory requirements: the nomenclature must be as up-to-date as possible and yet not be modified with excessive frequency, as this would necessarily incur drawn-out administrative and statistical duties and impede if not prohibit any long-term comparisons. However, problems such as those mentioned could be alleviated if, rather than applying a strict, meticulous nomenclature throughout, one were to adopt a system of open nomenclature, that is to say, a system of heading subdivisions. This would allow, without affecting the nomenclature's general framework, an up-to-date listing of new industries once they have acquired a certain standing. Without an open nomenclature system, such industries will continue to find themselves thrown under the headings "miscellaneous" or "other." Moreover, it is often these industries that experience the greatest growth rate.[2]

Issues of Frontiers

Services are defined quite differently from one country to the next. The main differences in drawing the line between goods and services are well known but raise difficulties for international comparisons.

The best-known example is that of *gas and electricity*, which are considered services in the United States and goods in most other countries. Cases like this are evidence of the great difficulty in defining both goods and services according to the usual criteria: material or nonmaterial, visible or invisible, storable or nonstorable. The latter, often evoked to defend the U.S. viewpoint, is not or no longer pertinent since gas is stored in underground vaults and sold to consumers as a stored item after liquefaction. *Repairs* (automobile, household appliances, shoes) are considered services in household consumer statistics in France and the United States and as goods (durable or semidurable depending on the nature of the goods being repaired) by other countries, such as Sweden, and by international organizations, like the OECD, and the EEC in conformity with the United Nations Statistics Organization classification of household consumption by purpose and durability (National Accounts System, United Nations, 1970); the material/nonmaterial criterion tends to justify the second choice, but then, why not extend the heading to include haircuts and surgical operations.[3]

The list of problems related to the frontier between goods and services or between the industrial and the service sector is a long one. To take two more examples, this time stated in the form of a question, when a business turns to *leasing* as a means of acquiring durable goods, should the investment be charged to the leasing company (a service industry) that bought the goods or to the business (manufacturer or service firm) that is to use the goods and that will, in most cases, become owner since a buying option is almost always exercised? Secondly, should *temporary employment* workers be placed under a same service sector—temporary placement agencies—or should they be placed under the heading of the industry in which they have been temporarily employed?[4]

It has also proven hard to draw frontiers *between services.* The well-known problem that most affects comparison among countries is the distinction between *market* services and *nonmarket* services. Though officially recognized by international organizations (UN, OECD, EEC), this distinction is, however, not accepted by all of the countries concerned, notably the United States, where only the distinction between public and private is taken into account. In the United States, services provided by private nonprofit organizations are not distinguished from other private services, while in the EEC they are placed under nonmarket services, along with a much more important service sector—public services. As it stands, the market/ nonmarket distinction itself is vague and avails diverse interpretations as is seen in the case of public hospitals considered as market services in the French National Accounts before 1986 and as nonmarket since then. The implementation of such distinctions leaves much room for interpretation in each country's particular covenant. Finally, and most important, even with identical covenants, varying judicial statutes and different financial modes of payment between countries cause the same services (health education) to be considered market services by one country and nonmarket services by another. It is not only the defined limits between market and nonmarket that vary from one country to the next, but also what is considered as household consumption, since the current rule is to ascribe the near totality of nonmarket services to collective consumption. Thus, for example, *health service* for 1985 represented 0.4 percent of household consumption in Great Britain, 0.7 in Denmark, and 2.4 in Italy, while as much as 7.7 in Belgium, 9.8 in France, and 11.1 in the Netherlands. The differences are less important though not insignificant for household expenditures related to *education* as seen in the figures in the OECD tables: 0.2 percent of household consumption in Sweden and Belgium, 0.3 in France, the Netherlands and Italy, while 2 percent in the United States and 2.8 in Canada.

When considering *financial services*, we are once more faced with the problem of breakdown, but this time between household and business consumption. Statisticians are generally at a loss when having to break down into user categories those services that correspond to the intermediary role of financial institutions, and that represent the majority of their service production. Instead, the sum of these intermediary functions is ascribed to intermediate consumption by either general business (as in the case of France) or by financial organizations (the solution adopted by the EEC for the presentation of input-output tables). Hence an extremely low level in the consumption of financial services by household, the only services taken into account being bank commissions, credit cards, and safe rentals. On the other hand, at least one country proceeds differently: the United States, where financial services represent 3.5 percent of household consumption, three-fourths of which are "furnished without payments" according to the 1985 National Accounts, whereas in France the figure is 0.5 percent and in Sweden, 0.7 percent. The ratio of business to household financial services (the published statistics only allow a measure for the whole of the credit and insurance services), is practically 1 in the U.S., whereas the ratio is 3.5 in Germany and the Netherlands, almost 6 in France, and over 20 in Italy. Such processing discrepancies affect, at least for the United States and the EEC countries, the evaluation of financial services for both households and businesses. But where business are concerned, the real obstacle is of another order.

A Problem of Measurement and Statistical Philosophy: The Input-Output Tables

With the exception of a few limited surveys, there are no *direct* measurements of intermediate consumption—expenditures by businesses of goods and services consumed during the production process. The only overall evaluations are those proposed in the input-output tables established by the national accounts that register the economic flow of goods and services from input to output and establish an equilibrium by category of goods and services, between total resources (production and imports) and both their final use (household consumption, collective consumption, gross fixed capital, exportation, and inventory changes) and their intermediate uses (business and government purchases).

Yet, the creation of an input-output tables (IOT), that is, the constraint to establish an equilibrium by "commodity" between resources and uses plays a fundamental role in the evaluation of annual national accounts for some countries such as France, where IOTs are established annually, and a lesser or insignificant role in other countries, such as the United States and the United Kingdom, where they are established at extended intervals. Two positions, almost two philosophies, on statistics confront each other here. Advocates of the first position undertake the regular upkeep of detailed, coherent statistical evaluations. For them, coherence is possible principally through the use of IOTs. Such a position is indeed ambitious given the variable quality of the data and the lack in the information available. Advocates of the second position, more pragmatic in nature, without ignoring the role of the IOTs in carrying out simulations— though not necessarily on an annual basis—do not place coherency in statistical evaluations as the top priority. They prefer to reveal "statistical divergences" rather than attribute them arbitrarily to an unknown entry, for example, changes in inventory. The best illustration of this attitude is found in the national accounts of the United Kingdom, which presents three distinct GDP figures: income-based, expenditure-based, and output-based. The United Kingdom National Accounts Department just uses their average for medium- and long-term analysis.

Without entering a debate on principles, it is important to note that the first approach does contribute to a significantly greater extent to the measurement of services through the annual assessment of intermediate consumption, given that service expansion in general is largely due to the rising purchase of services by the business sector.

LIMITS OF HARMONIZED INTERNATIONAL STATISTICS ON SERVICES

In light of the need for internationally harmonized statistics, a number of questions arise: What comparisons do international organizations propose? To what degree are the statistics reliable? And to what degree have the service headings been broken down?

A person turning to OECD publications on statistics should be warned from the start about their limited reliability.[5] Indeed, in practice, certain "standardized" statistics prove only in part, if at all, comparable. But it is above all the want in comparisons possible, even approximate ones, that become apparent during efforts to use international statistics as a basis for measuring and explaining the growth of services in developed countries.

In the remaining part of this chapter, we will examine the four main statistical categories: value-added by service sectors, household demand, business demand, and foreign demand.

Value-Added by Service Sector

The harmonized tables published by the OECD appear, at first, quite promising since the service sector is broken down into the following headings (along with their OECD number):[6]

Market Services

24–Wholesale and retail trade, restaurants and hotels
　25–Wholesale and retail trade
　26–Restaurants and hotels
　　27–Restaurants
　　28–Hotels and other lodging places
29–Transport, storage, and communication
　30–Transport and storage
　31–Communication
32–Finance, insurance, real estate, and business services
　33–Financial institutions
　34–Insurance
　35–Real estate and business services
　　36–Real estate except dwellings
　　37–Dwellings
38–Community, social, and personal services
　39–Sanitary and similar services
　40–Social and related community services
　　41–Educational services
　　42–Medical, dental, other health and veterinary services
　43–Recreational and cultural services
　44–Personal and household services

Nonmarket Services

47–Producers of Government Services
48–Other Producers

Note:
50–Less: Imputed bank service charge

Eighteen separate headings are provided for services (including those arrived at through deduction, such as business services). That is half the total headings and more than those provided for manufacturing, mining, and construction—an outstanding menu for international comparisons! However, a closer look at the actual statistics unfortunately leads to a more cautious assessment: numerous columns are left blank and one country, Switzerland, is not represented in any of the tables: there are no evaluations for value-added for either employment or gross fixed investment by kind of activity. Where they exist, figures do not always correspond to the heading content, as the numerous table footnotes indicate.[7] Basically, establishing comparisons based on these tables means running into numerous obstacles, only to find out by the end of this process, that the results actually offer limited possibility of comparisons. One comes out virtually empty handed. None of the countries have statistics for all of the headings nor do they conform 100 percent to the nomenclature or the evaluation rules adopted by the OECD.

Only *three countries*, Austria, Norway, and Sweden, provide data that allow in principle calculation, by subtracting, the value-added of those *business services* that have developed most over the past 20 years (engineering, computer services, auditing and accounting, cleaning services, caretaking and security, durable goods rentals—those services would be more appropriately labeled "other business services" to differentiate them from commercial services, transport, telecommunications, and insurance services). It was hoped that the same calculation would be possible for the United States and Finland, given that there was no footnote indicating that business services were classified elsewhere than under the heading number 35 for these two countries. However, the difference between heading 35 and the sum of headings 36 and 37 for these two countries is zero, implying the absence of business services (!) or their integration in "real estate." Even traditional sectors, such as transport, storage, and communication, are not isolated in 5 of 21 of the countries under consideration. A careful reading of the tables reveals such a degree of incoherence that a comparison limited to four regrouped service categories[8] is only possible for six countries: New Zealand, Austria, Denmark, France, the Netherlands, and the United Kingdom, and with reservations for four others: the United States and Finland as long as business services are really included under real estate, Sweden because value-added of financial institutions is reported net of imputed bank service charges, and Norway because the evaluations at constant price were only partially broken down by industry until 1979.[9] Two countries of major importance, Germany and Japan, are excluded from such comparisons.

The situation is even more discouraging for investment and employment statistics by service sector,[10] which greatly hinders prospects of international comparisons on the evolution of productivity in service sectors. This is possible only for the aggregate of services, market and nonmarket.

What criteria can be applied to determine whether national statistics have been transposed into the nomenclature according to the established norms? International statistics appear like a confusing mystery filled with blanks and exceptions to the rule. Cases do exist where the degree of detail in the national statistics renders trans-position impossible, but often poor international statistics can be attributed to the inadequate efforts on the part of the National Statistics Institutions in filling out the OECD's "National Accounts Questionnaire."[11]

The Statistics Office of the European Communities has had a more cooperative relationship with National Statistics Institutions, due its size, its vigilance, and its less ambitious scope.[12] The headings are fewer but more appropriate. Nevertheless, we still find cases of lack of disaggregation, in particular with "other market services" still too much of a catch-all residual category (45–50 percent of the total entries for the Netherlands, Germany, and France).

The Demand for Services by Households

International comparisons on household services consumption are either incomplete or only overall figures. Indeed, the EEC and the OECD favor classification by function (dwellings, health, transport, leisure), which fails to differentiate between goods and services consumption.[13] Eurostat would need to add just three headings to its 54 in order to present all the components of household consumption of services. Such a small effort would be justified by the major progress entailed.[14]

The OECD has adopted an even more concise version of the United Nation's nomenclature but adds a breakdown of household consumption expenditures by "durability," a classification with four entries, one of which is general services according to the UN definition of the term. However, this breakdown, i.e., the overall figure, does not exist for ten countries (West Germany, Belgium, Switzerland, Australia . . .).

As stated in the first part of this chapter, the varying delimitation between market and nonmarket services from one country to the next greatly impedes comparability. Table 15-1 illustrates this point by showing the negative correlation between household services consumption in the domestic market (column a) and the size of the government service sectors relative to the entire value-added of the service sector (column b). While, not surprisingly, the correlation is

Table 15-1. Market versus Public Services: The Crowding-Out Effect.

	(a) (%)	(b) (%)
Japan	51.6	14.4
United States	51.4	18.0
United Kingdom	43.6	24.8
Netherlands	42.5	21.1
France	40.3	22.9
Finland	37.8	30.2
Denmark	36.3	32.0
Sweden	34.5	39.5
Italy	31.9	25.5
Norway	31.7	28.5

Source: OECD Statistics for 1985.

not perfect (given the importance of factors like standard of living, cost of health services, role of government services), the table clearly stresses the bias introduced by excluding nonmarket services.

Comparison of overall household services consumption between countries is hence not meaningful, except in the cases where there is a degree of approximation at institutional level or in national accounting system. In this respect, the EEC efforts in singling out among nonmarket services what Eurostat calls "personal services" (consumed individually and free of charge like education, health, social security, and leisure) are very interesting. In a recent study, it was shown that Eurostat adds the value of these services to household income to calculate what is referred to as "personal" income.[15] It is just as possible to add it to final private consumption (household consumption and services furnished by private nonprofit organizations) in order to evaluate what can be qualified as "enlarged" consumption.[16]

Overall, a more detailed listing for the headings of household consumption by function is not the only prerequisite for a comparative analysis of service demand by households. What is also needed is to break up the mass of services rendered by the nonmarket branches of the public sector so as to distinguish these "personal" services which are not inherently nonmarket.

Service Demand by Business

In the discussion in the first part of this chapter on input-output tables (IOTs)—sole means for a global evaluation of services bought by businesses—the potential for comparison in this domain was considered limited; a look at the published data confirms this assertion.

The UN published harmonized input-output tables for approximately 15 Western nations—though not always the same nations—for the years 1959, 1965, 1970, 1975. The nomenclature, though modified in 1970, remained quite aggregated in that the headings for seven "services purchased by businesses" can be distinguished: 1) commercial, 2) hotels and restaurants, 3) transport and warehouse services, 4) communications, 5) financial, insurance, rental of immovable goods, and (other) business services, 6) other market services, 7) nonmarket services. The homogeneity of the IOTs by country is indeed mediocre: a large part of the services purchased by businesses and government agencies have been regrouped under the fifth category in France (47% in 1975), in Italy (45%) and in Sweden (40%), but the percentages drop to 21% in Canada and 17% in Germany. Conversely, in these countries the figure under "other market services" is quite high (20% and 45%, respectively) as opposed to the formerly mentioned countries (between 10% and 15%).

The EEC's standardized input-output tables offer a nomenclature twice as detailed, which allows, notably, distinguishing between credit and insurance services, rental of immovable goods, and (other) "business services."[17]

Taken globally, the evaluations appear coherent: the purchase of services represents from 13 percent to 16 percent of the production value of all branches of business or 27 percent to 34 percent of total intermediate consumption in the six most developed countries. Naturally the measures for Spain and Portugal are less at 24 percent and 21 percent, respectively. The detailed comparisons between countries show important differences that are doubtless real. For instance, it is surprising that "business services" constitute approximately 30 percent of the total intermediate consumption in Germany and France while only 13 percent in Italy, and to find the whole of credit and insurance services and business services at 25 percent for the United Kingdom and nearly 50 percent for France and Germany. Another example of heterogeneous classification is offered by the high variability of the scope of "other market services": 18 percent (United Kingdom), 10 percent (Denmark, Netherlands), 5-6 percent (Italy, France, West Germany).

The possibility for comparing trends over time is even more limited. Eurostat constituted an "IOT data base" for 1959, 1965, and 1970-80. For these 13 years, only France systematically provided Eurostat with data; Italy and the Netherlands provided for 10 of the years, Germany for 6, the United Kingdom for 5 years, and Belgium and Denmark for only 4. Hence, the data is less applicable than if gathered annually, given that continuity in evaluations is the best insurance for consistent acquisitions methods and stability in covenants. Also, the IOTs established at extended intervals are generally only evaluated *at current prices*.

Admittedly, there is a great need for a more regular standardized system since the analysis of IOTs shows that the total of services purchased by businesses and government agencies is on the average, for developed countries, almost equal to the services purchased by households, and that their growth rate is much higher due to the new patterns of demand by businesses for specialized services as analyzed in the rest of this book.

Service Demand from Abroad

Exporting services offers currently less prospects than serving households or business demands. Nevertheless, trade in services is on the upswing and may benefit a great deal from current multilateral attempts to ease trade restrictions in this field (see Part III of this book). The reference statistics are those of balance of payment and standard international comparisons proposed by the IMF.

It is not intended here to evoke the well-known problem of the general incoherence in statistics on foreign trade, that is to say, the situation in which the sum total of imports or sales figures exceeds that of the export or credit figures. The lack of balance in the world current account can be in large part ascribed to a poor census of service flows, notably financial. A less familiar frontier problem should be stressed here, that of comparing activities regrouped under the heading of "other goods, services, and income,"[18] which includes the services with the highest growth.

Comparison of the performances by major Western nations offers surprising conclusions. According to the statistics published by the IMF, France is the first exporter of these services (15 billion SDR (special drawing rights) for the year 1984–85) ahead of the United Kingdom (11 billion–13 billion) and Germany 11 billion), and far ahead of the United States (6 billion–7 billion). These exports create an excess of 6–8 billion SDR in France and the United Kingdom compared with 4 billion SDR in the United States. Yet, in sectors such as sale of engineering and construction services on the international marketplace, the United States is clearly far ahead.[19] The fact that France included an indistinct amount of "goods and services" under this heading does not explain such a statistical anomaly. Rather, this is above all due to the fact that revenues from major construction sites (over periods of one year or more) appear to be classified under direct investment income by the United States, conforming with the IMF instructions, while this is not the case for France and probably not for the United Kingdom or Germany.

In order to be significant, comparisons should be based on the sum of "other goods, services, and income" and direct investment income. But, other problems arise: the reinvested profits abroad represent approximately half of the direct investment income for the United States and the United Kingdom, while they are hardly taken into account by other countries who sometimes find themselves at a loss to distinguish direct investment income from other private capital income or from capital income in general.

One could argue that international bodies working on statistics could be more vigilant at times, but we must be aware that they have only limited control. An improvement in international statistics on services depends on an improvement in national statistics, greater international cooperation (nomenclature, covenants) and a joint effort by national organizations in providing complete, harmonized statistics, based on their available data. Users could also help by a more critical exploitation of statistical information as well as through demands and needs resulting from their works. The more statistics are used, the better they will become.

NOTES

1. Claude Fontaine, *L'expansion des services: un quart de siècle en France et dans le monde développé* (The Expansion of Services: A Quarter of a Century in France and the Developed World), 3 vols.: *Dynamics of Services, Demand for Services, Supply of Services.* (Paris: Rexervices, 1987).

2. The monthly surveys on business employment and earnings in the United States offer a good example of open nomenclature.

3. Another interesting case is that of restaurants and cafés. In France and in UN nomenclature, such expenditures are considered service expenses whereas in the United States, where the restaurant industry is not a distinct industry, but rather a branch of the retail trade, they are classified under household food consumption along with meat and vegetables bought in a retail store. As in many other instances (commercial services and transport included in the value of goods) ambiguity reigns. In the case of restaurants it is particularly apparent: goods and services are confused to varying degrees depending on whether the service is considered "real" restaurant or fast food. This perhaps explains why meals eaten out in the United States are considered goods that involve services, while in France they are considered services that involve goods. Sweden has chosen a middle road in subdividing expenditures on restaurants and cafés into two entries: one, the value of the drink and food consumed, the other, the service provided (the measure in services is evaluated as predominant at just over 60 percent).

4. Comparisons of employment by industry would still be misleading if all countries adopted the first solution, due to the unequal extent of temporary work. In the Netherlands it is twice that of France or the United Kingdom and three to four times that of Belgium and Germany.

5. In the foreword to *Labor Force Statistics*, the warning "for general public use" under the Economic Statistics and National Accounts Division of the OECD reads: "The standardized presentation of the tables does not imply that the series for the various countries are comparable. Important differences exist between countries in the matter of general concepts, classification and the methods used for obtaining the data. Consequently, comparisons must be approached with caution and should be regarded as approximate."

6. OECD, National Accounts, vol. 11, table 12: gross domestic product by kind of activity (and table 3: gross fixed capital formation, and 15: employment by kind of activity).

7. The most frequent infringements on the standard nomenclature are the including of restaurants and hotels or business services provided to enterprises under the heading, "Community, social and personal services."

8.   24: trade, hotels, restaurants; 29: transport, warehouses and communications; 32: banks, insurance, real estate, business services; 38: community services, personal and social services.

9.   The statistical discrepancy—5.7 percent total 1970—lessened and disappeared by 1980.

10. For instance, OECD tables for 1971–83 quoted for Japan only 0.4 percent of the total gross fixed capital formation attributed to service sectors! Subsequently, no OECD figures have been given for Japan.

11. This is flagrant in the case of France: OECD lacks published statistical data on France (only one heading for investment by market services and only six headings for value-added), and yet France has the means to evaluate a broad range of service sectors (at least 40 whose evolution we have followed since 1960 or 1970)!

12. The ESA is the community version of the UN system of National Accounts; it is, in effect, clearly less detailed than in the OECD tables for the same sector broken down into: Recovery and repair services, wholesale and retail trade; Lodging and catering services; Transport services (Inland; Maritime and air transport; Auxiliary); Communication services; Services of credit and insurance institutions; Other market services (refer to Eurostat, "National Accounts ESA: Tables by Kind of Activity," theme 2, series C).

13. Unless subject to exhaustive nomenclature subdivision, as is the case with the national accounts in the United States and in Sweden.

14. The headings of the UN nomenclature are the following:

     452: Home services less domestic services: dry cleaners, laundering, home appliance rentals, chimney sweeping, moving . . .

     623: Parking, tolls, auto insurance, driving lessons, car rentals . . .

     811: Hair dressers, beauty salons . . .

     It is also unfortunate that Eurostat continues to support that deplorable practice of publishing relative proportions at "constant prices" and not at current prices. The part of their budget that households put aside for a given expenditure is "real" only in relation to the price of the year, in other words, at current prices.

15. Eurostat, "Europe, United States, Japan, 1970–1986: main economic indicators," theme 2, series D, pp. 73 ff.

16. The enlargement for 1980 varies from + 8 percent in Japan and +11 percent in the United States and France, to +15 percent and +17 percent in Italy and the United Kingdom and + 32 percent in Denmark.

17. The IOTs for 1980 offer the following headings for a comparative analysis of services purchased by businesses and government enterprises: 1) Recovery and repair services, 2) Wholesale and retail trade, 3) Lodging and catering services, 4) Road transport services, 5) Inland waterway services, 6) Auxiliary transport services, 7) Maritime and coastal transport services,

8) Air transport services, 9) Auxiliary transport services, 10) Communications, 11) Credit and insurance, 12) Business services provided to enterprise, 13) Renting of immovable goods, 14) Market services of education and research, 15) Market services of health, 16) Market services n.e.c. (Eurostat, "National Accounts ESA: Input-Output tables 1980," theme 2, series C).

18.   The IMF nomenclature distinguishes within current account services transactions between the following categories: shipment, travel, direct investment income, other income from private and public sources, official and interofficial, property income, labor income and "other goods, services and income." Components of this last heading, which is a key one, differ greatly from one country to the next.

19.   Annual surveys carried out by *Engineering News Record* indicate that the foreign orders for U.S. engineering and construction firms were on the average four times that of French engineering and construction firms for the period 1981–85.

16 CAN WE MEASURE PRODUCTIVITY IN SERVICE ACTIVITIES?

Jacques de Bandt

The share of service activities has been increasing steadily and the economic stakes represented by these activities have become quite obvious. Nonetheless the idea still remains deeply rooted that service activities are not productive or are only marginally so. There is no real or effective production in the case of services, at least no objective production in the sense of a real or concrete content, leading to tangible, visible products. Nor, as a consequence, is there any effective productivity. A service is only a relation, something that is essentially of a subjective nature.

Of course everybody is ready to accept that this is not totally true for all services. Several activities produce a mixture of goods and services. It can even be said that all activities show this dualism: while in some cases the service component only "accompanies" the good, in other cases the service component becomes so dominant that the reference to physical, objective elements tends to disappear. And it is precisely in these cases that the productive character of services tends to be denied.

A widely held perception is that, because service activities do not correspond to "real" production, their development is to a very large extent fictitious, corresponding mainly to an increase in relative

An early version of this chapter was presented at the biennial Conference on Current Issues in Productivity, Rutgers University, New Brunswick, N.J., December 1987.

prices. This chapter shows instead that services, at least services to business, are productive. The following points will be developed:

1. When measuring value-added in constant prices in service activities, statisticians are only displacing the problem.
2. Contrary to the general observation concerning low productivity growth in service activities, it must be stressed that the *relative productivity of services is constantly higher.*
3. It is not easy to explain this higher relative productivity unless this is done on the basis *of quality differences and market imperfections.*
4. While the contradiction is solved in principle by taking *relative prices* into account (services being "capturing" activities) the contradiction is not so easily solved when considering the particular case of "higher" services to enterprises.
5. Is it possible to draw any conclusion from the relationship between the level of development and the share of services in gross domestic product? Even while statistical, the relationship does show that *the service activities play a productive role* in the development process.
6. It will be necessary, incidentally, to reject those theories—pushing the thesis of the low productivity growth in the service activities to its limits—which attempt to show that the *aforementioned relationship is only apparent* and that, as a matter of fact, the share of services is not increasing with the level of development.
7. When trying to measure productivity in service activities, it is thus necessary *to reject the notion of an autonomous and identifiable volume of production.* The productivity of (pure) services is indirect and is observable through the results obtained by the user.

Before going into these various points, it must be stressed that service activities are concerned only to the extent that the service component is dominant, with special emphasis on higher ("intellectual" or "information") services to business.

The Alleged Measurement of Value-Added in Constant Prices in Service Activities

The production of services[1] has always been measured by statisticians in terms of volume, that is, in constant prices. For national accounts purposes, there is a general presumption that, errors and approximations excepted, the measurement is correct. The OECD has indicated that value-added in constant prices can be measured by deflating current value-added, through "double deflation," or by extrapolating base year value-added.[2]

This is all very well. A measurement being needed, value added at constant prices is measured. But the question is left unresolved of what is the product in the case of services, the unit in which the product is measured, and the price of that unit. We are proceeding by analogy and do as if services were measured at constant prices. But this is not the case.

Is it necessary to stress in particular that no specific account is taken of the qualitative aspects of the problem? The analogy leads us to a kind of absurdity, given that services, in the absence of technical specifications, can only be characterized by their qualitative dimensions. When these are not taken into account explicitly, the measurement of production can only be arbitrary.

While we obviously know that the volume and the price of value-added are only accounting fictions, it is necessary to abandon such fictions when, as in the case of services, no element of reference exists on the basis of which these categories can be constructed in a nonarbitrary way. Hence we need to consider production and value-added of (pure) services only in current prices.

It must be underlined of course that this strong statement is only valid, strictly speaking, for the services, in which the nonmaterial and qualitative aspects are dominant. When it is possible to find, on the basis of physical quantities or of a combination of weighted physical quantities, an approximation of the quantity or the volume of production, the approximation can be considered acceptable. But this has to be decided on a case-by-case basis.

Most of the reasonings based on the current measures lead to a dead end, as the following section demonstrates.

The Dichotomy between Chronological and Cross-Sectional Comparisons

To start with, we must note the interesting contrast, in the case of services, between the low productivity growth over time and the higher relative productivity of services when compared with other activities.

The fact that productivity is growing more slowly in service activities than in other activities is generally accepted. There has been almost complete unanimity on this point, even though many observers do insist on the necessity for an acceleration of productivity growth in service activities or on the possibilities for such acceleration due to the new information technologies.

This observation does concern only labor productivity. We must take into account the fact that the growth of labor productivity in the manufacturing sector is, at least partly, due to the substitution of capital for labor and that total productivity is, for that reason, growing more slowly. Hence, it seems natural that the difference between services and manufacturing activities is smaller when considering the rates of growth of total productivity.

It must also be stressed that we are concerned with the growth rates of labor productivity and not with absolute levels. A priori we do not know anything about the relative productivity levels in industrial versus service activities. If, at least in principle, we can compare the inputs, in spite of their heterogeneity, we can compare neither "production efforts" nor products. A priori we do not know whether productivity levels are lower in services than in industry. Of course, if growth rates are lower in service activities, in the long run the level of productivity must necessarily also become lower.

But this is the point where the contradiction takes its full meaning. To compare heterogeneous products, we need to refer to the price system. But if we compare the productivity levels of services and industry with reference to the price system, the levels are not lower in the service activities.

This is precisely what relative labor productivities—productivities in terms of value (in current prices)—are measuring. Relative productivity for each activity is the ratio of the share of value-added in GDP and the share of employees in the total labor force.[3]

A situation in which relative productivities would all be everywhere equal to 1 would mean that for all activities 1 percent of the labor force produces 1 percent of GDP. Such a situation would correspond to the theoretical case in which all products would be evaluated at their labor-value, assuming of course the total labor content be taken into account both directly and indirectly (that is, the labor content in the upstream value-added corresponding to capital goods and to intermediate goods). But if the assessment of value-added is based on labor content (at average labor costs), then it is obviously the price system that is adapting itself, with real or physical productivity losing all relevance.[4] In other words, to a lower physical productivity (that is, a higher labor content) would simply correspond a higher value-added (hence, a higher price). The differences would be compensated.[5]

But, in fact, relative productivities are not identical, but systematically higher—above 1—in service activities[6] (Figure 16-1). In other words, even if "physical" productivities were lower, there would not be compensation, but overcompensation through prices and values added. In any case, this notion of physical productivity is itself flawed. Yet, we must stress that:

- While relative productivities are higher in the service activities in general, account must of course be taken of the wide dispersion within this very heterogeneous set of activities.

- The superiority of services would be higher in terms of relative total productivity than in terms of relative labor productivity.

- The differences between relative productivities generally tend to diminish with the level of development. These differences are markedly smaller in developed countries, where relative productivities are more or less converging towards 1.

- Since the beginning of the 1970s, the beginning of the crisis, the dispersion of relative productivities among service activities (as well as industrial activities) seems to have increased significantly.

The Higher Level of Relative Productivities in Service Activities

How can one try to explain the higher level of relative productivity in service activities? If we eliminate right away the idea that real productivity could be higher (things would be too simple in that case), it is possible to find some arguments that would explain differences in productivity. It is much more difficult to imagine arguments that would explain positive differences—that is, the higher level of relative productivity in services.

A first argument concerns the combination of production factors. Capital intensity is significantly higher in the industrial sector, capital-labor substitution explaining all or part of labor-productivity growth. This would seem to imply that, to the extent that the non-

Figure 16–1. Services Share in GDP versus Employment Relative to Level of Development (*1984*).

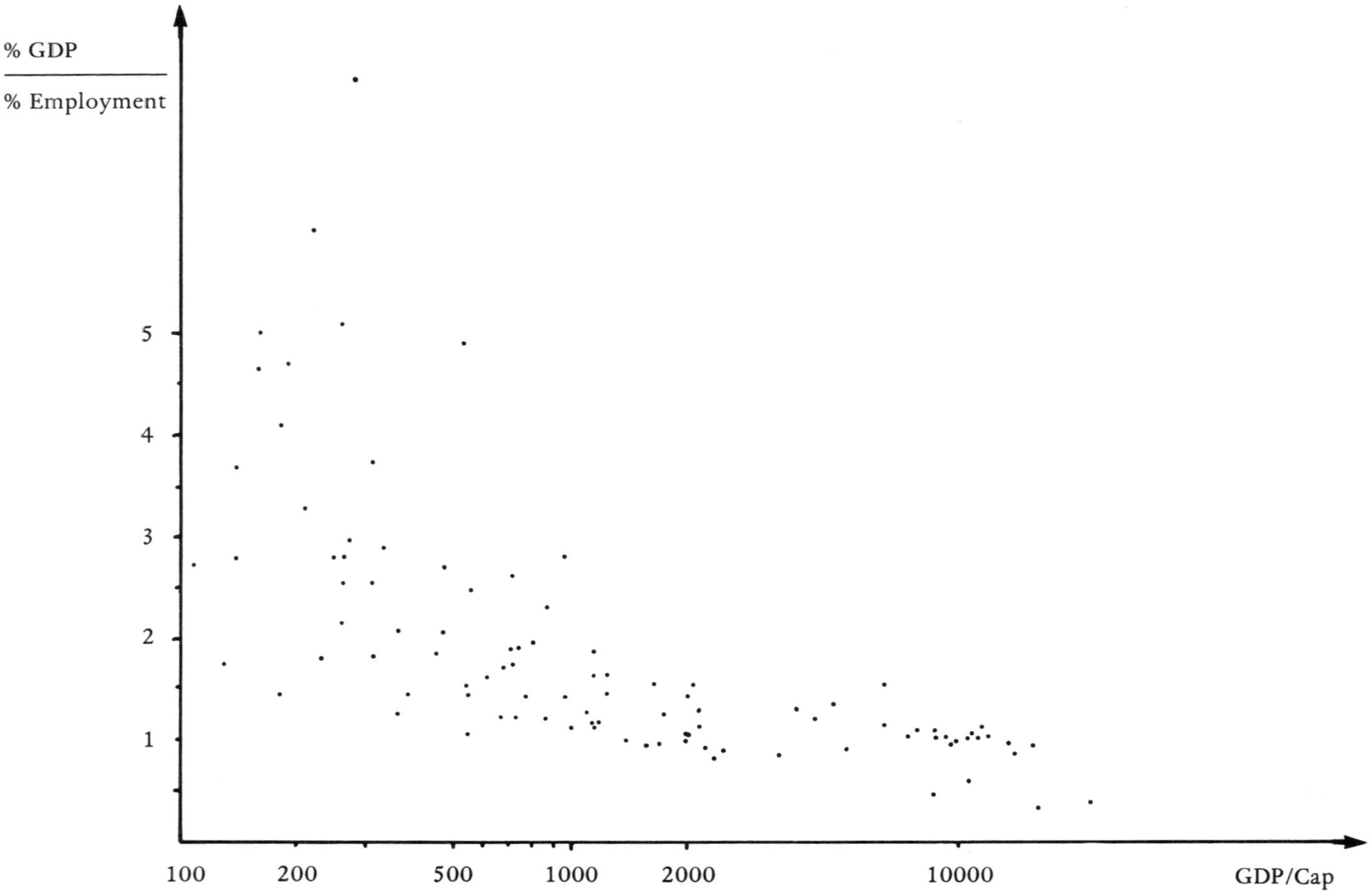

wage component of value-added is significantly higher in industry, relative productivity should also be proportionately higher than in services.

The second argument has to do with the structure of skills and wages. This cannot explain a higher relative productivity in services in general, where the levels of skills and wages are lower than average, but can nevertheless help explain it for some specific high-skilled services.

The third argument concerns the quality of services compared with that of goods. It is of course impossible to compare the quality of a service with the quality of a good. The question here is whether, taking into account the fact that the qualitative aspects are intrinsically part of the definition of services, qualitative variations (in terms of the continuous adaptation of services to users' needs) can explain the higher relative productivity of service activities.

This third argument is likely to support our proposition regarding productivity, but is only after all a working hypothesis. It seems unquestionable that the qualitative adaptation of services to needs that are specific and constantly evolving is one decisive aspect of the production of services and thus justifies higher prices for the user. If this is the case, then part of the production of the service has a chance of being registered as a price increase—that is, of being included in the value-added (in current prices), on the basis of which relative productivity is measured. But it risks being eliminated from value-added in constant prices, on the basis of which the evolution of productivity over time is calculated.

The fourth argument has to do with market power as opposed to the degree of competition, in particular international competition. The idea is that services being less traded (because they are less tradeable or because they are more regulated and thus more protected) are less exposed to international competition and thus able to maintain relatively higher prices and profit margins.

We are indeed obliged to note that rents or profits exist in a number of activities. This is particularly true for activities that are part of the "circulation sphere." A number of developing countries in particular are characterized by the importance of rents levied by the tertiary sector, mainly in the distribution sector. This is reflected by the high level of relative productivity of the tertiary sector on Figure 16-1.

This last argument is not negligible but is rather difficult to demonstrate. It is disconcerting to note, the available data not allowing for more precision, that a number of service activities with a high relative productivity (banking and insurance, consulting, engineering, marketing, and advertising, R&D) are also the most internationalized or in the process of being internationalized. This does not imply the rejection of the argument but makes it more difficult to prove.

To sum up:

- The first two arguments—capital intensity and the structure of skills and wages—would rather obviously seem to imply a lower relative productivity of service activities in general.

- On the contrary, the last two arguments would seem to imply, to a certain degree, a higher relative productivity for services.

- The heterogeneity of service complicates matters further, given that these four arguments do not play out in the same way for various services. For the "higher" services in particular, the second argument seems to be meaningful, while the fourth is not.

Relative Prices: Winners and Losers

This contradiction is easily solved if one takes into account the fact that in one case, the growth of productivity, the reasoning is in volume terms, while in the other case the reasoning is in value terms, including therefore relative prices. This leads us to attribute the observed difference to relative prices distortion, which in turn reflects a levying by service activities of other activities' value-added.

This is illustrated by the graph in Figure 16-2, which shows the relationship between productivity (or the reduction of costs for given factor prices) and price changes. The two axes represent alternatively changes in

- Global productivity (ratio of gross production over all the inputs) and prices (of the good or service)

- Total productivity (ratio of value-added in constant prices over the production factors) and the price of value-added

- Labor productivity (ratio of value-added in constant prices over labor) and the price of labor (that is, average labor costs)

Obviously, if the value of production is essentially made of value-added and if value-added is essentially made of wages, which is closer

Figure 16-2.   The Relationship between Productivity and Price Increases.

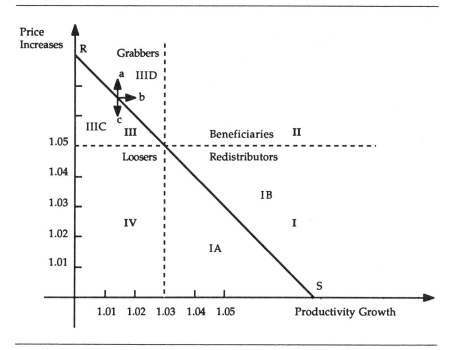

to reality for services, these three sets of relations tend to be the same.

Let us suppose that the average price increase has been of 5 percent and the average productivity increase of 3 percent. These average values serve to divide the graph into four quadrants within which we can plot the different products (or activities) according to their relative productivity and price growth rates.[7]

The four quadrants correspond to clearly different situations:

In I productivity is growing faster than average and relative prices are declining. Part of the productivity increase is thus distributed through lower prices. These activities are "redistributors."

In II productivity is growing faster than average, but prices also. These activities are (twice) "beneficiaries."

In III productivity growth is less than average, but prices rise faster than average. These activities are making up for their lack of productivity through higher prices; they are "grabbers."

In IV both productivity and prices grow below average. These activities are (twice) "losers," they are due to disappear unless they are willing to permanently accept lower incomes.

On the other hand, however, for given factor prices, the higher (the lower) productivity growth, the lower (higher) the price increase. For all activities along *RS*, price increases are inversely proportional to productivity growth.

RS divides quadrants I and III into two parts: the activities are differentiated according to whether they are more or less compensating their relative productivity growth rates:

In IA the activities are redistributing more than their productivity surplus.

In IB they are redistributing only part of their surplus.

In IIIC the activities are only partially compensating for their lower productivity growth by higher relative prices.

In IIID they are more than compensating for their low productivity growth. These are (twice) "grabbers."

On the basis of actual available, if not always reliable, data in different countries, a majority of service activities are located in quadrant III, and more particularly in IIID. In other words, service activities in general tend to belong to the category of twice grabbers, taking advantage of systematic distortions of relative prices in their favor. This means that one way or another they appropriate productivity surpluses from other sectors.

Needless to say, this all assumes a correct evaluation of the volume and price components of services. It must be recalled here that the "quality" component is not explicitly taken into account while integrated (for the largest part) in the price component.[8] If the quality component was shifted from price to volume, this would change the location of service activities both down and to the left.

But, in the more recent period, instead of being regrouped, for a majority, within the same quadrant, service activities have tended to be located in different quadrants, according to more differentiated situations:

1. A number of service activities tend to obtain higher price (and wage) increases, without actually being able to have higher productivity growth rates (in the traditional sense). In short, these are mainly "higher" services; they tend to move along (a).

2. Some of the service activities do register higher productivity growth rates. These are mostly activities that take advantage of the new technologies, for example, telecommunications.[9] These activities tend to move along (b).

3. Other service activities tend to be characterized by lower growth rates, both of productivity and of prices. These activities tend to move along (c). They are mostly traditional services, with low barriers to entry.

This leads to the observation that, while a certain number of service activities tend to leave quadrant III, the grabber aspect of service activities tends to be concentrated on a more limited number of activities, in particular on the so-called higher services. If this is the case, then the contradiction is not so easily solved, while in the case of those higher services, the demand and supply elements alone do not seem to justify the increase in relative prices.

If market imperfections are not negligible, it must be noted that these service activities have been affected, in the recent period, by the growing competitive pressures of internationalization and reduction of barriers to entry due to deregulation. At the same time, supply capacities are very important, and hence supply elasticities are very high.

Concurrently needs and demand are increasing fast, in connection with the transformation of the modes of production. This transformation implies that we are concerned here with the growth of an intermediate demand that is more subject to cost considerations, with firms willing to pay higher prices because these prices seem to correspond to "supplementary" services—services that are not quantitatively, but qualitatively superior (from the user's standpoint).

Services in the Growth Process

The gap between the low productivity growth and the high relative productivity of service activities must be related to the equally contradictory image resulting from the cross-sectional comparisons of the importance of service activities according to levels of development. It is well known that the share of services in GDP is systematically increasing with the level of GNP per head. On Figure 16–3 the relation is quite clear,[10] even if the variance is important.

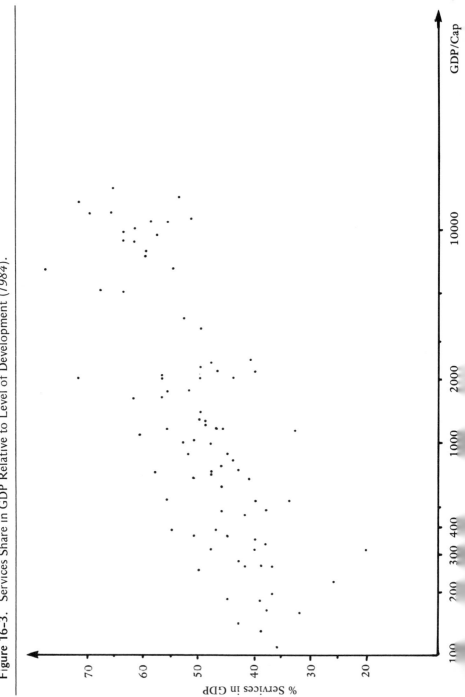

Figure 16-3.   Services Share in GDP Relative to Level of Development (1984).

Of course, the observed relations are only statistical, and by no means causal relations. They do not say anything about underlying mechanisms that have led to both the growth of GNP per head and of the share of services in GDP.

We can only observe that the share of services is greater in developed countries, and that higher levels of development cannot be attributed to higher growth rates of production and productivity in the industrial sector over the last decades. This means that services, in general, play a (positive) role in the growth process, even if this enables us to define neither the conditions, nor the ways and means, nor the extent of their impact.

We must finally stress that the relation is stronger in terms of employment (Figure 16-4) than in terms of GDP. But this reflects, for the main part, what was said earlier about the decrease of relative productivity in the tertiary sector with the level of development.

Of course, there are a number of elements that tend to mitigate or even to reverse this positive relationship. Beside errors and approximations in the data, the two main elements interfering with the relationship between services and overall growth are, on the one hand, the importance of nonmarket services[11] and, on the other hand, the importance and fluctuations of rent activities.

Not only is there no direct causal relationship, but service activities are linked with other activities through complementarity relations, such that only within the framework of consistency conditions—in terms of quantities and of prices—are services likely to contribute to development.

The Logic of Low Productivity Growth in Service Activities Pushed to the Limit of Absurdity

Part of the literature attempts to show that while the share of services in GDP increases with the level of development, this is due to price increase rather than "real" growth. I am referring here for instance to the work done on the basis of the United Nations' "system of international comparisons of gross product and purchasing power." On the basis of those data, R. Summers shows that substituting exchange rates referring to purchasing power parities for the data based on actual exchange rates, causes the positive correlation between the share of services and GNP per head to disappear.[12]

Figure 16-4. Services Share in Employment Relative to Level of Development (1984).

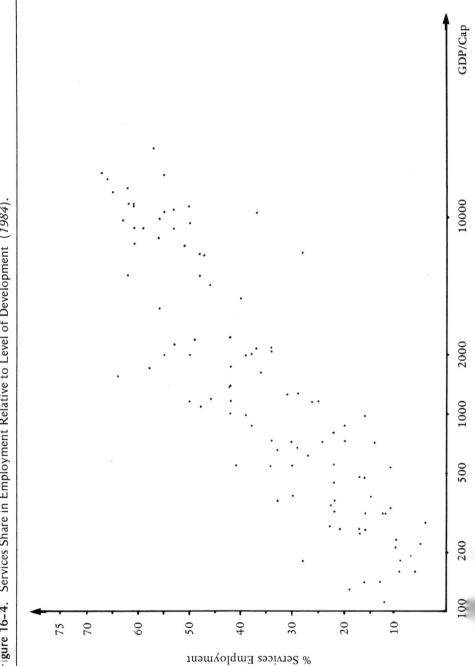

In the first case (actual exchange rates), the share of services ranges from something of the order of 20 percent to something of the order of 45-50 percent: 19.6 percent/6.6 (India); 20.5 percent/9.3 (Sri Lanka); 22.1 percent/13.2 (Philippines); 22.4 percent/4.9 (Malawi) to 49.3 percent/100 (United States); 47.8 percent/63 (United Kingdom); 45.1 percent/82.4 (Denmark).[13]

In the second case (purchasing power parities), both developed and developing countries are at the extremes in terms of the share of services in GDP: 27.8 percent/13 (Thailand); 29.9 percent/75.2 (Netherlands); 30.1 percent/68.4 (Japan) to 46.6 percent/63.9 (United Kingdom); 46.0 percent/24.0 (Jamaica); 45.6 percent/10.3 (Zambia).

Thus the relation is eliminated or even, to a certain extent, reversed. The difference is entirely due to the fact that relative prices of services are higher in developed countries.

The explanation given for the higher service prices in developed countries is simply as follows:

> In high income countries the general level of wages is pulled up by the greater weight of capital- and technology-intensive, high-productivity, high-wage industries. The high wages of these industries, which are mainly commodity producing, carry over to other industries, in which productivity is not so high.[14]

For these reasons, the price index of services do vary from 1 to 5 from the poorest to the richest countries.[15]

We will not discuss methodology here, except to point out that these comparisons are made—for those services for which no direct measure of output and/or price exist—on the basis of the evaluation of the outputs by the inputs, which means on the basis of the hypothesis that productivity is identical in the various countries, despite various attempts to avoid having to make this assumption.

We are obviously left with a contradiction. From the poorest to the richest countries, the share of services is increasing significantly faster in terms of employment than in terms of GDP. This essentially reflects the fact that, with development, relative productivity decreases, due to prices of services becoming increasingly consistent with other prices.

But it is not possible to consider simultaneously that the relative productivities are higher in developing countries (because of higher relative prices of services due to rents and other transfers) and that relative prices are higher in developed countries. In doing so the issue addressed in this chapter, that of measuring the volume of service activities, is thus assumed away.

Indirect Productivity

We need to abandon the idea that it is possible to identify and measure a production volume—that is, to isolate, by analogy, the price and volume components of service activities. Fundamentally, the problem is that the unit-specific production volume cannot be measured, to the extent that the service is integrated in the activity of another unit. Its product and hence its productivity are only indirect and can only be tackled through the user's activity.

What is at stake is more than trying to take into account the successive stages of the production process and thus the various elements that contribute to the production of cumulated value-added. Kuznetz has stressed the necessity to question the meaning of the separate measurement of products and productivities in the case of sectors that are closely integrated.[16] It is indeed of interest to observe how the elements that make up productivity (or competitivity) combine up to the level of the final product. But this comes down to taking into account the production volume and the own productivity of each stage of production and aggregating those to obtain a global picture.

The idea of indirect productivity goes much beyond this. The idea is that, taking into account the co-production aspect of service activities, productivity is not separable as such from use or consumption.

In the case of business services, the service is part of the production process and is not to be dissociated from the activities of the user that are accounted for as value-added. Although, for reasons of statute and accounting, the service activities—paid externally—are not integrated in the transformation activity, they belong, by their very nature, to this activity.

There is thus no possibility to identify the own product of the service activity. As a consequence the service inputs are to be considered as contributing to the product produced by the user. This comes down concretely to stating that service activities are part of the production process and are not different, from the point of view of production and productivity, from that of the internal service activities of the user enterprise and must be treated as such. As a consequence, these co-produced services should not be treated as intermediate consumption, but as elements of value-added.

This is the only way out of the arbitrariness of the methods currently used, which attribute the biggest part of observed variations to the price component while a more or less important part should be integrated in the volume component.

In order to evaluate this shift of value from the volume component to the price component, a parallel has to be drawn between the so-called increase of relative prices of business services and the relative increase of salaries of those employees who are producing, within the firms, the services bought externally. These increases are, of course, related.

Without even adhering to the "marginal productivity theory," it is indeed difficult not to establish a link between the productive contribution of services, be they internal or external, and this increase of relative prices and incomes. In other words, what is called price is, as a matter of fact, at least partly the recognition of the productive contribution of these factors—that is, of the volume of production resulting from their activity.

The only possibility left is thus to look at the product of the user and measure productivity at that level. In other words "indirect" productivity is measured at the level of the product, resulting from the activity of the user.

It is, however, necessary to reject any approach of indirect productivity, as long as it is based on an input-output table characterized by the same arbitrary distinction between price and volume of service activities, that was criticized above.

A study of productivity in the Canadian economy (1961–76) and more particularly of the direct and indirect effects of productivity, shows that notwithstanding their productivity growth, business services induced an increase (and not a reduction) of the labor coefficients in the other sectors.[17] Service activities are also shown to have had the lowest total productivity effects. These results have nothing to do with what we call here indirect productivity. They only show that the increase of services consumed by the enterprises has induced an increase of indirect employment, that is, of labor included in consumed services. In other words this is only an aggregation procedure: productivity is considered at the level of the production of items that are integrated in intermediate consumption.

Measuring indirect productivity means attributing the product of the "user" to the total of direct factors, including those factors that have contributed directly, although in the form of external services, to the production of this product and of its value.

Some Final Comments

The reasoning here concerns mainly the business services, to the extent that they are directly interfering with the production process.

Substituting a measure of indirect productivity to a measure of direct productivity of a service activity does not mean that no attempt can be made to measure the efficiency of the service production unit. But the only possibility is that of devising efficiency indicators in the organization and management of this unit.

A number (still limited) of studies do show the relationship between expenditures related to (internal or external) higher service activities and the performance of firms. While studies showing the effect of advertising have existed for a long time, more recent studies show the impact of research and development and, more generally, of nonmaterial investments.

CONCLUSIONS

All volume and price measures of services done by analogy are arbitrary. This arbitrariness is biased, in the sense that the separation of the volume and price components is usually done in favor of the price component and to the prejudice of the volume component. This obviously leads to both of the widespread assumptions regarding services, namely the drift of relative prices and the slow productivity growth of services.

Ultimately the reasoning based on current definitions leads to rejecting any relationship between the growth of services and of GNP and thus any positive role of services in the growth process. But such a conclusion is already contained in the starting hypotheses.

The relationship between the share of services and overall growth seems clear, except if strict complementarity conditions cease to exist. The productive contribution of services to business also seems quite clear, although much further empirical work is needed.

We must abandon any measurement of the production of services activities in constant prices. Instead we must develop reasoning in terms of value (that is, at current prices) and measure indirect productivity (at the level of the product of the service user).

NOTES

1. We are considering here only market services, and not the nonmarket services for which output is usually measured by the inputs. If what is coming out is measured by what is going in, this would tend to confirm that there is no "production."
2. OECD, "Measurement of Value Added at Constant Prices in Service Activities," in *National Accounts: Sources and Methods* (Paris: 1987).
3. To be more precise, account should be taken of both the number of hours worked and skill differences.
4. For the same reason that one should not estimate the parameters of a production function from value-added. See J. de Bandt, "La validité des fonctions de production intersectorielles," in J. de Bandt, ed., *Les proportions et intensités de facteurs: analyse sectorielle et intersectorielle* (Paris: CNRS, 1974).
5. This is necessarily true only in a closed economy. In an open economy, at least for tradeable goods, the price cannot adapt itself automatically (taking account of the average labor cost) to the labor content, to the extent that the product is exposed to the competitive pressure of productions made in the framework of other price systems.
6. Only a very limited number of exceptions exist: this is particularly the case of the Persian Gulf countries, in which oil rents reduce the relative share of the tertiary sector in GDP.
7. A. Bienayme, *Politique de l'innovation et répartition des revenus* (Paris: Cujas, 1966); P. Templé, "Déformation des Prix Relatifs et Gains de Productivité," *Economie et Statistique* 78 (May 1976): 29–39.
8. J. de Bandt, "La Productivité dans les Activités de Service: Sens et Non Sens," *Cahier "Services"* 1 (Ministère de la Recherche et de la Technologie, Paris, 1985).
9. A. Haid and J. Müller, "Measurement of Total Productivity Growth of the German Telecom Sector," paper, Berlin, 1987.
10. For the following variables:

    $X1$: GNP per head (1984)

    $X2$: Share of services in GDP (1984)

    $X3$: Share of services in GDP (1980)

    $X4$: Share of services in labor force (1980)

For 82 countries for which data are available (World Tables) the following regressions have been calculated:

(1) $X2 = 0.00075 \ X1 + 45.556$
    (3.38)   (36.57) $R^2 = 0.125$

(2) $X4 = 0.00276 \ X1 + 25.95$
    (9.4)   (15.81) $R^2 = 0.525$

(3) $X4 = 0.856 \quad X3 - 4.576$
    (5.27)   (-0.60) $R^2 = 0.258$

The weakest relation is in terms of the share of services in GDP, which is affected by a whole series of phenomena outside the relation considered here. If we exclude for example four eccentric countries, oil rent countries, the last regression becomes

$X4 = 1.43 \quad X3 - 33.6$
     (10.24)   (-5.02) $R^2 = 0.612$

11. N. Gemmell, *Structural Change and Economic Development: The Role of the Service Sector* (New York: Macmillan, 1986).

12. R. Summers, "Services in the International Economy," in R. Inman, ed., *Managing the Service Economy: Prospects and Problems* (Cambridge, England: Cambridge University Press, 1985).

13. The first figure is referring to the share of services in GDP, the second figure to GNP per head, the United States = 100. The figures are for 1975.

14. I.B. Kravis, A. Heston, R. Summers, *World Product and Income: International Comparisons of Real Gross Product* (Baltimore and London: John Hopkins University Press, 1982), p. 333.

15. Ibid., p. 337.

16. Simon Kuznetz, Comments (on V. Fuchs, *Economic Growth and the Rise of Service Employment*), in H. Giersch, *Towards An Explanation of Economic Growth* (Tubingen: J.C.B. Mohr, 1981).

17. H.H. Posner and L. Wesa, "Canadian Productivity Growth: An Alternative (Input-Output) Analysis," Economic Council of Canada, Ottawa, 1984.

17 AN OVERVIEW OF EXISTING STATISTICS AND NOMENCLATURES FOR SERVICES

Adrien Lhomme

There are numerous types of classifications by products, activities, occupation, education, geographic location, and so forth. However, there is no classification concerned solely with services. Service classifications that already exist or are in preparation are all part of classifications of products or activities combining goods and services.

This chapter, therefore, refers to classifications in general, including only a limited discussion of the goods dimension but showing how classifications of services fit into the gamut of classifications. In any case, most of the rules for drawing up classifications are universal and, given the well-known problems in clearly differentiating between goods and services (see Chapter 14), consistency requirements call for homogeneous structures. In spite of the current limited extent of comparability between service statistics, a description of existing service classifications may be a useful exercise if only because analysts are forced to rely on them. The second part of this chapter, dealing with the revision of classifications, will give researchers and economic analysts an idea of the tools that are available to them as of 1989.

DEFINITION

The words *nomenclature* and *classification* are generally used synonymously. French speakers prefer to use (the French word for) *nomenclature*, whereas English speakers prefer *classification*.

A classification is a finite and discrete series of objects or groups of objects that are all different from one another and belong to a specific field. The objects are collected together into groups or classes with a view to their specific characteristics and the objectives for which they are being classified. A classification may be simple or hierarchical (that is, with different levels); in the latter case each level constitutes a classification in itself. See Table 17-1, for example, where level 3, the most detailed, will constitute the reference level for production indexes; level 2, comprising some 60 branches, will be used to collect data for input-output tables, and level 1, with approximately 10 branches, will enable comparisons at a world level.

CURRENT INTERNATIONAL CLASSIFICATIONS

We shall examine two groups of existing classifications: products and activities, but there are others.[1]

International Product Classifications

A product classifications categorizes products according to their characteristics in order to draw up statistics on external trade, production, prices, consumption, or transport.

Products are transportable goods (merchandise), nontransportable goods (immovables), and services. The characteristics used to classify products include

- The origin of the product (fishery products, architects' services)

- The nature of the product (dangerous products, term deposits)

- The purpose of the product (textile machinery, agricultural services)

International product classifications are generally subdivided into goods and goods and services classifications. They deal with external trade (tariff or statistical), production, transport, or other special purposes.

Table 17-2 shows all the international product classifications currently in use. Table 17-3 gives further details for international prod-

Table 17-1. Hierarchical Classifications.

Level 1 (Classification no. 1)	Level 2 (Classification no. 2)	Level 3 (Classification no. 3)
1	11	111
		112
		119
	12	121
		129
2	20	200
.	.	.
.	.	.
.	.	.
.	.	.

Table 17-2. International Product Classifications.

	External Trade		Production	Transport	Other
	Tariff	Statistical	Production	Transport	Other
Goods	CCCN (CCC) CCT (CEC)	SITC-REV.2[b] (UNO) NIMEXE (CEC) SFTC (CMEA)	NIPRO (CEC) CCIAP (CMEA)	CSTE (CEE) NSTR (CEC)	CBEC (UNO) CCIO (UNO)
Services					
Goods and Services[a]			IGGS (UNO)		NACE-CLIO (CEC) CFCM (UNO)

Note: See Appendix 17-A for a glossary of abbreviations. Parentheses indicate the international bodies supervising the classification.
  a. See Table 17-3.
  b. REV.2: second revision of classification.

Table 17-3. International Product Classifications Dealing with Services.

	ICGS		NACE-CLIO		CFCM	
	Goods	Services	Goods	Services	Goods	Services
Level 1	6	4	133	55	8	
Level 2	18	15			33	
Level 3	42	32			34	16
Level 4	101	68				
Level 5	927	366				
Level 6	3.480	1,100				
Structure	Six-level numeric code (8 digits)		One-level numeric code (3 digits). The 186 codes can be regrouped in 44, 26, 25, 7, and 6 branches. Market and nonmarket services codified by a letter.		Three-level numeric code (3 digits). The 16 services codes are spread over the whole of the classification.	
Last version	1976		1971		1968	

Note: See Appendix 17-A for a glossary of abbreviations.

uct classifications dealing with services. (See Appendix 17-A for a glossary of the abbreviations used in the tables.)

International Classifications of Activities

Units of production can be classified according to the activity that they exercise, with a view to drawing up statistics on their outputs, factors of production (labor, capital and raw materials), and yields.

Units of production may be enterprises or organizations (legal units), groups of enterprises (legal-financial units), local units (firms), and units of homogeneous activity (subdivisions of firms).

In fact, the same production unit may have more than one activity, and in this case a distinction is made between principal, secondary, and ancillary activities. The principal activity is distinguished from the secondary activity (activities) on the basis of criteria such as turnover, total wages and salaries, numbers employed, and value-added. Henceforth, the principal activity obviously depends on the choice of criterion. An ancillary activity is one that produces identical services in all similar production units, for their own account.

The main characteristics used to classify activities are:

- The raw material (manufacture of leather goods)
- The production technique (printing, radio, and television)
- The use of the products (manufacture of textile machinery, business services)

In the Council for Mutual Economic Assistance (CMEA) member countries, the classification of activities takes account of the part played by the branches in the system of extended socialist reproduction of capital and of the social organization of labor reflected in specific organization forms (enterprises, farms, economic organizations, and local units).

There are three main international classifications of activities: The ISIC, NACE, and CBNE, *all three of which have a services section.* (See Table 17–4.)

Links between Classifications with a Service Section

Because classifications of activities and products have been developed separately by different bodies at different times, they are only comparable at levels 1 and 2 of the ISIC-REV.2—that is, for 15 and 4 classification headings (Table 17–5). The Customs Cooperation Council (CCC), the UN Statistical Office, and the European Communities are all working at strengthening their links.

CREATION, REVISION, AND HARMONIZATION OF CLASSIFICATIONS

Creation and Revision of Classifications

Classifications are constructed or revised empirically, although certain guidelines are followed.

Table 17-4. International Classifications of Activities.[a]

	ISIC-REV.2		NACE		CBNE	
	Goods	Services	Goods	Services	Goods	Services
Level 1	6	4	6	4	4	12
Level 2	18	15	32	48	27	40
Level 3	42	31	142	201	87	44
Level 4	101	68	441	317		
Level 5			570	317		
Structure	Four-level numeric code (4 digits)		Five-level numeric code (5 digits) distinction market/ nonmarket services codified by a letter		Three-level numeric code (6 digits)	
Last version	1968		1970		1983	

Note: See Appendix 17-A for a glossary of abbreviations.
a. Number of items by level.

First, the classificationist makes every effort to base his (or her) work on concrete data that he summarizes (inductive method) or for which he requests an analysis (algorithm). He avoids any kind of system leading to the creation of classes that would be justifiable in theory but useless in practice. He ensures that the contents of the classes do not overlap and that definitions are clear in spite of a certain arbitrariness inherent in any type of breakdown. The aim is to balance the classification, to give a more or less comparable economic weight to the various headings at the same level, while sometimes justifying exceptions. A given classification must tie in with others covering the same field and be fitted for a continued time series.

Next the classificationist respects certain rules of codification. He avoids equivocal headings and uses the words "and" or "or" where appropriate. He chooses a conventional vocabulary applied uniformly throughout the classification and prefers repeating the same words rather than using synonyms.

Table 17–5. Links between the Services Section of the Classifications of Activities and Products.

Finally, he will construct the classification in stages, drafting a prototype based on similar classifications and concrete observations which he then submits for criticism to experts, professional associations, and users.

While there is no general theory for constructing classifications, this way of making improvements interactively seems to ensure the availability of usable empirical classifications.

Harmonization of Classifications

Harmonization is the correspondence of two or more classifications. Correspondence implies that there is a set of links between the components of classification x and the components of classification y.

There are three possible types of correspondence:

1. n-to-1 correspondence: links n components of classification x with a single component of classification y.
2. 1-to-1 correspondence: links one component of classification x with one component of classification y, the result being symmetrical.
3. n-to-n correspondence: links n components of classification x with n components of classification y. N-to-n correspondence is not recommended for the harmonization of classifications.

More generally, working out the correspondence between two or more classifications often implies "losing" levels of disaggregation. The distinction between transport insurance and other insurance is of great value for trade classification but of little value for production classifications. The identification of branches of activity in an industrialized country might not carry on in a developing country. Finally, with one single service having several origins, it is not always possible to compare a classification of activities with a classification of products. (For instance, where does one include the renting of safe deposit boxes, which may be provided by banks or hotels or both?)

If classifications are to be comparable, they must be either constructed or revised at the same time, while taking into account the requirements of other classifications. Over the last 15 years, there has been great efforts to this effect. While the problems of harmonization should not be overestimated and experience has shown that a fairly restricted number of headings are affected in the long run, we must also be aware that perfect harmonization can never be possible, but that close correlation between classifications is an achievable aim.

CREATION AND REVISION OF INTERNATIONAL CLASSIFICATIONS

The multiplicity of classifications has caused a great deal of time and money to be wasted by economists, statisticians, carriers, and firms involved in external trade. Documents had to be filled in several times over, conversion tables and data processing programs had to be drawn up and updated. In the United States the lack of harmonization has been estimated to cost exporters up to 7.5 percent of the total export value of the products involved. In order to reduce costs and improve analyses and data sharing, major harmonization exercises at the world level began in 1973 under the supervision of the Customs Cooperation Council (CCC) and will probably be completed in 1989 with the revision of the United Nations' ISIC REV.3 and the SOEC's NACE (REV.).

Creation and Revision of International Product Classifications

The new classification of goods set up by the CCC is known as the Harmonized Commodity Description and Coding System (HS).[2] The HS will gradually be brought into use by all the countries in the world except for some Eastern bloc countries and has been used by the European Communities as of January 1988. Experts working on the HS have always taken into account, to the extent possible, the needs expressed by statisticians (external trade, production, and transport), importers and exporters, customs officials, and carriers, and for this reason the HS has now become the nucleus of all international goods classifications.

To sum up:

- The CCCN, the CCT, and special tariff classifications (such as those of the United States) will disappear.

• The SITC-REV.2 has now been revised (SITC-REV.3) and its basic headings (five digits) are drawn from HS headings. The NIMEXE has been replaced by the Combined Nomenclature (CN), the first six digits of which are the HS basic headings.

• New correlation tables will link the NSTR with the HS and the CBEC with the SITC-REV.3 (and thus with the HS).

• The Central Product Classification (CPC) has been set up, and is now linked to the HS, the SITC-REV.3, the ISIC-REV.3, and the NACE-REV. The NIPRO and the CCIO are now redundant.

• The European Communities are going to set up a Central Product Classification of the Communities (CPCCOM), which will probably include a sixth level.

• The NACE-CLIO is already linked to the Combined Nomenclature (CN) and thus to the HS, but this link will be used only for a transitional period until the NACE-REV and the CPCCOM are brought into use. There will certainly be a special level in the NACE-REV for input-output tables (probably level 2 comprising some 70 branches).

The classification of household goods and services has not been revised, but the statistical office of the European Communities has commissioned a study on the possibilities of improving links between the CPC and the classification of household goods and services. The final report of this study makes a few proposals for improvements but concludes that the project is difficult, if not impossible.

A new external trade statistic classification has been set up for balance-of-payments purposes: the Classifications of Exchange of Invisibles (CEI). It is a three-part classification including services, income, and transfers.

Table 17–6 shows all the new or revised international product classifications.

Table 17–7 gives further details for international product classification dealing with services.

Table 17-6. New or Revised International Product Classifications.

| | External Trade | | Production | Transport | Other |
	Tariff	Statistical	Production	Transport	Other
Goods	H.S. (CCC) C.N. (CEC)	SITC-REV.3 (UNO) SFTC (CMEA)	CCIAP (CMEA)	CSTE (CEE) NSTR (CEC)	CBEC (UNO)
Services					
Goods and Services[a]			CPC (UNO) CPCCOM (CEC)		CFCM (UNO)
Services Incomes Transfers[a]		CEI (CEC)			

Note: See Appendix 17-A for a glossary of abbreviations. Parentheses indicate the international bodies supervising the classification.
   a. See Table 17-7.

Table 17-7. New or Revised International Product Classifications Dealing with Services.[a]

	CEI		CPC		CPCCOM		CFCM	
	Incomes Transfers	Services	Goods	Services	Goods	Services	Goods	Services
Level 1	2	1	8	2				8
Level 2	7	10	53	18				33
Level 3	12	32	195	57			34	16
Level 4	40	62	1,020	178				
Level 5			1,551	383				
Structure	Four-level numeric code (4 digits).		Five-level numeric code (5 digits).		Probably six-level numeric code.		Three-level numeric code (3 digits). The 16 services classes are spread over the whole of the classification.	
Version	1989 (?)		1989 (?)		1990 (?)		1983	

Note: See Appendix 17–A for a glossary of abbreviations.
a. Number of items by level.

Revision of International Classifications of Activities

The revision of ISIC (ISIC REV.3) is being achieved by the end of 1988. Work on revision of the NACE (NACE REV) has only just begun and a description would be premature. The correspondence between NACE REV and ISIC REV.3 will be 1-to-1 or n-to-1 at each level. In NACE REV a distinction will be made between market and nonmarket services. It is also expected to have a fifth level. NACE REV will be one of the community statistical standards that will be vital for completion of the communitywide internal market (1992). CBNE will also be revised and linked with ISIC REV.3. (See Table 17-8.)

Table 17-9 summarizes the links between new classifications with a services section.

Table 17-8. Revised International Classifications of Activities.

	ISIC-REV.3		NACE-REV.		CBNE	
	Goods	Services	Goods	Services	Goods	Services
Level 1	6	11				
Level 2	33	26				
Level 3	85	74				
Level 4	154	138				
Level 5						
Structure	–First level is alphabetic (one letter) –Second level is numeric (2 digits) –Other levels are numeric (1 digit)					
Version	1989		1990		?	

Note: See Appendix 17-A for a glossary of abbreviations.

Table 17-9. Links between New Classifications with a Services Section.

Products — External Trade / Production

Levels — CEI: 1, 2, 3, 4 — CPC: 1, 2, 3, 4, 5 — CPCCOM: 1, 2, 3, 4, 5, 6

Number of Services Headings — CEI: 1, 10, 31, 62 — CPC: 2, 18, 57, 178, 383 — CPCCOM

Links

Number of Services Headings — ISIC.REV.3: 4, 24, 60, 122 — NACE.REV. — CBNE

Levels — ISIC.REV.3: 1, 2, 3, 4 — NACE.REV.: 1, 2, 3, 4, 5 — CBNE: 1, 2, 3, 4, 5, 6

Activities

WORK IN HAND ON SERVICE CLASSIFICATIONS

Services experts have not found the ISIC-REV.3 and the CPC described above entirely satisfactory. One criticism was that the two classifications were unbalanced. They considered, for example, that there was too much detail for products of the foodstuffs industries compared with products of data processing industries, which were too highly aggregated.

A group of experts from the statistical institutes of Australia, Canada, the Federal Republic of Germany, France, Hungary, Japan, the Netherlands, Sweden, the United Kingdom, the United Nations, the OECD, and the European Communities therefore met informally in Voorburg in January 1987, when they undertook to make contributions in the major services fields.[3]

The contributions have been examined by the joint United Nations Statistical Office/Statistical Office of the European Communities Working Party on the harmonization of classifications at world level and incorporated into the ISIS-REV.3 and the CPC (and thus into the NACE-REV and the CPCCOM).

In any case, the revision work for the ISIC and the CPC will have to be submitted to the United Nations Statistical Commission for approval in 1989. The NACE-REV and the CPCCOM are due in 1989 and 1990 respectively.

CONCLUSION

For well-known historical reasons, the goods section of the various classifications is the most detailed and has been most thoroughly tested, but current rethinking on services is bound to lead to improvements in classifications in this field, too. Yet we must learn from past errors: the arbitrary way in which classifications were first developed has made harmonization all the harder. As far as services are concerned, national institutes and international or private organizations must not be allowed to set up their own classifications without any concern for harmonization.

The importance of international cooperation cannot be overemphasized. In agreeing to take account of the requirements of other classifications, the Harmonized Commodity Description and Coding System (HS) has broken new ground and led the way. International reference classifications must be constructed or revised together.

Once there is harmonization, it can only be maintained if the bodies that set up the classifications and those that use them work together permanently. It is no longer possible to amend a classification without taking into account the effect on other classifications; neither is it any longer possible to allow divergent interpretations. Greater strictness will be required here, too, if we are not to be left with the same packages and different contents.

Consequently, the work of revising, interpreting, and updating classifications will have to be organized at a world level. In particular, data processing and automatic data transfer systems will have to be set up. This is the minimum price that will have to be paid if statisticians are to reduce to a significant degree the costs born by businesses and improve the work of researchers throughout the world.

Appendix 17-A. Glossary of Abbreviations in English and French.

	English		*French*
CBEC	Classification by Broad Economic Categories	CGCE	Classification par Grandes Catégorie Economiques
CBNE	Classification of the Branches of National Economy	CBEN	Classification des Branches d'Economie Nationale
CCC	Customs Cooperation Council	CCC	Conseil de Coopération Douanière
CCCN	Customs Cooperation Council's Nomenclature	NCCD	Nomenclature du Conseil de la Coopération Douanière
CCIAP	Common Classification of Industrial and Agricultural Products	CCIAP	Classification Commune des Products Industriels et Agricoles
CCIO	Classification of Commodities by Industrial Origin	CCIO	Classification des marchandises par Origine Industrielle
CCT	Common Customs Tariff	TDC	Tarif Douanier Commun
CEC	Commission of European Communities	CCE	Commission des Communautés Européennes
CEI	Classification of Exchange of Invisibles	CEI	Classification des Echanges d'Invisibles
CFCM	Classification of Household Goods and Services	CFCM	Classification des Fonctions de Consommation des Ménages
CMEA	Council for Mutual Economic Assistance	CAEM	Conseil d'Assistance Economique Mutuelle
COFOG	Classification of the Functions of Government	CFAP	Classification des Fonctions des Administrations Publiques

(Appendix 17-A. continued overleaf)

Appendix 17-A. continued

	English		French
CPC	Central Product Classification	CPC	Classification de Produits Centrale
CPCCOM	Future CPC for European Communities	CPCCOM	Future CPC des Communantés Européennes
CSTE	Commodity Classifications for Transport Statistics in Europe	CSTE	Classification des Marchandises pour les Statistiques des Transports én Europe
HS	Harmonized Commodity Description and Coding System	SH	Systèmé Harmonisé de Désignation et de Codification des Marchandises
ICGS	International Standard Classification of all Goods and Services	CIBS	Classification Internationale Type par produits de tous les Biens et Services
ILO	International Labor Organization	BIT	Bureau International du Travail
ISCED	International Standard Classification of Education	CITE	Classification International Type de l'Education
ISCO	International Standard Classification of Occupations	CITP	Classification Internationale Type des Professions
ISIC	International Standard Industrial Classification of all economic activities	CITI	Classification International Type par Industries de toutes les branches d'activités économiques
NACE	General Industrial Classification of Economic Activities within European Communities	NACE	Nomenclature Générale des Activités Economiques dans les Communautés Européennes
NACE-CLIO	Classification for Input-Output Tables	NACE-CLIO	Nomenclature des Tableaux Entrées-Sorties

NIMEXE	Nomenclature des Marchandises pour les statistiques du Commerce Extérieur de la Communauté et du Commerce Extérieur entre les Etats membres
NIPRO	Nomenclature commune des Produits Industriels
NSTR	Nomenclature uniforme des marchandises pour les statistiques des transports, revisée
CTCE	Classification Type du Commerce Extérieur
CTCI	Classification Type pour le Commerce International

NIMEXE	Nomenclature of goods for the external trade statistics of the Community and Statistics of the trade between Member States
NIPRO	Common Nomenclature of Industrial Products
NSTR	Standard Goods Classification for Transport Statistics, Revised
SFTC	Standard Foreign Trade Classification
SITC	Standard International Trade Classification

NOTES

1. There exist classifications such as the International Classification of Occupations of the ILO (ISCO), the International Standard Classification of Education created by UNESCO (ISCED), the United Nation's Classification of the Functions of Government (COFOG), and the European Communities' Nomenclature of Territorial Units for Statistics (NUTS), to name a few.
2. It is composed of 5,019 basic subheadings structured as 1,241 headings and 96 chapters.
3. Post and telecommunication; banking, insurance; real estate; renting of machinery and equipment without operator and renting of personal and household goods; computer and related activities; legal, accounting, bookkeeping, and auditing activities, tax consultancy, business and management consultancy; technical services; research and development; advertising; press agencies; other services; social services; recreational, cultural, and sporting activities; industrial services.

REFERENCES

Beekman, M. "Harmonization of Economic Classifications." Paper for the 44th Session of the ISI, Madrid, September 1983.

C.C.C. International Convention on the Harmonized Commodity Description and Coding System. 26–38 rue de l'Industrie, B-1040 Brussels.

CMEA. Conversion key between the classification of branches of the national economy of the CMEA member countries and the U.N. International Standard Industrial Classification of All Economic Activities, CMEA Secretariat, Moscow, May 1983, GE. 83–33225.

CMEA. Conversion key between the U.N. International Standard Industrial Classification of All Economic Activities and the classification of branches of national economy of the CMEA member countries, CMEA Secretariat, Moscow, 1983, GE. 83–33406.

Conference of European Statisticians. Classification of national economy branches countries, members of the Council for Mutual Assistance, Conf. Eur. State/WG.22/GR.2/3/add 1, December 22, 1965.

Ebensberger, Dr. Hans. Internationale Wirtschaftszweig und Gütersystematiken und Ihre Harmonisierung, Wirtschaft und Statistik, 2/1986, pp. 77–96.

EUROSTAT. REGIO, Regional Data Bank, Division B2, January 1987.

_____ . Nomenclature Commune des produits industriels NIPRO, Edition 1975, Luxembourg, 1976.

_____ . European System of Integrated Economic Accounts, ESA, Second Edition, Luxembourg, 1979.

_____ . N.A.C.E., General Industrial Classification of Economic Activities within the European Communities, Luxembourg, 1975.

Hoguet, J. Plaidoyer pour une nomenclature internationale des marchandises, Lecture for Basle University, 1976.

INSEE, Division Nomenclatures. Notes de Méthode, Construction et coordination des Nomenclatures, F.2, 1981.

INSEE. Note rapide sur quelques aspects des méthodes de construction des nomenclatures, 28 janvier 1983, n° A4294/943.

_____ . Note sur quelques structures de base dans le domaine des nomenclatures et tables (note de travail), Paris, 2 février 1983, n° A4301/943.

_____ . Normalisation: Représentation des éléments de données. Codification, Fascicule établi par la division nomenclatures, F.8, 1983.

_____ . Les nomenclatures statistiques, 14 mai 1984, n° A4872/943.

Lenstang, Ph. Le nouveau système français de nomenclatures d'activités et de produits, Economie et Statistique, décembre 1973.

_____ . Réflexions sur la construction des nomenclatures, Sociologica Ruralis, XVIII/4, van Gorcum, Assen, 1978.

_____ . Les nomenclatures de produits et d'activités, situation actuelle et travaux en cours, Courrier des Statistiques, n° 21, janvier 1982, pp. 33–42.

Lux, Michael. The Harmonized Commodity Description and Coding System—current situation and consideration—internal publication of EUROSTAT.

Mesnage, M. Un graphisme et une notation symboliques pour les structures de classifications économiques, OSCE, OS/13/71-F.

N.C.C.D. Nomenclature du Conseil de Coopération Douanier (NCCD), 26-38, rue de l'Industrie, B-1040 Brussels.

O.S.C.E. NST 1968, Luxembourg, 1968.

Rousseau, R. Pourquoi change-t-on de nomenclature? Economie et Statistique n° 70, septembre 1975.

_____ . Le nomenclature détaillée de produits, bloc note de l'O.E.P., juillet-août 1981.

U.N. Classification by Broad Economic Categories, Statistical Papers, Series M, n° 53, REV. 1, New York, 1976.

_____ . International Standard Industrial Classification of All Economic Activities, Series M, n° 4, REV. 2, New York, 1968.

_____ . International Standard Classification of All Goods and Services (ICGS), Draft, E/CN.3/493, 22 juin 1976.

_____ . Classification of Commodities by Industrial Origin, Series M, n° 43, REV. 1, New York, 1971.

_____ . Standard International Trade Classification, Series M, n° 34 REV. 3, New York, 1986.

_____ . First draft of the Central Product Classification Provisiona, ST/ESA/STAT/SER.M/77*, June 30, 1986.

_____ . First complete draft of the revised International Standard Industrial Classification of All Economic Activities (ISIC), Provisional, ST/ESA/STAT/ SER.M/4/REV. 3*, June 30, 1986.

_____ . Système de compatabilité nationale, Etudes Méthodologiques, Series F, n° 2, REV. 3, New York, 1970.

_____ . Classification of the functions of government, Series M, n° 70, New York, 1980.

Wilson, B. Une classification internationale de frêt pour l'établissement de statistiques des transports (recommandation n° 21 de l'ONU-CEC), Information de l'EUROSTAT, 2ème trimestre 1987, pp. 28–35.

BIBLIOGRAPHY

Aho, C. Michael and Aronson, Jonathan D. 1985. *Trade Talks: America Better Listen!* Council on Foreign Relations, Inc.

Aho, C. Michael and Levinson, Marc. 1987. "A Canadian Opportunity." *Foreign Policy*, No. 66, Spring, pp. 143–155.

Albert, Michel and Boissonnat, Jean. *Crise Krach Boom.* Paris, Seuil.

Albrecht, K. and Zemke, R. 1985. *Service America, Doing Business in the New Economy.* Homewood, Ill., Dow Jones Irwin.

Allen, F. 1984. *Reputation and Services.* Wharton School, University of Pennsylvania, Discussion Paper No. 3, November.

Aronson, J.D. and Cowhey, P.F. 1984. *Computer, Data Processing and Communication Services.* Ann Arbor, University of Michigan, Research Seminar in International Economics, October, 27 p.

_____. 1984. *Trade in Services: A Case for Open Markets.* Washington, D.C., American Enterprise Institute for Public Policy Research, 46 p.

Aronson, J.D. 1986. *Trade in Services, An Agenda for International Trade Negotiations.* Washington, D.C., mimeograph, February, 10 p.

Aronson, Jonathan D. and Cowhey, P.F. 1988. "When Countries Talk: International Trade in Telecommunications Services." Cambridge, Mass., Ballinger.

Ascher, Bernard and Whichard, Obie G. 1987. "Improving Services Trade Data, in Balassa, Carol. Negotiation of Services in the U.S.-Israel Free Trade Area. *Journal of World Trade Law*, forthcoming.

Atinc, A. et al. 1984. "International Transactions in Services and Economic Development." *Trade and Development*, No. 5, pp. 141–214.

319

de Bandt, J. et al. 1985. *La Productivité dans les Services.* Paris. Ministère de la recherche et de la Technologie, November.

de Bandt, J., ed. 1985. *Les Services dans les Sociétés Industrielles.* Paris. Economica.

de Bandt, Jacques. 1988. "Le Débat sur la productivité dans les services: des problèmes mal posés." *Revue d'Economie Industrielle,* Special issue: Le dynamisme des services aux entreprises, No. 43, Paris, 1st Semester.

Bannon, M. and Blair, S. 1985. *Services Activities, The Information Economy and the Role of Regional Center.* Dublin, University College, January, 173 p.

Barcet, André and Bonamy Joël. 1988. "Services et transformation des modes de production." *Revue d'Economie Industrielle,* Special issue: Le dynamisme des services aux entreprises, No. 43, Paris, 1st Semester.

Baumol, W. J. 1985. "Productivity Policy and the Service Sector," in Inman, R.P., ed., *Managing the Service Economy, Prospects and Problems.* Cambridge University Press, pp. 301–318.

Bavishi, V. B. and Wyman, H. E. 1983. *Who Audits the World: Trends in the World Accounting Profession.* Storrs, Conn., Center for Transnational Accounting of Connecticut School of Business Administration, 1109 p.

Beca, R. 1985. *Les Flux de Données d'Accompagnement du Commerce International: Elements pour une Négotiation Internationale.* Paris, Ministère du Développement Industriel et du Commerce Extérieur, 11 p.

Beniger, James R. 1986. *The Control Revolution: Technological and Economic Origins of the Information Society.* Cambridge, Mass., Harvard University Press.

Benz, S. 1985. "Trade Liberalization and the Global Service Economy." *Journal of World Trade Law,* March-April, pp. 95–120.

Bergsten, C. Fred. 1987. "Economic Imbalances and World Politics." *Foreign Affairs,* Vol. 65, No. 4, pp. 770–794.

Berthelot, Yves. 1988. "Quatre idées sur les services, la croissance et le développement." *Revue d'Economie Industrielle,* Special Issue: Le dynamisme des services aux enterprises, No. 43, Paris, 1st Semester.

Bhagwati, J.N. 1984. "Splintering and Disembodiment of Services and Developing Nations." *World Economy,* June, pp. 133–144.

_____. 1987. "International Trade in Services and Its Relevance for Economic Development," in Giarini, Orio, ed., *The Emerging Service Economy.* Oxford, Pergamon Press for the Services World Forum, Geneva.

Black, F. 1985. "The Future for Financial Services," in Inman, R.P., ed., *Managing the Service Economy, Prospects and Problems.* Cambridge University Press, pp. 223–230.

Boehme, H. 1978. *Restraints on Competition in World Shipping.* London, Trade Policy Research Centre, 86 p.

_____. 1983. "Current Issues and Progress in European Shipping Policy." *World Economy,* Vol. 6, No. 3, September, pp. 325–352.

Brand, Stewart. 1987. *The Media Lab: Inventing the Future at MIT.* New York, Viking Penguin, Inc.

Brender, A., Chevallier, A. and Pisani-Ferry, J. 1980. *Etats-Unis: Croissance, crise, changement technique dans une économie tertiare.* Paris, Centre d'Etudes Prospectives et d'Informations Internationales.

Bressand, A. 1985. *Le Prochain Monde.* Paris, Seuil, 316 p.

_____. 1985. *Services in the New Worldeconomy. In Search of a Conceptual Framework.* Hannover, International Symposium on the Services Sector, 12-13 May, 12 p.

_____. 1986. *Services, Corporate Strategies and GATT Negotiations: A New Challenge for Europe.* Ditchley Park Conference, 14-16 February, 21 p.

_____. 1987. "Wealth Creation and the Role of Financial Markets in the Early Twenty-First Century." *Finance and The International Economy.* The Amex Bank Review, Oxford University Press, New York.

_____. 1987. "Currency Chaos. The Newest Strategic Tool." *The International Economy,* Paris, October-November.

_____. 1988. "Regulation in the Age of Network Strategies." *Project PROMETHEE Perspectives,* No. 5, Paris, PROMETHEE, March.

Bressand, Albert, Distler, Catherine and Nicolaïdis, Kalypso A. 1988. "European Interconnection and the "OGI" Dilemmas." *Project PROMETHEE Perspectives,* No. 6, Paris, PROMETHEE, June.

Bressand, Albert and Nicolaïdis, Kalypso A. 1988. "Les Services au coeur de l'économie relationelle." *Revue d'Economic Industrielle,* Special issue: Le dynamisme des services aux entreprises, No. 43, Paris, 1st Semester.

Brochand, B. and Lendrevie, J. 1983. *Le publicitor.* Paris, Dalloz, 568 p.

Brock, W.E. 1982. "A Simple Plan for Negotiation on Trade in Services." *World Economy,* Vol. 5, No. 3, November, pp. 229-240.

Broclawski, J.P., de Gaulle, Y. and Miermont, A. 1981. "De Bons Résultats pour l'Economie Française: Les Echanges de Services." *Paris, Economie, Previsions Statistiques et Etudes Financières,* No. 49, April, pp. 25-48.

Bulthuis, R., van Holst, B. and de Wit, G.R. 1985. *The Service Sector and Technological Developments.* Rotterdam, The Netherlands Economics Institute Foundation, April.

Butler, Richard E. 1988. "Interconnection and Trade: Priorities for WATTC-88." *Project PROMETHEE Perspectives,* No. 7, Paris, PROMETHEE, July.

Canton, I.D. 1984. "Learning to Love the Service Economy." *Harvard Business Review,* May-June, pp. 89-97.

Carter, R.L. and Dickinson, G.M. 1979. *Barriers to Trade in Insurance.* London Trade Policy Research Centre, 84 p.

Chamoux, J.P. 1980. *L'Information sans Frontière.* Paris, Documentation Française, 179 p.

Channon, D.F. 1978. *The Service Industries: Strategy, Structure and Financial Performance.* London, MacMillan, 292 p.

Chant, J.F. 1984. *The Canadian Treatment of Foreign Banks: A Case Study in the Workings of the National Treatment Approach.* Ann Arbor, University of Michigan, Research Seminar in International Economics, October 44 p.

Clark, M.G. 1986. *Services and the General Agreement on Tariffs and Trade.* Discussion Paper Commissioned by the International Economics Program of the Institute for Research on Public Policy, Ottawa, January, 40 p.

Cohen, M. and Morante, T. 1981. "Elimination of Non-Tariff Barriers to Trade in Services: Recommendations for Future Negotiations." *Law and Policy in International Business*, Vol. 13, No. 2, pp. 495-519.

Cooper, Richard N. 1987. "Survey of Issues and Critical Review of the Conference on International Trade in Services." Paper delivered at the Pacific Trade and Development Conference, Wellington, New Zealand, January, Mimeograph. Harvard University.

Deardorff, A.V. 1984. *Comparative Advantage and International Trade and Investment in Services.* Ann Arbor, University of Michigan, Research Seminar on International Economics, November 7, 35 p.

Diebold, W. Jr. and Stalson, H. 1983. "Negotiating Issues in International Service Transactions, in Cline, W.R., ed., *Trade Policy for the 1980s.* Washington, D.C., Institute for International Economics.

Diebold, William, Jr., ed. 1988. *Bilateralism, Multilateralism and Canada in U.S. Trade Policy.* Cambridge, Mass., Ballinger for Council on Foreign Relations.

Distler, Catherine, ed. 1988. "La Déréglementation dans les années 90." *Le Communicateur*, Special issues, No. 5, Paris, July.

Dizard, Wilson P. and Turner, Lesley D. 1987. "Telecommunications and the U.S.-Canada Free Trade Talks." Paper published by the International Communications Project of the Center for Strategic and International Studies, Washington, D.C., Mimeograph.

Dobell, R., McRae, J.J. and Desbois, M. 1986. *The Service Sector in Canadian Economy: Government Policies for Future Developments.* Halifax, Institute for Research on Public Policy.

Drake, William. 1988. "WATTC-88: Restructuring the International Telecommunication Regulations." *Telecommunications Policy*, September.

Dwyer, D.F. Jr. 1984. *Trade Barriers to United States Motion Picture and Television Pre-Recorded Entertainment, Publishing and Advertising.* New York, CBS Inc., September, 33 p.

Eken, S. 1985. "Integration of Domestic and International Financial Markets: The Japanese Experience." *World Bank Staff Paper*, March, pp. 499-548.

Eward, R. 1985. *The Deregulation of International Telecommunications.* Dedham, Mass., Artech, 400 p.

Ewing, A.F. 1985. "Why Freer Trade in Services Is in the Interest of Developing Countries?" *Journal of World Trade Law*, Vol. 19, No. 2, March-April, pp. 147-169.

Faulhaber, G.R., Noam, E. and Tasley, R., eds. 1986. *The Impact of Information Technology on the Service Sector.* Cambridge, Mass., Ballinger.

_____. 1986. *Services in Transition: The Impact of Information Technology on the Service Sector.* Cambridge, Mass., Ballinger.

Feketekuty, G. 1984. *Negotiating Strategies for Liberalizing Trade and Investment in Services.* Ann Arbor, University of Michigan, Research Seminar on International Economics, October, 17 p.

Feketekuty, G. and Aronson, J.D. 1984. "Meeting the Challenges of the World Information Economy." *World Economy*, Vol. 7, No. 1, March, pp. 63–86.

Feketekuty, G. and Hauser, K. 1985. "The Impact of Information Technology on Trade in Services." *Transnational Data Report*, Vol. 8, No. 4, pp. 220–224.

Feketekuty, G. 1986. "Trade in Professional Services: A Trade Policy Perspective." *Barriers to International Trade in Professional Services.* University of Chicago Legal Forum, Vol. 1, Summer.

_____. 1987. "About Trade in Tourism Services," in Giarini, O., ed., *The Emerging Service Economy.* Oxford, Pergamon Press for the Services World Forum, Geneva.

_____. 1987. "Trade Policy Objectives in Telecommunications." Paper published by the International Telecommunications Union in connection with the Legal Symposium of Telecom 87, a conference organized by the International Telecommunications Union in Geneva, Switzerland, October.

_____. 1988. "International Trade in Services: An Overview and Blueprint for Negotiations." Cambridge, Mass., Ballinger.

Findlay, C.C. 1983. *Australian International Civil Aviation Policy and the ASEAN-Australia Dispute.* ASEAN-Australia Joint Research Project, Kuala Lumpur and Canberra, 61 p.

_____. 1985. *A Framework for Services Trade Policy Questions.* Canberra, Australia-Japan Research Centre, Research Paper No. 16, 54 p.

Fitzpatrik, J. 1985. *Technology and Economic Development: The Role of Private Services.* Dublin, Regional Studies Association, March.

Foucher, Michel. 1988. *Fronts et frontières: Un tour du monde géopolitique.* Paris, Fayard.

Fraser, Donald R. and Cooper, S. Kerry. 1984. *Banking Deregulation and The New Competition in Financial Services.* Cambridge, Mass., Ballinger.

Freeman, Harry. 1987. "The Importance of Services," in Fried, E.R. and Tresize, H.P., eds. *Building a Canadian-American Free Trade Area.* Washington, D.C., Brookings Institution.

_____. 1985. *Potential of the Services Sector in Job Creation.* Hannover, International Symposium on the Services Sector, 12–15 May, 32 p.

Fuchs, V.R. 1964. *Productivity Trends in the Goods and Services Sectors 1929–1961: A Preliminary Survey.* Study No. 89, New York, National Bureau of Economic Research, 42 p.

_____. 1968. *The Services Economy.* New York, National Bureau of Economic Research, 280 p.

_____. 1969. *Production and Productivity in the Service Industries.* New York, Columbia University Press, 395 p.

_____. 1980. *Economic Growth and the Rise of Service Employment.* New York, National Bureau of Economic Research, 30 p.

_____. 1985. "An Agenda for Research on the Service Sector, in Inman, R.P., ed., *Managing the Service Economy, Prospects and Problems.* Cambridge University Press, pp. 319-326.

Gershuny, J. and Miles, I. 1983. *The New Service Economy: The Transformation of Employment in Industrial Societies.* London, Frances Pinter, 283 p.

Gershuny, Jonathan I. 1987. "The Future of Service Employment," in Giarini, O., ed., *The Emerging Service Economy.* Oxford, Pergamon Press for the Services World Forum, Geneva.

Giarini, O. 1981. "Some Considerations in the Activity of Insurance Business and Its Relevance for a General Reassessment of Economic Theory." *The Geneva Papers on Risk and Insurance.* Geneva, Vol. 6, No. 21, October, pp. 44-103.

_____. 1984. "The Notion of Economic Value in Post-Industrial Society." *Cycles, Value and Employment.* Oxford, Pergamon Press, 43 p.

_____. 1985. "The Consequences of Complexity in Economics: the Vulnerability, Risk and Rigidity Factors in Supply." *The Theory and Practice of Complexity.* Tokyo, The United Nations University, pp. 133-145.

Giarini, Orio, ed. 1987. *The Emerging Service Economy.* Oxford, Pergamon Press for the Services World Forum, Geneva.

Giarini, Orio. 1988. "Les Nouvelles conditions du progrès économique: de la rigidité de l'offre à l'économie de service." *Revue d'Economie Industrielle,* Special issue: Le dynamisme des services aux entreprises, No. 43, Paris, 1st Semester.

_____. *The Limits to Certainty-Facing Risks in the New Service Economy.* Forthcoming.

Gibbs, M. 1985. "Continuing the International Debate on Services." *Journal of World Trade Law,* Vol 19, No. 3, May-June, pp. 199-218.

Goldfinger, Charles. 1986. *La Géofinance.* Paris, Odyssée/Seuil.

Gosser, Alfred, ed. 1987. "Les Pays d'Europe occidentale." *Notes et Etudes Documentaires.* La Documentation française, Special issue, No. 4837-38.

Gramlich, E.M. 1985. "Government Services," in Inman, R.P., ed., *Managing the Service Economy, Prospects and Problems.* Cambridge University Press, pp. 273-289.

Gray, P.H. 1983. "A Negotiating Strategy for Trade in Services." *Journal of World Trade Law,* Vol. 17, No. 5, September-October, pp. 377-388.

Grey, R. de. 1983. *Trade Computer Services.* Montreal, Royal Bank of Canada, Mimeograph.

_____. 1984. *Negotiating About Trade and Investment in Services.* Ann Arbor, University of Michigan, Research Seminar in International Economics, October, 17 p.

_____. 1986. *A Not-So-Simple Plan for Negotiating on Trade in Services.* London, Mimeograph, 20 p.

Griffiths, B. 1975. *Invisible Barriers to Invisible Trade.* London, MacMillan, 178 p.

Gunn, Thomas G. 1987. *Manufacturing for Competitive Advantage: Becoming a World Class Manufacturer.* Cambridge, Mass., Ballinger.

Hart, Jeffrey A. 1987. "The Employment Impact of International Trade in Services." Mimeograph forthcoming in volume to be published by the National Academy of Sciences.

Herman, B. and van Holst, B. 1985. *International Trade in Services: Some Theoretical and Practical Problems.* Rotterdam, Netherlands Economic Institute, September, 32 p.

Hindley, B. and Smith, A. 1984. "Comparative Advantage and Trade in Services." *World Economy*, Vol. 7, No. 4, December (1985), pp. 369-389.

Hindley, Brian. 1987. "Introducing Services into the GATT." Trade Policy Research Centre, London, Mimeograph.

Hindley, G. 1982. *Economic Analysis and Insurance Policy in the Third World.* London, Trade Policy Centre, 62 p.

Holmstrom, B. 1985. "The Provision of Services in a Market Economy," in Inman, R.P., ed., *Managing the Service Economy, Prospects and Problems.* Cambridge University Press, pp. 183-213.

Imaï, Ken-Ichi. 1988. "International Corporate Networks: A Japanese Perspective." *Project PROMETHEE Perspectives*, No. 6, Paris, PROMETHEE, June.

Inman, R.P., ed. 1986. *Managing the Service Economy: Prospects and Problems.* Cambridge, Cambridge University Press, 336 p.

Jackson, John H. 1987. "Potential Umbrella MTN Agreement on Services." American Enterprise Institute, Washington, D.C., Mimeograph, forthcoming.

Jussawalla, M. 1985. "Constraints on Economic Analysis of Transborder Data Flows." *Media, Culture and Society*, Vol. 7, No. 3, London, Sage, pp. 297-312.

_____. 1987. "The Information Revolution and Its Impact on the World Economy." Paper prepared for the international seminar, Toward an International Service and Information Economy: A New Challenge for the Third World, sponsored by the Friedich Ebert Foundation, Mimeograph, forthcoming.

Kakabadse, Mario A. 1987. "International Trade in Services: Prospects for Liberalization in the 1990's." Atlantic Paper 64. New York, Croom Helm, for the Atlantic Institute for International Affairs.

Kane, E.J. 1984. "Technological and Regulatory Forces in the Developing Fusion of Financial Services Competition." *Journal of Finance*, Vol. 39, No. 3, July, pp. 759-806.

Karunaratne, N.D. 1985. "The Information Revolution, Australia and the Developing Neighbours." *Economia Internazionale*, Vol. 38, No. 2, March, pp. 179-196.

Kasper, Daniel M. 1988. *Deregulation and Globalization: Liberalizing International Trade in Air Services.* Cambridge, Mass., Ballinger.

Kendrick, J.W. 1985. "Measurement of Output and Productivity in the Service Sector," in Inman, R.P., ed., *Managing the Service Economy, Prospects and Problems.* Cambridge University Press, pp. 111-123.

Keohane, Robert and Nye, Joseph. 1977. *Power and Interdependence.* Boston, Little, Brown.

Kierzkowski, H. 1984. *Services in Development Process and Theory of International Trade.* Geneva, Graduate Institute of International Studies, June, 40 p.

Kravis, I.B. 1983. *Services in the Domestic Economy and in World Transactions.* University of Pennsylvania, National Bureau of Economic Research Working Paper, No. 1124, May (1984), 39 p.

_____. 1985. "Services in World Transactions," in Inman, R.P., ed., *Managing the Service Economy, Prospects and Problems.* Cambridge University Press, pp. 135-161.

Krommenacker, R.J. 1975. *Les Nations Unies et l'Assurance-Réassurance.* Paris, Librairie Générale de Droit et de Jurisprudence, 215 p.

_____. 1984. *World-Traded Services: The Challenge for the Eighties.* Dedham, Mass., Artech House, 222 p.

_____. 1979. "Trade-Related Services and the GATT." *Journal of World Trade Law*, Vol. 13, No. 6, November, pp. 510-522.

_____. 1986. "Services, Their Regulatory and Policy Framework in the Light of the Emerging Integrated Services Digital Networks (ISDN)." *Proceedings of the Pacific Telecommunications Conference.* Honolulu, January.

_____. 1986. "Discussions on Services in GATT." *Transnational Data and Communications Report*, February, pp. 15-16.

_____. 1986. "The Impact of Information Technology on Trade Interdependence." *Journal of World Trade Law*, Vol. 20, No. 4, July-August, pp. 381-400.

_____. 1987. "Services and Space Technology: The Emergence of Space Generated, Highly Integrated Goods and Services (IGS," in Giarini, O., ed., *The Emerging Service Economy.* Oxford, Pergamon Press for the Services World Forum, Geneva.

Krommenacker, Raymond J. and Roulet, Jean Rémy. 1987. "Bibliography, Research Programmes and Institutions Related to Services," in Giarini, O., ed., *The Emerging Service Economy.* Oxford, Pergamon Press for the Services World Forum, Geneva.

Kodjo, Edem. 1988. *L'Occident: du déclin au défi.* Paris, Stock.

Langdale, J.V. 1984. *Information Services in Australia and Singapore.* ASEAN-Australia Joint Research Project, Kuala Lumpur and Canberra, 37 p.

Lanvin, Bruno. 1987. "International Trade in Services, Information Services and Development: Some Issues." UNCTAD, Discussion Paper 23. Geneva, Mimeograph.

_____. 1988. "Services intermédiares et développement." *Revue d'Economie Industrielle*, Special issue: Le dynamisme des services aux entreprises, No. 43, Paris, 1st Semester.

Lanvin, B. and Prieto, F. 1986. "Les Services, Clé du Développement Economique?" *Revue Tiers Monde*, Vol. 27, No. 105, January-March, pp. 97-108.

Larrera de Morel, B. and Dubarry, J.P. 1981. *Le Tertiaire Exposé: Situation et Perspectives des Echanges Invisibles.* Paris, Documentation Française, 109 p.

Legris, P. and Jegon, A. 1983. "La Contribution des Services à l'Equilibre Extérieur: Le Cas Français et quelques exemples étrangers." *Banque*, No. 426, March, pp. 323-340.

Leveson, I. 1985. *The Service Economy in Economic Development.* New York, Hudson Strategy Group Inc., 10 p.

_____. 1985. "Services in the U.S. Economy," in Inman, R.P., ed., *Managing the Service Economy, Prospects and Problems.* Cambridge University Press, pp. 89-102.

Lowenfield, A. 1986. "GATT Principles and an Agreement on Services." *Barriers to International Trade in Professional Services.* University of Chicago Legal Forum, Vol. 1, Summer.

MacDonald, S. and Mandeville, T. 1984. *Telecommunications in ASEAN and Australia.* ASEAN-Australia Joint Research Project, Kuala Lumpur and Canberra, 32 p.

Madec, A. 1981. "Aspects Economiques et Juridiques des Flux Transfrontières des Données. *Problèmes Economiques et Sociaux.* January, pp. 5-16.

Maitland, Donald (Sir). 1988. "Sequel to 'The Missing Link.'" *Project PROMETHEE Perspectives*, No. 7, Paris, PROMETHEE, July.

Malka, B. and Prin, E. 1985. *Du Secteur Tertiaire à l'Economie des Services: Une Bibliographie Internationale de 1979 à nos Jours.* Paris, Centre National de al Recherche Scientifique, 374 p.

Martinez, L. 1985. *Communications Satellites: Power Politics in Space.* Dedham, Mass., Artech, 320 p.

Malmgren, H.B. 1985. "Negotiating International Rules for Trade in Services." *World Economy*, Vol. 8, No. 1, March, pp. 11-26.

Meyer, N. Dean and Boone, Mary E. 1986. *The Information Edge.* Holt, Rinehart & Winston of Canada, Ltd.

Momigliano, F. and Siniscalco, O. 1983. "The Growth of Service Employment: A Reappraisal." *Banca Nazionale del Lavoro, Quarterly Review*, No. 142, September.

Nayyar, D. 1986. *International Trade in Services, Implications for Developing Countries.* New Delhi, Export-Import Bank of India, 33 p.

Nicolaïdis, Kalypso A. 1988. "Contactors vs. Contractors: Towards an Integrated Approach to Defining Trade in Services." Working Paper 39, PROMETHEE, Paris.

_____. 1988. "Deregulation vs. Liberalization: Old Synergies, New Dilemmas." *Project PROMETHEE Perspectives*, No. 5, Paris, PROMETHEE, March.

Nora, S. and Minc. A. 1978. *L'Informatisation de la Société*. Paris, Documentation Française, 152 p.

Nusbaumer, J. 1983. "Some Implications of Becoming a Services Economy." *Communication Regulation and International Business*. J. Rada and G. Russel Pipe, eds. Amsterdam, North-Holland, pp. 23–37.

_____. 1985. "L'Economie des Services: Nouvelle Donne de l'Economie." *Le Secteur des Services: Quel Avenir pour le Luxembourg?* N. von Kunitzki, ed., Luxembourg, Institut Universitaire International, pp. 13–27.

_____. 1985. "Services and the International Economic Agenda." *International Geneva*. Graduate Institute of International Studies, pp. 100–106.

_____. 1986. "Services in the International Economy: Issues and Prospects." (Forthcoming, J. Rada, ed., North-Holland.)

_____. 1986. "Services in the World Economy: the Issues." *Kuelgazdasag*, pp. 3–10 (*Hungarian Economic Journal*—in Hungarian).

_____. 1986. *Les Services: Nouvelle Donne de l'Economie*. Paris, Economica, 1984, 142 p. English version forthcoming: *Services, the New Deal*. Boston, Kluwer-Nijhoff.

_____. 1987. *Services in the Global Market*. Boston, Kluwer Academic Publishers.

_____. 1987. *The Services Economy: Lever to Growth*. Norwell, Mass., Kluwer Academic Publishers.

Organization for Economic Cooperation and Development. 1987. *Elements of a Conceptual Framework for Trade in Services*. Paris.

Oulton, N. 1983. *International Trade in Services and the Comparative Advantage of EC Countries*. Ditchley Park, Trade Policy Research Centre Meeting, April. Mimeograph.

Petit, Pascal. 1986. *Slow Growth and the Service Economy*. London, Frances Pinter (Publishers) Limited.

_____. 1988. *La Croissance tertiaire*. Paris, Economica.

_____. 1988. "Tertiarisation, croissance et emploi: quelles nouvelles logiques?" *Revue d'Economie Industrielle*, Special issue: Le dynamisme des services aux entreprises, No. 43, Paris, 1st Semester.

Philipps, A. and Berlin, M. 1985. *Technology and Financial Services: Regulatory Problems in a Deregulatory Environment*. Wharton School, University of Pennsylvania. Discussion Paper.

Pipe, Russ. 1987. "The Ultimate Bypass." *Datamation*, August 1.

Porter, M.E. and Millar, V.E. 1985. "How Information Gives you Competitive Advantage." *Harvard Business Review*, No. 4, July-August, pp. 149-160.

Rada, J. 1984. "Advanced Technologies and Development: Are Conventional Ideas about Comparative Advantage Obsolete?" Geneva. *Trade and Development*, No. 5.

_____. 1987. "Information Technology and Services," in Giarini, O., ed., *The Emerging Service Economy*. Oxford, Pergamon Press for the Services World Forum, Geneva.

Reboud, L. 1984. "L'Importance Economique des Services." *Le Marché Commun des Services*. Grenoble, Centre Universitaire de Recherche Européenne et Internationale, March 1, pp. 3–35.

_____. 1985. "Signification d'un Marché Commun dans le Domaine des Services au Regard de la Libéralisation des Echanges et du Protectionnisme." *Le Protectionnisme*. Lassudrie-Duchéne, B. and Reiffers, J.L., eds. Paris, Economica, pp. 335–346.

Richardson, John. 1987. "A sub-sectorial Approach To Services' Trade Theory," in Giarini, O., ed., *The Emerging Service Economy*. Oxford, Pergamon Press for the Services World Forum, Geneva.

_____. 1987. "Tourism Services," in Giarini, O., ed., *The Emerging Service Economy*. Oxford, Pergamon Press for the Services World Forum, Geneva.

Riddle, D.I. *Services-Led Growth: The Role of the Service Sector in World Development*. New York, Praeger, 290 p.

Rimmer, P.J. 1984. *Consulting Services: Supply to South-East Asia from Australia*. ASEAN-Australia Joint Research Project, Kuala Lumpur and Canberra, 92 p.

Robinson, Peter. 1987. "An International Policy Framework for Trade in Services and Data Services: The Current Debate in International Organizations." Paper prepared for the international seminar, Toward an International Service and Information Economy: A New Challenge for the Third World, sponsored by the Friedrich Ebert Foundation, Mimeograph, Forthcoming.

Rosenfield, S.B. 1984. *The Regulation of International Commercial Aviation*. Dobbs Ferry, N.Y. Oceana Publications.

Rutkowsky, A. 1985. *Integrated Services Digital Networks*. Dedham, Mass., Artech, 300 p.

Rutkowski, Anthony M. 1988. "The Global Information Fabric." *Project PROMETHEE Perspectives*, No. 6, Paris, PROMETHEE, June.

Ruyssen, O. 1985. "Les Services à Marée Montante, in Lesournes, J. and Godet, M., eds., *La Fin des Habitudes*. Paris, Seghers, pp. 326–347.

Sampson, G.P. and Snape, R.H. 1985. "Identifying the Issues in Trade in Services." *World Economy*, Vol. 8, No. 2, June, pp. 171–182.

Sapir, A. 1982. "Trade in Services: Policy Issues for the Eighties." *Columbia Journal of World Business*. Fall, pp. 77–83.

_____. 1983. "North-South Issues in Trade in Services." *World Economy*, Vol. 8, No. 1, March, pp. 27–42.

Sapir, A. and Lutz, E. 1981. *Trade in Services: Economic Determinants and Development-Related Issues.* World Bank. Staff Working Paper, No. 480, 38 p.

_____ . 1980. *Trade in Non-Factor Services: Past Trends and Current Issues.* World Bank, Staff Working Paper, No. 410, 137 p.

Satterthwaite, M.A. 1985. "Competitiveness and Equilibrium as a Driving Force in the Health Services Sector," in Inman, R.P., ed., *Managing the Service Economy, Prospects and Problems.* Cambridge University Press, pp. 239-267.

Sauvant, K.P. 1986. *The International Transactions in Services.* Westview Press, Boulder, Col., 224 p.

_____ . 1986. *Trade and Foreign Direct Investment in Data Services.* Westview Press, Boulder, Col., 220 p.

Saxonhouse, G.R. 1983. *Services in the Japanese Economy.* Ann Arbor, University of Michigan, Research Seminar in International Economics, Paper No. 129, December, 50 p.

Schaumburg-Mueller, H. 1983. *A Study of Trade in Services: Some Theoretical Considerations and Trends in Denmark's Trade in Services in the 1970's.* Copenhagen, School of Economics and Business Administration.

Schott, Jeffrey J. and Smith, Murray G., eds. 1988. *The Canada-United States Free Trade Agreement: The Global Impact.* Washington, D.C., Institute for International Economics.

Schott, J.J. 1983. "Protectionist Threat to Trade and Investment in Services." *World Economy*, Vol. 6, No. 2, June, pp. 195-214.

Schrier, E., Nadel, E. and Rifas, B. 1984. "Forces Shaping International Maritime Transport." *World Economy*, Vol. 7, No. 1, March, pp. 87-102.

Schultz, S. 1984. "Trade in Services: Its Treatment in International Forums and the Problems Ahead." *Intereconomics*, November-December, pp. 267-273.

Self, R. 1982. "The Importance of Trade in Services." *Economic Impact*, No. 2.

Semkow, B.W. 1985. "Japanese Banking Law: Current Deregulation and Liberalization of Domestic and External Financial Transaction." *Law and Policy in International Business*, Vol, 17, pp. 81-155.

Shapiro, I. 1986. "Opportunities for U.S. Lawyers in Asia." *Barriers to International Trade in Professional Services.* University of Chicago Legal Forum, Vol. 1, Summer.

Sharp, Eric (Sir). 1988. "The Need for Global Alternatives." *Project PROMETHEE Perspectives*, No. 7, Paris, PROMETHEE, July.

Shelp, R.K. 1981. *Beyond Industrialization.* New York, Praeger, 234 p.

Shelp, R., Stephenson, J.C., Truitt, N.S. and Wasow. B. 1984. *Service Industries and Economic Development: Case Studies in Technology.* New York, Praeger, 150 p.

Shelp, R.K. 1985. *Entrepreneurship in the Information Society.* Washington, D.C., Conference on Entrepreneurship in the American Economy. Heritage Foundation, 16 April, 17 p.

Smith, Murray G. with Aho, C. Michael and Horlick, Gary N. 1987. *Bridging the Gap: Trade Laws in the Canadian-U.S. Negotiations.* Toronto and Washington, Canadian-American Committee.

Snape, Richard H. 1987. "Prospects for Liberalizing Services Trade." Paper to be published in the proceedings of the Pacific Trade and Development Conference on Trade and Investment in Services in the Pacific, Wellington, New Zealand, January.

Soros, George. 1987. *The Alchemy of Finance: Reading the Mind of the Market.* New York, Simon and Schuster.

Spero, J.E. 1985. *International Trade and the Information Revolution.* Cambridge, Harvard University, Center for Information Policy Research, 17 p.

Stalton, H. 1985. "U.S. Trade Policy and International Service Transactions," in Inman, R.P., ed., *Managing the Service Economy, Prospects and Problems.* Cambridge University Press, pp. 161-178.

Statement by Thirty-Three Economists from Thirteen Countries. 1987. *Resolving the Global Economic Crisis: After Wall Street.* Special Report 6. Washington, D.C., Institute for International Economics, December.

Steger, Debra P. 1987. "Constitutional Implications of the Implementation in Canada of a Trade-In-Services Agreement." Discussion Paper in Series on Trade and Services, Institute for Research on Public Policy, Victoria, June.

Stern, R.M. 1984. *Global Dimensions and Determinants of International Trade and Investment in Services.* Ann Arbor, University of Michigan, Research Seminar in International Economics, October, 43 p.

Sternlieb, G. and Hughes, J. 1985. *A Note on Information Technology, Demographics and the Retail Response.* Wharton School, University of Pennsylvania, Discussion Paper No. 9, June.

Summers, R. 1985. "Services in the International Economy," in Inman, R.P., ed., *Managing the Service Economy, Prospects and Problems.* Cambridge University Press, pp. 27-48.

Tanaka, K. 1986. *On the Criticism of Japan's Distribution Mechanisms.* Tokyo, Keidanren, January, 22 p.

Thomas, D.R.E. 1978. "Strategy Is Different in Service Business." *Harvard Business Review*, July-August, pp. 158-165.

Tisdell, C. 1984. *Tourism, the Environment, International Trade and Public Economics.* ASEAN-Australia Joint Research Project, Kuala Lumpur and Canberra, 46 p.

Trade and Development Report. 1988. UNCTAD, New York.

Trigano, G. 1983. "Une Multinationale des Loisirs," in Cotta, A. and Ghertman, M., eds., *Les Multinationales en Mutation.* Paris, Presses Universitaires de France, pp. 133-140.

Tucker, K. 1979. *Structural Determinants of the Size of the Services Sector: An International Comparison.* Canberra, Working Paper No. 4, Bureau of Industry, 32 p.

_____ . 1981. *Traded Services in the World Economy.* Canberra, Working Paper No. 16, Bureau of Industry, 37 p.

Tucker, K., Seow, G. and Sundberg. M. 1983. *Services in ASEAN-Australian Trade.* ASEAN-Australia Joint Project, Kuala Lumpur and Canberra, 44 p.

_____ . 1984. *ASEAN-Australian Trade in Tourist Services.* ASEAN-Australia Joint Research Project, Kuala Lumpur and Canberra, 60 p.

U.S. Congress, Office of Technology Assessment. 1987. *International Competition in Services.*

_____ . 1988. *Technology and the American Economic Transition: Choices for the Future* OTA-TET-283. Washington, D.C., U.S. Government Printing Office, May.

Vernon, Raymond and Spar, Deborah. 1989. *Beyond Globalism.* Traeger.

Walter, I. 1985. *Barriers to Trade in Banking and Financial Services.* London, Trade Policy Research Centre, 123 p.

White, Lawrence J. 1988. *International Trade in Ocean Shipping Services: The United States and the World.* Cambridge, Mass., Ballinger.

Wildman, Steven S. and Siwek, Stephen E. 1988. *International Trade in Films and Television Programs.* Cambridge, Mass., Ballinger.

Yoshino M.Y. and Lifson, Thomas B. 1986. *The Invisible Link: Japan's Sogo Shosha and the Organization of Trade.* Cambridge, Mass., MIT.

Young, D.N. 1985. *Technology Impacts on the Structure of the Insurance Industry.* Wharton School, University of Pennsylvania. Discussion Paper No. 10, June.

INDEX

Labor:
  developing countries and cross-
    border movement of, 87–88
  export of services and cost of, 93–94
  productivity measurement and, 280,
    284
  trade in services negotiations on
    migration of, 186
  trade in services specialization and,
    97, 112, 113, 114–115, 129
  trade liberalization and, 96
Langeard, E., 32 n. 2
Lanvin, Bruno, 81–82, 105–117,
    117 n. 7
Larson, E., 117 n. 9
Lassudrie-Duchéne, B., 135 n. 12
Latin America:
  foreign trade and, 139
  services in, 141
  trade in services negotiations and,
    174
Lawrence, Robert Z., 101 n. 6
Lempérière, J., 117 n. 5
Lhomme, Adrien, 297–315
Liability insurance companies, 241,
    244
Liberalization of trade, see Trade
    liberalization
Life insurance companies, and risk:
  risks faced by, 241–242
  risk management and, 245, 248
Lindert, P.H., 179 n. 3
Loan risks, 240
Loan syndication, 243
Local area network (LAN), 39, 43
Logica, 74, 75, 77
London Stock Exchange, 3, 5, 6–7, 8,
    9, 246
Lutz, E., 134 n. 2

Macroeconomics, and trade in services,
    108, 115, 128–133
Malpractice, 230
Management:
  intracorporate networks and styles
    of, 26
  producer services and, 92–93
  risks and, see Risk management
  thoughtware and challenges to,
    41–42

Manufacturing:
  basic services and value-added
    services differentiated in, 11
  computer-aided (CAM), 34, 37, 43,
    77, 140
  Mexican services sector and,
    145–149
  "productivity frontier" in, 17–18
  relationship-based processes in, 20
  research and development (R&D)
    in, 72
Maquiladoras, 143, 218
Market access fact-finding (MAFF)
  telecommunications talks,
    212–213, 217
Marketing, and producer services, 92
Market-oriented sector-selective
  (MOSS) telecommunications talks,
    210–212
Markets:
  information technology and changes
    in, 3–4
  networks and, 23
  producer services in development
    and, 90, 92
  thoughtware information flows in,
    43
Marshall, Alfred, 230
Marshall, Colin, 57
Mass customization:
  integration and, 21–23
  productivity gains and, 21–22
MCI, 216–218
Media, deregulation of, 10
Merciai, P., 134 n. 7
Mergers and acquisitions (M&As), 29,
    241
Merrill Lynch, 165
Metacorporate networks, 29–30, 45
Mexico:
  export income of, 139, 143
  foreign direct investment (FDI) in
    services in, 151–152
  import income of, 142, 143
  oil industry in, 142, 145
  producer services growth in,
    145–149
  productivity in, 150–151
  services and development of,
    142–153

comparative advantage approach to, 85–86, 192
fundamental concepts of, 223–316
growth of, 84
networked economy as, 25–26
risk and, 228–231
risk management and, 225–234
as a system, 226–227
trade liberalization and, 84–85
Services:
  basic services and value-added services differentiated in, 10–11
  business environment changes and, 34–35
  definition of, 7
  developing countries and impact of, 138, 139–142
  "hollow companies" in, 34
  impact of revolution in, 138–140
  Mexican economy and, 142–145
  network infostructure and, 25
  productivity measurement in, 277–295
  research and development (R&D) and market for, 72–73
  strategic determinants of value-adding in, 35–37
  strategic positioning within networks and, 59–61
  technical complexity of production and, 34–35
  trade in, *see* Trade in services
  Uruguay Round negotiations on, *see* Trade in services negotiations in GATT
  wealth-creation process and, 17
Services Enquiry Points (SEP), 187
Services measurement:
  demand for services by household in, 268–269
  establishing relevant measure in, 260
  financial services and, 263–264
  frontiers and, 261–264
  input-output tables (IOT) in, 264–265
  international heterogeneity in, 260–265
  international organizations and, 253–254, 259, 272
  limits of, 265–272
  nomenclature in, 260–261
  productivity measurement in, 277–295

service demand by business in, 270–271
service demand from abroad in, 271–272
value-added by service sector in, 265–268
Settlement networks, 6
Shavell, S., 235 n. 7
Shelp, Ron, 117 n. 6
Singapore, 38, 175, 246
Sistema Economica Latino-Americano (SELA), 141, 152, 154 n. 9, 155 n. 10
Sitkin, J., 32 n. 3
SKF, 42–43
Smith, Adam, 232
Software:
  labor cost advantages of developing countries and, 94
  research and development (R&D) for, 74–75
  risk management with, 248–249
  suppliers of, 44
  trade in services and, 129
Sogeti, Cap, 73, 75
Spain, telecommunications talks in, 212, 213
Specialization:
  nonfactor services and, 126, 127
  risk and, 229
  strategy in trade in services with, 112, 113, 114–115
Spriano, Giorgio, 32 n. 9, 32 n. 10, 65–79, 67, 79 n. 1
Stanback, T.M., 135 n. 15
Statistical Office of the European Community (SOEC), 254, 268, 305, 311
Statistics:
  classification issues in, 297–315
  international heterogeneity in, 260–265
  international organizations and collection of, 253–254, 259, 272
  productivity in service activities in, 277–295
  services measurement in, 259–272
Stiglitz, Joseph, 235 n. 12, 235 n. 15
Stock Exchange Automated Quotation System (SEAQ), 6, 7
Stock exchanges:
  deregulation of, 3, 5, 8, 10
  London Big Bang and, 3, 5, 6, 8, 9

SERVICES WORLD FORUM MEMBERSHIP LIST AS OF DECEMBER 1988

Julian Arkell, Chairman of the Working Party of the European Community Services Group, London

Jonathan Aronson, Professor, School of International Relations, University of Southern California

Association Internationale pour l'Etude de l'Economie de l'Assurance (dite "Association de Genève")

Claude Barfield, Director of Trade Policy Studies, A.E.I., Washington

Emmanuelle Baudet, Compagnie Européenne de Publications, Paris

Anders Bergquist, University of Lund, Dep. of Economics

Joël Bonamy, Chercheur, CEDES—Economie et Humanisme, Lyon

Meriel Bradford, Services Negotiator, Government of Canada

Albert Bressand, Director, PROMETHEE, Paris

Robert Bruce, Partner, Debevoise & Plimpton, Washington

Arthur A. Bushkin, President, Telemation Association, Inc., Washington

Jean Buursink, University of Nijmenger

Juan R. Cuadrado Roura, Fundation FIES, University of Alcalà, Madrid

Roy Damary, MBA Coordinator, Webste University, Switzerland

Gerard Dickinson, Professor, City University Business School, London

Catherine Distler, Deputy Director, PROMETHEE, Paris

Wilson P. Dizard, Senior Fellow in International Communications, CSIS, Washington

J.-Marc Duvoisin, Marketing Department, Nestlé, Lausanne

Geza Feketekuty, Counsellor, Office of the U.S. Trade Representative, Washington

Claude Fontaine, REXECO, Paris

Guadalupe Freymond, C.A.S.I.N., Geneva

Jean Gadfrey, Université de Lille I, Villeneuve d'Ascq

Orio Giarini, Secrétaire Général, Association Internationale pour l'Economie de l'Assurance, Geneva

Murray Gibbs, Economic Affairs Officer, UNCTAD, Geneva

Charles Goldfinger, Manager, Global Electronic Finance, Brussels

Kathryn Hauser, Bell Atlantic, Arlington, Virginia

Bas van Holst, Head of the Division Society and Policy, Netherlands Economic Institute, Rotterdam

Stef J.-M. Chr. de Jong, Executive Search Consultant, Boyden

Horst Keppler, Volkswirtschaftliches Seminar, University of Goettingen

Henryk Kierzkowski, Graduate Institute of International Studies, Geneva

Raymond Krommenacker, GATT Counselor, Group of Negotiations Services Division, Geneva

Bruno Lanvin, Office of the Secretary General, UNCTAD, Geneva

François Muller, Transport Division, Economic Commission for Europe, Brussels

Kiyo Nanao, Mission Permanente du Japon, Geneva

Phedon Nicolaides, Chatham House, London

Kalypso Nicolaïdis, Research Associate, PROMETHEE, Paris

Thierry Noyelle, Columbia University, New York

Gunter A. Pauli, President, European Service Industries Forum, Keebergen

Russell Pipe, Publisher, Transnational Data Report, Amsterdam

Juan RADA, Director, International Management Institute (IMI), Geneva

Louis Rebound, Directeur CUREI, Université des Sciences Sociales, Grenoble

John B. Richardson, Directorate General for External Relations, EEC Commission, Brussels

Dorothy I. Riddle, President, ISI, Tempe, Arizona

Jean Rémy Roulet, Chercheur, Association Internationale pour l'Etude de l'Economie de l'Assurance, Geneva

André Sapir, Professor, Université Libre de Bruxelles

Jeffrey Schott, Research Fellow, Institute for International Economies, Washington

Walter R. Stahel, Directeur de L'Institute de la Durée (Environment), Geneva

Sandra Vandermerwe, Senior Faculty Member, International Marketing, IMI, Geneva

Peter Zweifel, Professor, Institüt für Eupirische, Wirschafforschung, Zurich

ABOUT THE CONTRIBUTORS

Albert Bressand is director of PROMETHEE, a Paris-based international research group. PROMETHEE specializes in the study of the emerging global information economy (with an emphasis on telecommunications, financial markets, and trade in services) as well as its implications for corporate strategies, corporate alliances, and regulatory frameworks. He is also chairman of Services World Forum, a Geneva-centered network of experts on international services issues, and a board member of a number of research and professional groups, including Futuribles (Paris), the Association Française des Analystes de Risques-Pays (AFAR, Paris), and the panel of experts on competitiveness advising the French Minister for Industry. Dr. Bressand has served as economic adviser to the French foreign minister, as deputy director of the French Institute of International Affairs (IFRI), and as a member of the policy planning staff of the World Bank. Dr. Bressand's publications include *Le Prochain Monde* (Paris, Editions du Seuil, 1985, with Catherine Distler) and the 1981 and 1982 editions of the *RAMSES* report on the state of the world economy. His articles have appeared in *Foreign Affairs, Le Monde, Revue Tiers-Monde, Politique Internationale*, and *Daedalus.* Dr. Bressand holds engineering degrees from Ecole Polytechnique and Ecole Nationale des Ponts et Chaussées and a Ph.D. in political economy from Harvard University.

Kalypso Nicolaïdis is a Ph.D. candidate in political economy and government at Harvard University, where her research focuses on trade in services, and a research associate at PROMETHEE. She has served as a consultant for UNCTAD and as research associate at the OECD and other international organizations. Ms. Nicolaïdis holds a master's degree in public administration from the Kennedy School of Government, Harvard University, and a graduate degree in international economics (DEA) from the Institut d'Etudes Politiques, Paris.

Jonathan D. Aronson is a professor in the School of International Relations and in the Annenberg School of Communications at the University of Southern California. His publications include *When Countries Talk: International Trade in Telecommunications Services* (with Peter Cowhey, 1988); *Trade Talks: America Better Listen!* (with Michael Aho, 1985); *Profit and the Pursuit of Energy: Markets and Regulation* (1983); *Debt and the Less Developed Countries* (1979), and *Money and Power: Banks and the World Monetary System* (1977). With Peter Cowhey, he is currently completing an edited volume on Mexican telecommunications and a volume for the Council on Foreign Relations on international corporate alliances. He was an International Affairs Fellow of the Council of Foreign Relations in the Office of the U.S. Trade Representative in 1982–83. Professor Aronson received his B.A. from Harvard University and his Ph.D. in political science from Stanford University.

Joël Bonamy is a senior researcher at the CNRS in Lyon, France, where he is in charge of the Center of Exchange and Documentation on Services Industries (CEDES). His research is focused on the service economy and especially the role of services in the transformation of the productive system. He has written many articles and contributed to several books, including *Les Services, Problèmes Théoriques et Méthodologiques* (1984), *Les Services aux Entreprises dans les Sociétés Industrielles* (1985), *La Productivité dans les Services* (1986), and *Business Services and the Transformation of the Production System* (1988).

Françoise Carner received her master's degree in history from El Colegio de México and has published a number of articles on the services economy, the latest of which deals with services and trade liberalization in Mexico. She has served as an official at the Mexican Institute of Foreign Trade, and was a consultant to the United Nations Center on Transnational Corporations. She is presently a Ph.D. candidate at El Colegio de México.

Peter F. Cowhey is an associate professor in the Graduate School of International Relations and Pacific Studies and in the department of political science at the University of California in San Diego. His research focuses on the international communications and information industries. Professor Cowhey's books include *When Countries Talk: International Trade in Telecommunications Services* (with J. Aronson) and *The Problems of Plenty: Energy Policy and International Politics*. His articles have appeared in such journals as *Regulation, International Organization*, and the *International Journal.*

Jacques de Bandt is research director at the National Center for Scientific Research (CNRS) in Paris, and professor of industrial economics at the University of Paris, 10 Nanterre. He is also director of the cooperative research group in industrial economics and editor of the French *Review in Industrial Economics (Revue d'Economie Industrielle)*. He recently served as a contributing editor for *Traité d'Economie Industrielle*, published by Economica in 1988. Professor de Bandt has doctorates in law and economics.

Fernando De Mateo is an expert in both trade policy and the economy of the services sector, and has published a number of books and articles on the subject. From 1971 to 1974 he served as economic counselor of Mexico in charge of economic affairs in Geneva, and was coordinator of the Effective Protection Study in Mexico, advisor to the Minister of Trade and Industrial Development, as well as consultant to UNCTAD and ECLAC. He is presently in charge of the National Study on Services in Mexico and Mexican negotiator to the Uruguay Round in the Negotiating Group on Services. He received his B.A. in economics from the National University of Mexico and his master's degree in economics from El Colegio de México and Johns Hopkins University.

Gerard M. Dickinson is professor of insurance and director of studies in the Centre for Insurance and Investment, City University Business School, London. He is an adviser to PROMETHEE, Paris. He has been a professor at the University of British Columbia and in 1983–84 was visiting C. V. Starr professor of international insurance at the American Graduate School of International Management (Thunderbird Campus). Professor Dickinson has published widely in the areas of insurance and risk management and is author or co-author of four books. His most recent publication, written with R. L. Carter, is *Obstacles to the Liberalization of Trade in Insurance*, published in 1988 by the Trade Policy Research Centre, London. He received his Ph.D. from the University of Sussex.

Catherine Distler is deputy director of PROMETHEE, with a special interest in telecommunications-related issues—technology, national and international regulations, and corporate strategies. She also serves as the coordinator of the *World Technology Report*, prepared at the request of the French Minister of Research by the Centre de Prospective et d'Evaluation, and as a member of the advisory board of *Transnational Data Report*. Her publications include *La Déréglementation dans les années 1990* (Paris, Editions PROMETHEE, 1988), *Le Prochain Monde* (Paris, Editions du Seuil, 1985, with Albert Bressand); her articles have been published in *Politique Internationale, Le Nouvel Observateur, la Revue de l'Energie*, and *Globe*. Catherine Distler is an alumna of Ecole Normale Supérieure. She holds an engineering degree from Ecole Nationale Supérieure des Télécommunications and a graduate degree in applied mathematics (DEA, Université de Paris IX Dauphine).

Leif Edvinsson, president of Consultus International, has been actively engaged in international business consulting for fifteen years. Consultus International is part of the Consultus Group, which specializes in the upgrading and value-added process for services organizations. Mr. Edvinsson works with clients in Europe, the United States, Japan, Singapore, and Australia on the subject of know-how and technology. He is special adviser to the Committee of Trading Services in Sweden and founding member of the board of the Swedish Coalition of Service Industries. He also serves as business adviser and on the board of directors for various service and thoughtware exporters. He is also engaged by the United Nations International Trade Center as an adviser on systematic export growth. Mr. Edvinsson holds a master's degree in business administration from the University of California, Berkley, and the University of Lund, Sweden. He is actively involved in research and development on the export and international marketing of services and thoughtware together with CTF, Sweden.

Geza Feketekuty is counselor to the U.S. Trade Representative, where since 1976 he has developed and coordinated U.S. trade policy, including trade in services. He played a key role in coordinating U.S. participation in the Tokyo Round of Multilateral Trade Negotiations and in planning the next round of multilateral trade negotiations. He was formerly senior staff economist for international finance and trade with the Council of Economic Advisers and an economist and budget examiner with the Office of Management and Budget. He has also been an instructor in economics at Princeton University, a visiting professor at Cornell University, and an adjunct professor at the School of Advanced International Studies of Johns Hopkins University. From 1962 to 1966, Mr. Feketekuty was editor in chief of *The American Economist.* He is also the author of *Trade in Services: An Overview and Blueprint for Negotiation*, published by Ballinger in 1988.

Claude Fontaine is an economist at REXECO, an organization providing macroeconomic analysis and forecasts to its 80 member firms. He graduated from the Institute of Political Studies in Paris with a master's degree in economics and was assistant professor, working with Jean Fourastié for ten years. His major publications are "Les Mouvements de Prix et Leur Dispersion, 1892–1963" ("Price Movement and Deviations, 1892–1963") Armand Colin, 1967; "Chroniques de Conjoncture Sociale" ("Social Climate Chronicles") SEDEIS, three times a year, 1977; "L'expansion des Services: un Quart de Siècle en France et dans le Monde Développé" ("The Expansion of Services: a Quarter of Century in France and the Developed World") (REXERVICES, 1987).

Orio Giarini is secretary general and director of the International Association for Insurance Economics Research, known as the Geneva Association, formed by sixty-five CEOs of the leading insurance companies in all European countries, including also eight leading companies in the United States, Canada, and Brazil. He is also associate professor of service economics at the Graduate Institute of European Studies of the University of Geneva, cofounder of the Services World Forum, and a member of the Club of Rome. Professor Giarini is the author of *Dialogue on Wealth and Welfare*, published by Pergamon, Oxford, in 1980 and of other books on the transition from the industrial to the service economy. He is also editor of a quarterly journal on the economics of risk, uncertainty, and insurance.

Murray Gibbs is chief of the International Trading System Unit in the UNCTAD Secretariat. This Unit is responsible for the implementation of UNCTAD's mandate on services and development, as well as more general trade policy issues.

Raymond J. Krommenacker is a counselor at the General Agreement on Tariffs and Trade (GATT) and a lecturer at the Institut d'Etudes Politiques of Paris (Cycle Supérieur de Sciences Economiques). His publications include *World-Traded Services: The Challenge for the Eighties*, published by Artech House, Norwood, Massachusetts in 1984 and *Les Nations Unies et l'Assurance-Reassurance*, published by the Librairie Générale de Droit et de Jurisprudence, Paris, 1975. His articles include "Providing a Multilateral Legal Framework to Modern High Technology Services," "The Emergence of Space-Generated, Highly Integrated Goods and Services," and "Telematics in the Multilateral Negotiations on Trade in Services." Dr. Krommenacker has a Ph.D. from the Geneva Graduate Institute of International Studies.

Bruno D. Lanvin, currently an economist in the Office of the Secretary-General of the United Nations Conference for Trade and Development (UNCTAD) in Geneva, has been with the United Nations for ten years, specializing in economic research and analysis in the area of international trade. He holds a B. A. in Mathematics and Physics, an M.B.A. from the Ecole des Hautes Etudes Commerciales in Paris, and a Doctorat d'Economie from the University of La Sorbonne, and has taught international economics in various universities in the United States and in Europe. He is the author or co-author of numerous publications on services, including:

1. "Les services, clé du développement économique?" (with F. Prieto) *Revue Tiers-Monde*, No. 105, Paris, January-March 1986.

2. "La société d'information en suspens," *Futuribles*, Paris, October 1986.

3. "Réseaux et compétitivité," in "Les services de communication du futur," *Bulletin de l'IDATE* No. 25, Montpellier, November 1986.

4. "Information Technology and Competitiveness in the Service Industry," *Bulletin de l'IRES* No. 119, Université Catholique de Louvain, October 1987.

5. "The impact of trade and foreign direct investment in data services on economic development: Some issues," UNCTAD Discussion Paper No. 23, Geneva, January 1988.

6. "Les services avancés, infrastructure du développement," *Mondes en Développement*, No. 60, January–March 1988.

7. "Una sfida dagli effetti ancora imprevedibili," *Politica Internazionale*, No. 1–2, IPALMO-Milan, January-February 1988.

8. "Services intermediaires et développement," *Revue d'Economie Industrielle*, No. 43, March 1988.

9. "Information, commerce international des services et développement," in *L'Europe face à la nouvelle économie de service*, O. Giarini and J. R. Roulet eds., PUF, Paris, 1988.

10. "Services et nouvelles stratégies industrielles: quels enjeux pour le Sud?" *Revue Tiers-Monde* 29, No. 115, Paris, July-September 1988.

11. "La dynamique internationale des services d'information: de la double inconstance à la double fracture," *Futuribles*, January 1989.

Adrien Lhomme is principal administrator at the European Community's Statistical Office, where he is in charge of the nomenclatures sector. His work involves coordinating activities and products nomenclatures within the European Community and worldwide in conjunction with other international organizations, particularly the Statistical Office of the United Nations. He has a master's degree and teacher's diploma in economics from the University of Liège.

Pascal Petit is director of research at CNRS and a research officer at CEPREMAP, Paris, a centre linked with the French Commissariat du Plan, which works on long-term issues in economic growth and planning. He has published in the areas of macroeconomic modeling, productivity employment, and technology and industrial relations.

He is the author of *Slow Growth and the Service Economy*, published by Frances Pinter, London, 1986.

John Richardson, who has been an official with the Commission of European Communities since 1973, has been responsible since September 1982 for the development of the Commission's policy on external trade in services. Since the start of the Uruguay Round he has been the Commission's negotiator in the Group for Negotiations on Services.

Giorgio Spriano is an economist in the Economic Research Department of Sanpaolo Bank in Turin. He was a Rockefeller fellow at the Centre for European Policy Studies in Brussels and a research associate with the PROMETHEE in Paris. He received his Ph.D. from the London School of Economics and was graduated in Economics at the University of Turin.